The External History of English:
Stories of English

The External History of English: Stories of English

1판1쇄 발행 2019년 8월 31일

지 은 이   이필환
펴 낸 이   김진수
펴 낸 곳   **한국문화사**
등   록   제1994-9호
주   소   서울특별시 성동구 광나루로 130 서울숲 IT캐슬 1310호
전   화   02-464-7708
팩   스   02-499-0846
이 메 일   hkm7708@hanmail.net
홈페이지   www.hankookmunhwasa.co.kr

책값은 뒤표지에 있습니다.

잘못된 책은 구매처에서 바꾸어 드립니다.
이 책의 내용은 저작권법에 따라 보호받고 있습니다.

ISBN 978-89-6817-791-0 93740

이 도서의 국립중앙도서관 출판예정도서목록(CIP)은 서지정보유통지원시스템
홈페이지(http://seoji.nl.go.kr)와 국가자료공동목록시스템(http://www.nl.go.kr/kolisnet)에서
이용하실 수 있습니다.(CIP제어번호: CIP2019032029)

The External History of English:
Stories of English

PIL-HWAN LEE

한국문화사

PIL-HWAN LEE is Professor in the Department of English Language and Literature at Keimyung University, where he has taught since 2000. Before that, he worked for Chonbuk Sanup University for more than six years (1994-2000). He has held visiting appointments at the University of Manchester (supported by the British Council Fellowship, 1998-1999) and the California State University (Fresno, 2005). He graduated from the Department of English Language and Literature at Seoul National University (1986), and did his PhD there, too (1993, *A Diachronic Study on Word Order in English: The Minimalist Approach*).

He is the author of *English Diachronic Syntax* (1999, Excellent Authorship by the Korean Ministry of Culture, Sports and Tourism) and *Syntactic Changes in English* (2007, Excellent Authorship by the Korean Ministry of Culture, Sports and Tourism). He was the chief-editor of the journal *English Language and Linguistics* and was the president of the English Linguistics Society of Korea (2015-2017). His research efforts have focussed on English historical syntax and English grammar. He has written more than forty articles on these subjects.

■ Preface

Why do we have to study the history of English?

There are already so many books on the history of English, both large and small, that this book seems redundant and unnecessary. What is more, this book does rarely give new academic findings on the topic. Nevertheless, I decided to make this book to be brought into the world, since it was written for pedagogical purposes, not for strictly academic ones. The main readers of this book will be Korean university students. These days, we, Korean professors, are forced to take such 'practical' classes like TOEIC, English Composition, English Grammar, etc., as the major courses of the Department of English and, at the same time, are pressed to give up teaching the so-called 'academic' subjects, including the history of English. "Most English-language courses, nowadays, are either concerned with developing a practical competence or with understanding the synchronic structure of English" (Rastall 2002: 31).

There is a prediction that artificial intelligence will overcome language barriers as a tool beyond what we can imagine in a near future. The barriers of language will soon disappear, and the day of liberation from the difficulty and boredom of learning foreign languages is not far. Then we may not have to waste time and effort in studying English. The purpose of language education is not to secure 'communication tools', however, but to provide an opportunity for the mutual understanding of the culture and the promotion of the individual's cultivation to alleviate the conflict and to eliminate its cause. From this point of view, the meaning of learning the history of English is revealed. It is an attempt to understand the whole English-American culture.

Nevertheless, the history of English was taught too atomistically without the proper connection with contemporary English. So I believe that what matters is not the course itself but the teaching method and textbooks for the course. For "English in Historical Perspective", advocated by Rastall (2002), the history of English should be taught at a university-level, at least for the students of English major. In spite of the need to seek for the explanation of contemporary English usage in a historical light, we did not achieve this goal at the courses of the Department of English. This situation is severely observed in the non-native environment, as at Korean universities. It is a greatly worrying situation that the students' interest in English linguistics (not the study of the so-called 'practical' English), English literature, or the humanities in general, has recently been weakening in Korea. However, I am confident that the study of the history of English will be of great help in studying contemporary 'practical' English, too.

This book was written to be used as a(n easy) textbook for the course of the history of English at Korean Universities. Therefore, the contents of the book should be a little different from those of the books written for English-native students. We cannot help taking outsiders' perspectives. So this book is mostly concerned with the external history of English, for Korean students to be more familiar with the history of England (or the United Kingdom), the western Europe, and North America (the United States of America and Canada).

Lastly, I should confess that I feel uneasy in publishing this book, because I am greatly worried about the possibility of infringing copyright. This book contains not a few direct quotations. I have tried to reveal all the primary sources of the quotations, but it was limited and not always possible. I apologize for any infringement of copyright, if any.

Pil-Hwan Lee
Youngam Hall, Keimyung University, January 2019

C·O·N·T·E·N·T·S

Preface __ 5

I. Backgrounds to the History of English

CHAPTER 1. English: Its Present and Future __ 13

    1.1. English Today ·· 13
    1.2. Why is English so Important? ·· 22
    1.3. Strengths and Weaknesses of English ······································ 25
    1.4. English Tomorrow ··· 35

CHAPTER 2. Language Change and History of English __ 41

    2.1. Language Change and English ·· 41
    2.2. Internal History vs. External History ······································· 42
    2.3. Chronological Division of English ·· 43
    2.4. Changes in English ·· 45
    2.5. English is Still Changing ·· 54
    2.6. Reasons for the Study of the History of English ················ 72

CHAPTER 3. The Pre-Old English Period (before 449) __ 80

    3.1. Ancestor of English: Proto-Indo-European Language ············ 80
    3.2. Language Families within the Indo-European Group ············ 84
    3.3. Germanic Language Family ·· 90
    3.4. Celtic and Romance Language Families ·································· 95
    3.5. Typological Classification of English ·· 97

II. The History of English: External History

CHAPTER 4. The Old English Period (449-1100) __ 105

    4.1. Before the English: Celtic and Roman Britain ·················· 106
    4.2. The Early Old English Period (c. 450-900) ····················· 110
    4.3. The Late Old English Period (900-1100) ························ 130
    4.4. Old English Literature ·· 138

CHAPTER 5. The Middle English Period (1100-1500) __ 141

    5.1. The Early Middle English Period (1100-1300) ················· 143
    5.2. The Late Middle English Period (1300-1500) ·················· 150
    5.3. Middle English Dialects ·· 155
    5.4. The Rise of Standard English ··· 158
    5.5. Middle English Literature ··· 162

CHAPTER 6. The Modern English Period (1500-1800) __ 165

    6.1. The Early Modern English Period (1500-1650) ················ 165
    6.2. The Late Modern English Period (1650-1800) ················· 186
    6.3. Modern English Literature ·· 196

CHAPTER 7. Expansion of English around the World __ 201

    7.1. Expansion of English within the British Isles and
         to Ireland ·· 201
    7.2. Expansion of English to America ····································· 208
    7.3. Expansion of English to Canada ····································· 212
    7.4. Expansion of English to Australia ··································· 216
    7.5. Expansion of English to New Zealand ···························· 219
    7.6. Expansion of English to Other Areas ····························· 221

CHAPTER 8. The American English __ 222

  8.1. Language Variation in America ······································ 223
  8.2. Differences between British and American English ············ 226

Cited Bibliography __ 264
Index __ 268

I.

Backgrounds to the History of English

Chapter 01

English: Its Present and Future

1.1. English Today

1.1.1. English as a World Language

Nobody will deny that English is the world's most important language. In fact, it is regarded as the only global language nowadays.

 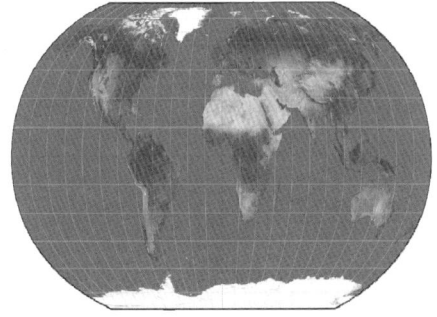

Figure 1.1. Two Versions of World Atlas
("World Atlas" In *Wikipedia*. Retrieved July 31, 2018)

But its history as a separate language is not long. It was one of the various dialects of Germanic tribes who lived in the western part of Europe and became an independent language roughly in the middle of the 5th century. So it has the history of at most about 1500 years. Nevertheless, it could become a global language over the last few centuries, mainly after the 16th century.[1)]

No one will deny that English is a world language. English is used all around the world by professionals and academics in international encounters. It is often the official language of international and multinational companies and industries. Also, it is the language of the Internet. "The present-day world status of English is primarily the result of two factors. One is the expansion of British colonial power, which peaked towards the end of the 19th century. The other is the emergence of the United States as the leading economic power of the 20th century" (Crystal 1997b: 53).[2)] In fact, the latter

---

1) Because of the status of the English language as the communicative medium of the global information society, it is called *a world language*, *a global language*, *a world common language* or *an international language*. Refer to McArthur (2004) and Erling (2005) for the histories and meanings of, and similarities and contrasts among the diverse labels of English. *English as an International Language* (abbreviated as *EIL*) refers to "the specific use of English for international, professional and academic purposes, which is mostly carried out in the written language," while *global English* means "the English used worldwide by people of any ethnicity in any kind of international setting." (Erling 2005: 42)

Since the differences between *a world language*, *a global language*, *a world common language* and *an international language* are not clear and delicate, however, the terms are used indiscriminately in this book.

2) "So what made English the world language? Behind its success story there are two main factors: first, the expansion and influence of British colonial power ... ; second,

factor is more important to understand the status of English as a world language today. The role of the US will be greatly influential even for the future of English. To fully understand the globalization of English, its history should be considered, but we will survey the present status of English before going back to its past.

Probably all peoples or nations of the world will think that their language has intrinsic advantages or strengths over other foreign languages because they do not have any difficulty in maintaining their life through their native tongue. Meanwhile, a foreign language is much more difficult to learn and use. Everybody loves their own language,[3] and their language will seem to be perfect and superior to any other foreign language.

We, Koreans,[4] are also very proud of our language, Korean, and its writing system, Hangeul, which means 'The Great Letters'.[5] We love Korean and try to polish our language more elegantly. In spite of our pride, however, we are being forced to learn and study English more than our language. In a near future, English will be taught in more classes at schools

---

the status of the United States of America as the leading economic, military and scientific power of the twentieth century." (Svartvik and Leech 2006: 6)

[3] I used the plural pronoun *their* in referring to *everybody* not to follow the so-called sexist usage *his*. This will be an instance showing that English is still changing. The plural form has been generally accepted even in the written English. Refer to Lee (2006, 2007: Chapter 6).

[4] This book is written to be used as a(n easy) textbook for the course of the History of English at Korean Universities. Therefore, the contents of the book should be a little different from those of the books written for English-native students. We cannot help taking outsiders' perspectives.

[5] Hangeul is the only writing system in the world that was invented by a single person in a short period, i.e. during a few decades.

than Korean.

But it should be noted that a mother tongue is perfect only in terms of internal purposes. For example, the Korean language perfectly functions only between Koreans. In fact, every language has its own internal advantages. The internal functioning is not the whole story, however. The situation is quite different in the international affairs. A language does not attain importance because of what are assumed to be purely internal advantages. A language can be important only when the nation where it is spoken can exert its cultural, political, economic and military power among nations.

There are 6,000 or so languages spoken in the world (Davidson 2007: 48, Barber 1993: 53).[6] Among such a large number of languages, only the half-dozen or so most widely spoken languages could attain the position of international importance because the external conditions were met. Specifically, English, French, German and Spanish are important languages because of the history and influence of their populations in modern times; for this reason, they are widely used outside their mother tongue territories. Sometimes the cultural importance of a nation was so great at some former time that its language remains important long after it has ceased to represent political, commercial or other greatness. Greek and Latin, for

---

[6] It is a serious problem in terms of cultural diversity that a lot of languages are disappearing every year. "... some 90% of the world's 6,000 or so languages are currently threatened, not least by the domination of English, ..." (Davidson 2007: 48) "Languages are dying at an unprecedented rate." (McArthur 2001: 61) Meanwhile, Hook's (2002: 36) figure about the number of the world languages is a little lower; "Nobody knows exactly how many languages there are, or have been, but there are probably about 5,000 languages spoken in the world today."

example, are studied in their classical forms because of their great civilization preserved and recorded in their literature. But ancient Greek and Latin do not serve as a language of wider communication because they are 'dead' now.[7] Meanwhile, a new language is getting a new prestigious status because of the emerging power of its nation. Recently, for example, Chinese draws new attention because of the political and economic roles that China has been playing. There are predictions that China will be the world number-one economic power within a few decades. However, Chinese is rarely accepted and used beyond China and a few vicinity countries that have been strongly influenced by the Chinese culture for a long time, for example, Malaysia. Japanese is the same. It is rarely used outside Japan, either. Japanese can be said to be underestimated considering Japan's economic power and contribution to the world economy. But notice that the status of a language is not determined only in terms of the economic might of its mother tongue country. In a sense, cultural aspects are more important, since languages are understood culturally rather than economically.

Language is always changing internally. Likewise, the status or importance of a language is also changing. This book is to survey the external history of the English language. This is to understand the importance of Present-day English and to study the present state of English more comprehensively.

---

[7] "To say that a language is 'dead' is like saying that a person is dead. ... A language dies when nobody speaks it any more." (McArthur 2001: 61)

1.1.2. English, England, Britain and the United Kingdom

Before talking about English, we need to know exactly what nation Britain is, who are the British and what are the differences between *England*, *Britain* and *the United Kingdom*. "Lying off the north-west coast of Europe, there are two large islands and several much smaller ones. Collectively, they are known as *the British Isles*. The largest island is called *Great Britain*. The other larger one is called *Ireland*. In the British Isles there are two states. One of these governs most of the island of Ireland. This state is usually called *the Republic of Ireland*. It is also called *Eire* (its Irish language name). Informally it is referred to as just *Ireland* or *the Republic*. The other state has authority over the rest of the British Isles (the whole of Great Britain, the northeastern area of Ireland, and most of the smaller islands). Its official name is *the United Kingdom of Great Britain and Northern Ireland*, although it is usually known by a shorter name (*the United Kingdom* or *the UK*). In other contexts, it is referred to as *Great Britain* (shortly, *GB*). Unofficially, *the UK* is often simply called *Britain*, and its people are called *British*.[8] The normal adjective, when talking about something to do with *the UK* is also *British*, as in *the British Embassy* or *the British Council*. However, people often refer to *Britain* by another name. They call it *England*. But this is not strictly correct, and it can make some people angry. *England* is only one of the four nations of *the British Isles* (*England*, *Scotland*, *Wales* and *Northern Ireland*). The

---

[8] "The people of the UK are *British* citizens. Not everybody likes the modern label *Briton* or *Britons*, although this is the correct way of referring to the ancient Celtic people of Britannia." (Svartvik and Leech 2006: 15) Refer to Section 4.1.

political unification of these four nations was a gradual process that took several hundred years, which will be explained below in detail."9)

1.1.3. English as L1, L2 or a Foreign Language10)

There are a number of ways of looking at the role of English in different countries of the world. Basically, we can divide up countries according to whether they have English as a native language (ENL), English as a second language (ESL), or English as a foreign language (EFL). We can use another terms such as L1 (for the people who have a variety of English as a first language, or mother tongue) and L2 (for the people who have learned a variety of English as a second language, in addition to their mother tongue). The first category is self-explanatory. The difference between English as a foreign language and English as a second language is that in the latter instance only, English is actually used for the communicative purpose within the country.11) According to Crystal (1997b: 54), there is a total of 75 territories where English functions as L1 or L2. The US linguist Kachru, an Indian-American scholar, has divided these English-speaking countries of the world into three broad types, which he symbolizes by placing them in three concentric circles. That is, the ways in which English has been accepted and used around the world can be

---

9) This paragraph is the summary of the several pages of O'driscoll (1995: 8-13).
10) This section is based on Crystal (1997a: 92-115; 1997b: 53-63; 2002: 233-63), Barber (1993: 234-42), Baugh and Cable (1993: 283-85), Svartvik and Leech (2006: 71-149) and Fisiak (1995: 134-35).
11) There is a view that, today, a distinction between ESL and EFL is not clear, nor relevant.

understood as three concentric circles, as in Figure 7.1 (Crystal 1997b: 54):[12]

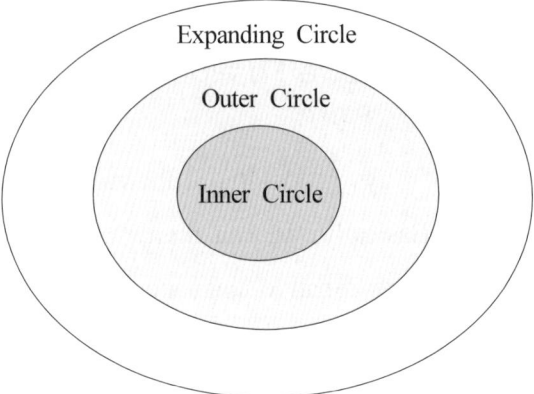

Figure 1.1. The Three 'Circles' of English
(Kachru (1985) through Crystal (1997b: 54))

1. The Inner Circle (L1 or ENL): These countries are the traditional bases of English, where it is the first language. It includes the US, the UK, Ireland, Canada, Australia and New Zealand.

---

12) Mesthrie (2008: 31) gives the following numbers of English speakers or users of each country:

The Inner Circle: e.g. the US (242,200,000), the UK (56,458,000), Canada (25,625,000) and New Zealand (3,305,000)

The Outer Circle: e.g. Bangladesh (104,204,000), Ghana (13,552,000), India (783,940,000), Kenya (21,044,000), Malaysia (15,820,000), Nigeria (105,448,000), Pakistan (101,855,000), Philippines (58,091,000), Singapore (2,584,000), Sri Lanka (16,638,000), Tanzania (22,415,000), Zambia (7,054,000)

The Expanding Circle: e.g. China (1,045,537,000), Egypt (50,525,000), Indonasia (176,764,000), Israel (4,208,000), Japan (121,402,000), Korea (43,284,000), Nepal (17,422,000), Saudi Arabia (11,519,000), Taiwan (19,601,000), the former USSR (279,904,000), Zimbabwe (8,984,000)

2. The Outer or Extended Circle (L2 or ESL): These countries represent the earlier spread of English in non-native contexts, where the language plays an important second-language role in a multilingual setting. In many of these countries, English is an official language and widely used in administration, education and the media. It includes Singapore, India, Malawi, and over 50 other territories.
3. The Expanding Circle (EFL): This includes countries that recognize the importance of English as an international language though they have no history of colonization. English has no special administrative status in these countries, e.g. Korea,[13] China, Japan, Poland, and a growing number of other states.

According to Crystal (1997b: 60-63), the number of those who have learned English as a first language (L1) is roughly 337 million, and the total of 235 million represents an estimate of those who have learned English as a second language (L2). This is a rough estimate of more than twenty years ago (around in 1995). For the members of the expanding circle, who have learned English as a foreign language,[14] the estimate varies enormously. They have been as low as 100 million and as high as 1,000 million. It is clear that this expanding circle is greatly contributing

---

[13] We, Koreans, learn English as a foreign language. We do not normally use English to communicate with other Koreans, but generally with foreigners. Meanwhile, for example, Indians learn English as a second language. They will expect to use it to communicate with other Indians, and will hear it used in the speech-community as a matter of course. (cf. Barber (1993: 238)).

[14] Barber (1993: 238) says, however, that "the distinction between second language and foreign language is not a sharp one, and there are cases, like Indonesia, where classification is disputable."

to the global status of English. It is here that English is used primarily as an international language, especially in the business, scientific, legal, political and academic communities.[15] According to Crystal's (1997b: 61) cautious estimate, there are 670 million native or near-native speakers of English (having 'native-like fluency') in the lowest. The most extreme estimate is that there are 1,800 million speakers (having 'reasonable competence'). The 'middle-of-the-road' or 'neutral' estimate is that there are from 1,200 to 1,500 million English speakers around the world. Now the English-speaking countries are not restricted to a single continent or to a single region. It spreads all over the world geographically.

1.2. Why is English so Important?

Every language is important to its native speakers,[16] so the importance of a language cannot be evaluated in terms of its internal communicative value. But there are some "objective standards of relative importance" among various languages (Quirk *et al.* 1985: 3).

The first criterion will be the number of speakers of the language. In the number of its speakers, English is one of the most important languages of the world. Spoken by more than 380 million people as a first or native language in the United Kingdom (the UK), the United States of America (the US) and the former British Empire,[17] it is the largest of the western

---

15) The reason why English is accepted as an essential qualification in getting a good job in Korea can be understood in this vein.

16) "A native speaker is one whose *first language* and *language of thought* are the same." (Hook 2002: 35)

(more technically, will be later referred to as Indo-European) languages. Some of the other European languages are comparable with English in reflecting the forces of history, especially with regard to European expansion since the 16th century. Spanish, next in size to English, is spoken by about 240 million people, Russian by 210 million, Portuguese by 125 million, German by 110 million, French by 85 million native speakers (and a large number of second-language speakers), Italian by 65 million.[18]

But the speakers of English far exceeds the speakers of these languages. English, however, is not the most widely used language in the world. Chinese is spoken by more than a billion people in China alone. So the number of speakers do not determine all about the importance of a language. In any case, it is an undeniable fact that English is a language having a great number of speakers. More importantly, the number of its speakers, especially, the second language (i.e. ESL) or the foreign language (i.e. EFL) speakers are steadily growing.

The second criterion is "the geographical dispersal of the language" (Quirk *et al*. 1985: 3). As is well known, the English-speaking territories spread all over the world. It is the historical legacy of the British Empire of the 18th and 19th centuries. "About 1500 million people - over a third of the world population - live in countries where English has some official

---

17) There is no way to determine the exact number of the speakers of a language. But there are several estimates studied by linguists. According to Davidson (2007: 48), for example, there are 380 or so million Anglophones (a broader term than 'native' or 'mother tongue' speakers of English).
18) These figures are from Baugh and Cable (1993: 4). So the numbers have been clearly increasing since then.

status or is one of the native languages, if not dominant native language" (Quirk *et al*. 1985: 3). "Geographical extent plays a significant part in a language's worldwide importance, and here English wins over all others. There is no other language that is spoken as an official or semi-official language in 80 or more countries on all continents, as a first or second language, by more people than English" (Hook 2002: 36).

The third criterion will be the role in the fields of culture, science and technology played by the language. English is undoubtedly the primary medium leading the development in these fields.[19] The unrivalled status of English is based on its use as a means of international communication, including the Internet. English is the only universal language used internationally on the Internet. During the 1990s the explosive growth of the Internet established English as a world language in ways that could not have been foreseen only a few years earlier. In a world where econo-technical superiority is what counts, the real 'powerhouse' is English. If econo-technical superiority is important, we might wonder about the relative status between English and Japanese. Although spoken by 125 million people in Japan, a country that has risen to economic and technical dominance since World War II, the Japanese language has yet few of the roles in international affairs that are played by English. Cultural consideration is also important. For example, major broadcasting and film industries in the UK and the US have greatly contributed to the spread of English worldwide. Think about the great

---

[19] "English is the world main language of communication in books, learned journals, newspapers, e-mail, air-traffic control, international conferences, science and technology, diplomacy, broadcasting, advertising, music, and so on." (Hook 2002: 36)

successes of such films produced in English as *Harry Potter* series or *The Lord of the Rings*. The stories of these films are based on the literary works written in English with the same titles. Therefore, it will be the combined effect of economic and cultural forces that determines the world language.

The last criterion will be the political connotation of a language. English is not the language of a certain single nation. It is the language of the UK, but it is the language of the US, Canada, Australia and New Zealand at the same time. And it is one of the languages spoken in the United Nations. In a diplomatic setting, English is the only language which will be adopted as a communicative medium without arousing any political hesitation, since it is not the language of a certain specific country.[20]

Besides these language-external factors, English also has its intrinsic advantages or strengths to occupy a prominent place in international communication.

1.3. Strengths and Weaknesses of English

According to Baugh and Cable (1993: 8-11),[21] English possesses several intrinsic "assets" (i.e. strengths) by which it could be a world language in a rather short time span.

To begin with,[22] English has cosmopolitan vocabulary, i.e. the mixed

---

20) "... in countries or groups of countries where people have several or many different first languages, English may be the preferred lingua franca because it is felt to be neutral ground." (Svartvik and Leech 2006: 7)
21) Besides Baugh and Cable (1993), there are more linguistic experts who advocate the intrinsic pre-eminence of English to be a world language.
22) Section 1.3 contains the summary of Baugh and Cable (1993: 8-13).

character of its vocabulary. It is the most prominent among the assets of the English language. English is classified as a Germanic language. That is to say, it belongs to the group of languages to which German, Dutch, Flemish, Danish, Swedish and Norwegian also belong.[23] It shares with these languages similar grammatical structure and many common words. On the other hand, more than half of its vocabulary is derived from Latin. Latin is not a Germanic language but the ancestor of Romance or Italic languages such as French, Spanish, Portuguese, Italian and R(o)umanian. Some of the borrowings from Latin have been direct, a great many through French, some through the other Romance languages. As a result, English also shares a great number of words with those Romance languages. To a lesser extent, the English vocabulary contains borrowings from many other languages. Instead of making new words by the combination of existing elements, as German often does, English has shown a marked tendency to go outside its own linguistic resources and borrow from other languages. So cosmopolitan a vocabulary is an undoubted asset to any language that seeks to attain international use.[24]

The second asset that Baugh and Cable (1993) argue that English possesses to a preeminent degree is inflectional simplicity. English has undergone the progressive simplification of its inflections within the

---

[23] The genealogical classification of English will be dealt with in Chapter 3.
[24] However, there may be a disagreement on the argument that the cosmopolitan character of English vocabulary is an "asset" of English. The cosmopolitan feature of English vocabulary means the vastness of its word stock. English has so many words that no native speaker knows them all and non-native learners have a great burden of memorizing them one by one. Thus this may be regarded as an obstacle, rather than an asset, for English to become a world language.

historical period. Instead, it employed various prepositions, especially during the Middle English period (roughly from 1100 to 1500),[25] and developed the fixed word order. In this process of simplification English has gone further than any other language in Europe. Inflections in the noun have been reduced to a sign of the plural and a form for the possessive case.[26] The elaborate Germanic inflection of the adjective has been completely eliminated except for the simple indication of the comparative and the superlative degrees.[27] The verb has been simplified by the loss of practically all the personal endings, the almost complete abandonment of any distinction between the singular and the plural, and the gradual discard of the subjunctive mood.[28]

There is an opinion, however, that the simplicity of inflections is not always a merit of English. Because of the loss of a great part of inflections, a considerable amount of ambiguity arose. Now we should rely on almost exclusively on word order to identify the grammatical functions (e.g. subject, object, (predicative) complement, etc.) within a given sentence. And we have another burden of distinguishing and properly using English's extravagant prepositions.[29]

---

25) For the chronological division of English, see Section 2.3.
26) For details, see Section 3.5.2.
27) An Old English (roughly from the middle of the 5th century to 1100) adjective agrees with the noun it modifies. Germanic languages, in general, had developed this distinctive adjective paradigm of inflections. Adjectives were inflected according to its position as well as to the gender, case and number of the noun it modifies. Fortunately to us, however, all the adjectival endings were lost completely after the Old English times. Only the inflections for the comparison still remain.
28) For details, see Section 3.5.1.

In the third place, English enjoys an exceptional advantage over all other major European languages in having adopted natural (rather than grammatical) gender. Gender in English is determined by meaning or real sex in the natural world. All nouns naming living creatures are masculine or feminine according to the sex of the individual, and all other nouns are neuter. Attributive gender, as when we speak of a ship as feminine, sun and moon as masculine or feminine, is personification and a matter of rhetoric. Since English follows the natural sex of the referred noun, we do not have to memorize the gender of each noun as in German. It will be a greatly vexing work for foreigners to memorize the gender of each noun which does not match up with the real world sex.

Whereas the three features just described are arguably of great advantage in facilitating its acquisition, English also presents some difficulties that the foreign student inevitably encounters in learning it (Baugh and Cable 1993: 11-13).[30] Smith (2005: 57) also says that "English has certain strengths which make it attractive to those who know it well, but it also has a number of weaknesses which - though mostly of no great consequences to native speakers (spelling being a major exception) - make it difficult to learn and understand and therefore unsuitable as a global lingua franca."[31]

---

29) This is very difficult for foreign learners of English. For example, the proper choice of English prepositions constitutes an important part in English (grammar) tests.
30) "English did not become a world language on its linguistic merits. The pronunciations of English words is irritatingly often at odds with their spelling, the vocabulary is enormous and the grammar less learner-friendly than is generally assumed." (Svartvik and Leech 2006: 6)
31) A *lingua franca* (Italian literally meaning Frankish language) means any language widely used beyond the population of its native speakers. Any given language

For instance, English has a disadvantage that it employs too many idioms or idiomatic expressions.32) Because an idiom is a form of expression peculiar to one language, non-native learners should memorize one by one. It will be difficult and tedious. Of course, all languages have their special ways of saying things. However, English possesses too many idioms.33)

Another and more serious disadvantage or weakness of English as a world language is the chaotic character of its spelling and the frequent lack of correlation between spelling and pronunciation. English spelling do not properly represent the pronunciation of the word. To put it another way, there is a big discrepancy between spelling and pronunciation. The spellings of Present-day English are not fully regularized. English spelling is not always phonetic. There is no simple one-to-one correspondence between sounds and the letters that represent them. Thus the same sound can be spelled so differently. For example, the [ei or eɪ] sound is spelled

---

normally becomes a lingua franca primarily by being used for international commerce, but can be accepted in other cultural exchanges, especially diplomacy. A synonym for lingua franca is *vehicular language*. Whereas a *vernacular language* is used as a native language in a single speaker community, a vehicular language goes beyond the boundaries of its original community and is used as a second language for communication between communities. For example, English is a vernacular in England, but is used as a vehicular language (that is, a lingua franca) in Pakistan. ("Lingua Franca" In *Wikipedia*. Retrieved July 31, 2008)

32) So the dictionary of idioms and the dictionary of phrasal verbs are essential to English learning.

33) "It is doubtful whether idiomatic expressions are so much more common in English than in other languages - for example, French - as those learning English believe, but they undoubtedly loom large in the minds of non-native speakers." (Baugh and Cable 1993: 12)

so differently,34) as in h*ate*, d*ay*, r*ai*n, g*ao*l, g*au*ge, f*e*te, neglig*ee*, sl*eigh*, th*ey*, br*ea*k, m*é*tier, and still others. Likewise, the [ʃ] sound is spelled in the 11 different ways, as in *sh*oe, na*ti*on, *s*ugar, man*si*on, mi*ssi*on, suspi*ci*on, o*ce*an, cons*ci*ous, *ch*aperon,35) *sch*ist and *f*u*ch*sia. The [ou] sound has 10 different spellings, too, as in s*o*, s*ew*, s*ow*, *oh*, *ow*e, d*ough*, d*oe*, b*eau*, s*oa*k and s*ou*l. Conversely, the same spelling can be pronounced so differently, as in thr*ough* [-u:], b*ough* [-au], th*ough* [-ou], b*ough*t [-ɔ:-], c*ough* [-ɑf or -ɔf], r*ough* [-ʌf], hicc*ough* [-ʌp], and others. Consider the sound difference between the two word groups in the following:

h*ear*d vs. b*ear*d	m*ea*t vs. gr*ea*t vs thr*ea*t
m*oth* vs. m*oth*er	h*ere* vs. th*ere*
d*ear*, f*ear* vs. b*ear*, p*ear*	d*ose*, r*ose* vs. l*ose*
g*oose* vs. ch*oose*	d*o* vs. g*o*
d*ea*d vs. b*ea*d	w*or*d vs. sw*or*d, etc.

In the meantime, English has words pronounced identically but spelled differently (called homonyms), such as *flower/flour, tale/tail* and *to/too/two*. On the other hand, there are such words as spelled identically but pronounced differently; *lead* (the metal)/*lead* (the verb), *dove* (the bird)/*dove* (the past form of the verb *dive*), *bow* (a weapon for shooting arrows)/*bow* (to bend your head), *wind* (a current of air moving)/*wind* (the

---

34) The symbol in [ ] is a sound or a pronunciation, whereas the one in < > is a spelling or a letter.
35) In French <ch> is pronounced as [ʃ], so the English words having <ch> of [ʃ], like *ch*aperon, *ch*ef and *ch*auffeur, are in most cases borrowed from French.

verb), and *bass* (the lowest range of musical notes)/*bass* (a type of fish).36)

There are a lot of reasons for this chaotic situation. In Old English (roughly from the middle of the 5th century to 1100), the pronunciation of a word was relatively transparent and rule-governed. So we can easily determine the sound only by seeing the spelling. However, English spellings began to be intermingled with foreign spelling conventions and so became disorderly after the Middle English period. The spelling complexity is surely a disadvantage of English as a world language, since English learners (even native learners too) should spend a lot of time and energy in trying to master the complex spelling system.37)

According to Smith (2005), English cannot be a good international language, since it is not a language which can achieve unambiguous communication between people with mutually unintelligible tongues. There are at least four reasons: unpronounceability, irregularity, over-complexity and ambiguity.

For the unpronounceability of English, we can say English has an unusually large number of vowels and consonants. There are at least 12 vowels and 10 diphthongs. And English has not a few consonant sounds which a foreign learner cannot pronounce properly. For example, we, Koreans, cannot distinguish, without special training, the differences between [f] and [p] (or [h]), [v] and [b], [d] and [ð], and [t] and [θ]. It

---

36) Technically, these words are called *heteronyms*. Two words are *heteronyms* if they are spelled the same, but pronounced differently, and have different meanings.
37) There are some defenders of English spellings. They emphasize the useful way in which the spelling of an English word often indicates its etymology. This is one of the reasons for the failure of most spelling reforms.

is not easy for us to pronounce the consonant clusters such as *-ngths* as in *stre<u>ngths</u>*, *spl-* as in *<u>spl</u>it*, and *-sps* as in *cri<u>sps</u>,* because the Korean language does not tolerate such complex syllable structures like CCCVCCC. The general pattern is CVC. The extreme case is Japanese, which permits only the CV syllable structure, so Japanese learners of English habitually insert a vowel between each consonant. In any events, to be a fluent English speaker, we need to take special pronunciation training.

English has another weakness that it shows a great deal of irregularity, particularly with regard to inflection and orthography. Orthographic irregularities and the striking mismatch between sound and spelling were sufficiently dealt with in the above. It is well-known that English verbs and nouns permit a large number of irregular forms. According to Smith (2005: 59), "about 70% of verb use in everyday speech involves an irregular verb." A lot of plural forms of English nouns are also irregular. These irregular forms require the monotonous process of memorizing one by one through endless repetition exercises and this is not helpful for English learners, especially foreign learners.

English has a weakness that its grammar is too complex and too ambiguous, so English grammar is a great obstacle for English learning.[38]

---

38) "True, English grammar has few inflectional endings compared to languages like German, Latin or Russian, but its syntax is no less complex than that of other languages. ... So it is totally wrong to suppose, as some native speakers of English actually do, that English has no grammar. The grammar of English not only exists but has been subjected to more detailed study than that of any other language." (Svartvik and Leech 2006: 6)

A few grammar topics, exemplified as follows, clearly shows that English grammar is not easy for foreign learners to acquire:

① Tenses and aspects
(e.g. distinction between simple past and present perfect, distinction between *will* and *be going to*, etc.)

② Modal auxiliaries
(e.g. distinction between *can* and *may* in the sense of 'possibility', distinction between *must, have to, should* and *ought to* in the sense of 'obligation', ambiguity between *will* and *shall* as a future auxiliary, etc.)

③ Gerunds (or Verbal Nouns) and infinitives: How to distinguish the two constructions?

④ How to judge the countability of nouns, whose distinction does not correspond to the real world situation in many cases? The countability of nouns governs the use of articles and relevant modifiers in its front.

⑤ The various relativizers: *who, that, which, what,* etc.

⑥ the highly confusing *some / any* and other relevant contrasts
(e.g. *still, yet* and *already*)

⑦ various prepositions and conjunctions

⑧ a lot of phrasal verbs, etc.

Thus Smith (2005) concludes that "English is a poor lingua franca," since it possesses not a few language-internal intrinsic weaknesses. On the country, the linguists like Hook (2002: 35) argue that "just as English is the world's easiest language, it is also the world's most useful language." He (p. 38) also says that "English has become an easily acquired, ultra-useful international language as no other in the past." To him, the paucity of grammatical inflection, the easy grammatical conversion (i.e. the same form used for different parts of speech), even English spelling are the advantages of English. It does not strike on him that these factors can create ambiguities and complexities in other areas. So all the judgements on the strengths and weaknesses of English are mostly subjective.

Our conclusion is that the choice of an international language, or lingua franca, is never based on linguistic or aesthetic criteria but always on language-external factors like political, economic and demographical criteria (Quirk et al. 1985: 3). Every language serves for its speakers as a perfect medium of communication, which means that it has a perfect internal system with both its own advantages and disadvantages. In other words, all languages are adequate for the needs of their culture, properly expressing various ideas and the refinements of thought. Thus the evaluation of the importance of various languages cannot take place in terms of the internal structure of the language, e.g. the number of vocabulary, inflection, word order, and the like. We do not learn English because it is somehow intrinsically superior or because it is the best language in the world, but just because it is generally accepted as the world common language.[39] If another language(s) take(s) the position of a world language instead of or along with English, we will have no choice but to learn the language(s), too, irrespective its or their linguistic strengths and weaknesses. The status of a world language is not a matter of language itself but an uncontrollable language-external matter.

1.4. English Tomorrow

We wonder how long English will keep on functioning as a world language and what probable position it will occupy in the future. There are predictions about the future of English, mostly optimistic but often gloomy,[40] although it is admittedly hazardous to predict the future of a nation and its language. Nevertheless, we are curious about what will happen to the present status of English as the single international language.

---

[39] "The reason is not that the language (i.e. English, author's addition) is easy, beautiful or superior in linguistic qualities. Most people who want to learn it do so because they need it to function in the world at large." (Svartvik and Leech 2006: 2)

[40] "English is here to stay as a world language, for the time being at least. The global information society need a lingua franca, and English, despite its imperfections, is the unchallenged incumbent ... However, if they (the Chinese) feel that economic prowess should be matched by linguistic strength, not only to make their lives easier in international liaisons but also as a vehicle for their culture, English will cease to be the single world language and will have to share the stage with Chinese, or revert to being a merely regional linguistic power." (Smith 2005: 62)

In Section 1.2 we suggested four criteria to judge the relative importance among languages. The first criterion was the number of speakers of the language. If the future of a language is closely bound up with the influence and prestige of its speakers, the most important question to ask is if the speakers of English will increase or decrease. "If the future of a language were merely a matter of the number of those who use it as a first language, English would appear to be entering a period of decline after four centuries of unprecedented expansion. What makes this prospect unlikely is the fact that English is widely used as a second language throughout the world. The number of speakers who have acquired English as a second language with near native fluency is estimated to be between 350 million and 400 million. If we add to first and second language speakers those who know enough English to use it more or less effectively as a foreign language,[41] the estimates for the total number of speakers range between one and one and a half billion. In some of the developing countries that are experiencing the greatest growth, English is one of the official languages, as it is in India, Nigeria and the Philippines. In some countries English is a neutral language among competing indigenous languages, the establishment of any one of which would arouse ethnic jealousies. In most developing countries communications in English are superior to those in the vernacular languages." (Baugh and Cable 1993: 6). In terms of the criterion of the number of its speakers, therefore, the future of English is bright.

Secondly, English-speaking territories will not be reduced,[42] since there

---

[41] To English native speakers, English is principal, while it is auxiliary for the ESL or EFL speakers.

[42] English has "a special place in seventy-five territories" (cf. Crystal 1997b: 109-110)

is no possibility that the present English-speaking communities will give up their present language, English, to adopt another language for their everyday conversation. Rather, there are countries where their indigenous languages are being abandoned and being driven into demise, as in Ireland and Scotland, where Irish and Scottish Gaelics are 'dying'.[43] So it can be said that English has a bright future in terms of the second criterion, i.e. the geographical dispersal of the language.

We can say without much hesitation that the status of English as a world language will not be much lowered in the fields of culture, science, technology and the international politics, since the US is believed to exert superpower in these fields for a long time in the future.[44] Since the breakup of the Soviet Union, the US has been the only superpower in the world and its supremacy is not shaking. Recently, China's challenge is strong, but we need to watch more.

Nevertheless, the future of English is not bright in all aspects. In recent years doubts have arisen whether English will remain as a single international language and whether its use as an international language will

---

and is "likely to serve in some form, for some time yet, as the global auxiliary language". (Davidson 2007: 48)

43) "The loss of Gaelic was so significant that death was the only possible expression for it. That loss was - still is - for me, as for my dad, a kind of death in the family." (McArthur 2001: 60)

44) "Latin became the dominant cultural language of Western Europe, not because it was intrinsically superior to Greek or Arabic or the local languages, but because of the political, military and administrative achievements of Imperial Rome. Similarly, the wealth and power of the United States make her a creditor nation in linguistic matters." (Barber 1993: 263)

continue at the present level. The doubts come from the fear, especially among English native speakers, that "national varieties of English are rapidly growing further apart and will finally separate into mutually incomprehensible languages" (Quirk *et al.* 1985: 8). That is, new varieties of English are rapidly developing in different parts of the world. In particular, newly independent nations (mainly from the former British Empire) need "further language change in order to provide a badge of political, social and literary identity" (Crystal 2002: 293). So the worry is that "within a generation or two international standard English will have fragmented into a range of only partly intelligible dialects" (Crystal 2002: 293).[45] "Varying levels of unintelligibility already exist, with variations in vocabulary, grammar and pronunciation being introduced which cumulatively can make a local form of English impenetrable to the outsider" (Crystal 2002: 294).[46]

There is a regional variation between varieties of English, each of which is recognized as a standard in its own sphere of influence. Thus many new (national) varieties of English have emerged during the last few decades, e.g. Malenglish ('Malayan English'), Japlish (Japanese + English), Singlish (Singapore + English), Spanglish (Spanish + English), Chinglish (Chinese + English), Taglish (Tagalog [spoken in the Philippines] + English, cf. Englog [English + Tagalog]), Denglish (Deutsch + English), Frenglish

---

[45] Crystal (1997a, b) maps the development of eight main, if overlapping, standard(izing) varieties of regional English: 1) British and Irish, 2) American and Canadian, 3) Australian and New Zealand, 4) African, 5) Caribbean, 6) South Asian, 7) East Asian, 8) South Pacific.

[46] "... many of the 'New Englishes' are already or may yet become new languages: the evolutionary process goes on." (McArthur 2001: 62)

(French + English, cf. Franglais [Français + Anglais]), and so on. Of course, Konglish (Korean + English) can be added to this list. However, Crystal argues that these new varieties are actually more expressive than either of the standard forms of English, i.e. British and American Standard English.[47] Since these varieties meet the needs of group identity, they should not be oppressed. To get the pan-national (through the national or local variety) and international intelligibility, however, standard English(es) will be and should be taught. Crystal (2002: 294) says that "so maybe in a century or so we (i.e. English native speakers) shall all be bilingual in our own language, with our home variety of English co-existing with an English international lingua franca." "It is after all the monolingual 'native' speaker of a single variety of a standard global language who is the most linguistically disadvantaged of all - socially, culturally, emotionally and intellectually" (Davidson 2007: 49). Davidson argues that we should be plurilingual in the future, with most speaking one or more forms of more than one language.

Considering all the matters, the emergence of new local and national varieties will not function as an obstacle to the status of English as a world language. Rather, it will exert positive influences on the increase of English speakers worldwide.

However, some scholars like Smith (2005) condemns the globalization of English as "Curse", not seeing as "Gift". Smith says that the worldwide use of English reflects the imperialism of the British Empire in the 18th and 19th centuries and "the view that what is good for America is good for

---

[47] Davidson (2007: 48) regards the ideas of the monolingual 'native speaker' and a single uniform 'standard English' as myths.

the rest of the world, including the English language". To him the 'English-only' does not have enough cause, so it is just a paraphrase of the monolingual linguistic imperialism. But we should say that it is not objective to see the spread of English on a global scale as a linguistic form of imperialism. Likewise, it is not proper to consider English as a successful language because of its inherent linguistic superiorities. We do not learn English due to the merits of the language itself or the merits of its speakers. The desire for us to be a fluent English speaker is not from the love for the language but for the better opportunities it can give us. Therefore, we need to avoid value judgements in discussing language matters, since the status of a language is generally determined by language-external factors. Anyway, it seems that we cannot reverse the strong flow of language history which has strengthened the status of English as a global language. Nevertheless, this does not mean that we think that English is the best language in the world.

Language Change and History of English

2.1. Language Change and English

All living languages are in a state of change. It is one of the prominent features of human languages. In this sense, languages are like living creatures, which are born, get old, and finally die. The rate of change varies from time to time and from language to language. Changes can be observed in all levels of language; in pronunciation, spelling, word form, syntactic structure and meaning. Language changes may be at a different pace and with different intensity in these various areas of their structure. It is a little difficult to notice language change because change is generally very slow and gradual. However, change is real and always present. Indeed, it would be strange if language did not change while everything else in its surrounding undergoes constant modification.

English is not an exception to this. Since its birth or establishment as an independent language from one of the Germanic dialects roughly in the middle of the 5th century,[1] English has undergone more changes than any other language spoken in Europe. And the changes reflect the external history of the English people. This book is concerned with such changes as English has undergone for over a millenium and with the history of the people who have used the language as their mother tongue.

2.2. Internal History vs. External History

As was already mentioned above, the formation and change of any language is inseparably related to the environment of its speakers and of the society in which it is spoken. Thus, a broad picture of the history of a language must include not only the development of the structure of the language but also an account of the external forces, such as cultural, political, social, scientific and technological, which influence this evolution. Thus, we need the division between the internal history and the external history of a language. The internal history means the changes occurring in the structure of a particular language. It includes the changes of its spellings and lexicon, pronunciations (i.e. phonological change), inflections or word-forms (i.e. morphological change), word order or structures (i.e. syntactic change), and its meaning (i.e. semantic change).

By contrast, "the external history of English deals with all non-structural factors which have exerted influence on the evolution of English and directed its course of change" (Fisiak 1995: 23). There are various external factors. They include the political (e.g. the formation of states, wars,

---

[1] For the ancestry of English, see the next chapter.

invasions, etc.), social (e.g. changes in social structure, social prestige, etc.), economic (e.g. economically-motivated social movements, uprisings, industrialization, etc.), and scientific and cultural factors (e.g. the introduction of printing and several cultural movements like Renaissance, etc.). The impact of Christianization is especially important for the history of English. It has a profound influence on the English language and literature. "The extent to which these kinds of external factors contribute to the development of a language varies from one period to another and from one place to another" (Fisiak 1995: 23).

2.3. Chronological Division of English

Before proceeding to see the changes English has undergone, we need to say about the chronological division of English for the easy understanding of the development of English. It is a kind of convention to divide the history of English into several (commonly four) periods. It is to facilitate the description of its evolution. Of course, time division is arbitrary because there cannot be a stopping in the flow of time. Nevertheless, we can have some clear and major turning points or departures for each period, correlated with major linguistic changes (language-internal factors) as well as major cultural, social and political changes (language-external factors). Although there are some minor disagreement for the division,[2] the

---

[2] Different scholars often put the boundaries in slightly different places. According to Culpeper (1997: 11), for example, Early ModE spans the years 1500 to about 1750, and Late ModE spans the remaining years. The Norman Conquest of the year 1066 is often regarded as the dividing point between OE and ME.

following is generally accepted as the chronological division of English (Fisiak 1995: 24-25, Barber 1993: 39):[3]

Table 2.1 Chronological Division of English

Old English (OE)	Early OE	(c.[4] 450 - 900)
	Late OE	(900 - 1100)
Middle English (ME)	Early ME	(1100 - 1300)
	Late ME	(1300 - 1500)
Modern English (ModE)	Early ModE	(1500 - 1650)
	Late ModE	(1650 - 1800)
Present-day English (PDE)	(1800 - Today)[5]	

The division between OE and ME is based on both the internal and external changes of English. Internally, at the end of the OE period the vowels in word-final unstressed syllables were all reduced into <e>, which again caused the weakening of complex inflectional system of English. Externally, with the Norman Conquest (1066) and its aftermath, OE evolves into ME. The Norman Conquest is a political incident by which England became to be governed by French-speaking Norman kings and nobles. As a consequence, English was strongly influenced by French and adopted a

---

[3] The terms like Old English, Middle English and Modern (or New) English were established by the late-19th-century scholars Henry Sweet and Julius Zupitza.

[4] Here, 'c' is the abbreviation of Latin *circā* meaning 'about, around, roughly'. This means that we do not know or cannot determine the exact time of the beginning of the English language. It began the life of an independent language roughly in the middle of the 5th century.

[5] The chronology of PDE as from 1800 to today might give the impression that no change occurred after the 19th century, which is not the case at all. English is still changing. It is not fixed.

huge amount of French words.

The beginning of ModE began with the introduction of printing at the later part of the 15th century (exactly, in 1476) and the English Renaissance of the 16th century. Internally, the weakened vowel of the word-final syllables mostly disappeared in this period, so English lost most of its inflections.

The start of PDE roughly corresponds to the time of the American Revolution at the end of the 18th century. There was no particular notable internal change between ModE and PDE.

2.4. Changes in English

When we look at the following short passages (Texts 1-4), which represent the four different periods of the history of English, we can easily notice how dramatically English has changed. The passages are all from the Bible, the parable of the Prodigal Son (*Gospel of Luke*; Chapter 15, Verses 11-17):[6]

[Text 1: from Old English]
   11. Sōðlīce sum man hæfde[7] twēgen suna. 12. Þā cwæð se gingra tō his fæder, "Fæder, syle mē mīnne dǣl mīnre ǣhte þe mē tō gebyreþ."

---

6) Barber (1993: 33-38) also quotes the passages on the story of the Prodigal Son (Verses 25-32) from the four different periods.

7) We will see later that the letter <æ> (called "ash") is the combination of <a> and <e>, and <Æ> is its capital letter (i.e. a+e=æ, A+E=Æ). But these two letters <æ> and <Æ> disappeared from English spellings in the ME period. Now the letter <a> represents [a] for some words (e.g. *f<u>a</u>r*) and [æ] for others (e.g. *f<u>a</u>t*).

þā dǣlde hē him his ǣhta. 13. Ða æfter fēawum dagum ealle his þing gegaderode se gingra sunu and fērde wræclīe on feorlen rīce and forspilde þǣr his ǣhta, lybbende on his gǣlsan. 14. Ðā hē hȳ hæfde ealle āmyrrede, þā wearð mycel hunger on þām rīce and hē wearð wǣdla. 15. Þā fērde hē and folgode ānum burshsittendum men þæs rīces; ðā sende hē hine tō his tūne þæt hē hēolde his swīn. 16. Ða gewilnode hē his wambe gefyllan of þām bēancoddum þe ðā swȳn ǣton, and him man ne sealde. 17. Þā beþōhte hē hine and cwæð, "Ēalā hū fela yrðlinga on mīnes fæder hūse hlāf genōhne habbað, and ic hēr on hungre forwuðe! ..."

This text is from OE, more specifically from the main dialect of OE, West Saxon. This is one part of the translation of the New Testament by Ælfric (c. 950 - c. 1010), the greatest prose writer of the OE period.[8] So this passage is written in the English of the 10th century. It will not look like (a form of) English at all to non-specialists in this field. It is nearly impossible for even an English native speaker to read this passage without special training. So we need the translation of the passage to understand it. The following is the word-for-word translation and Text 4 is the PDE translation:

11. Sōðlīce sum   man hæfde twēgen suna. 12. Þā   cwæð se
    Truly   a-certain man had   two   sons.   Then said   the

---

8) Ælfric of Eynsham (c. 950 - c. 1010) was one of the most learned scholars of late Anglo-Saxon England and a prolific and elegant writer of vernacular prose whose works were widely read in his own time. (Lapidge *et al.* 1999: 8)

gingra   tō his fæder, "Fæder, syle mē mīnne dǣl   mīnre
younger to his father, "Father, give me my   share of-my

ǣhte   þe mē tō gebyreþ." Þā   dǣlde   hē him his ǣhta.
property, that me to belongs." Then divided he him his property.

13. Ða   æfter fēawum dagum ealle his þing gegaderode se gingra
    Then after a-few   days   all his thing gathered   the younger

sunu and fērde wrǣclīe on feorlen rīce   and forspilde þǣr his
son and went abroad to distant kingdom and wasted   there his

ǣhta,   lybbende on his gǣlsan. 14. Ðā   hē hȳ   hæfde ealle
property, living in his luxury.   When he them had   all

āmyrrede, þā wearð   mycel hunger on þām rīce   and
wasted,   then happened a-great famine in that kingdom and

hē wearð   wǣdla. 15. Þā   fērde hē and folgode ānum
he became   poor.   Then went he and followed one

burhsittendum men þæs rīces;   ðā sende hē hine tō his
city-dwelling man of-this kingdom then sent he him to his

tūne   þæt   hē hēolde his swin. 16. Ða   gewilnode hē his
estate so-that he kept his pigs.   Then desired   he his

wambe   gefyllan of   þām bēancoddum   þe   ðā   swȳn ǣton,
stomach filled   with those bean-pods   that those pigs ate,

and him man ne   sealde. 17. Þā   beþōhte   hē hine and cwæð,
and him man not(hing) gave.   Then bethought he him and said,

"Ĕalā hū   fela yrðlinga on mīnes fæder   hūse hlāf genōhne
"Alas! how many laborers in my   father's house bread enough

habbað, and ic hēr on hungre forwuðe! ..."
have,   and I   here in hunger perish! ..."

This passage clearly shows that English has greatly changed since the 10th century when it was written. It is beyond our purpose to read and understand this passage accurately.9) Suffice it to say that the English language spoken roughly from the 5th century to the 11th century was quite different from the English we hear everyday. It employed such spellings as are now obsolete, like <ð>, <þ>, <Ð>, <æ> and <Æ>.10) To represent the vowel

---

9) So the detailed morphological and grammatical accounts of the passage are not given here. This book is not to steer students to read and understand OE and ME texts in its original. But I want you to try to understand the English texts written after the Early ModE period, since the most valuable literary works in English, e.g. Shakespeare's plays, appeared in and after this period.

10) <ð> (called "thorn") and <þ> (called "eth") are the spellings corresponding to the present-day <th>, which have the pronunciations of either [ð] or [θ]. The two letters could be used interchangeably. And <Ð> is the capital letter of <ð> or <þ>. But all these letters disappeared from English roughly at the same time of the disappearance of <æ> and <Æ>. Now [ð] and [æ] are found in the inventory

length, the macron was adopted, as in <ā>, <ē>, <ī>, <ō> and <ū>.[11] And a lot of words, such as *sōðlīce* 'truly', *cwæð* 'said' and others, are not used any more. Word order was quite different. Here we see three different types of word order; different arrangements of Subject-Verb-Object. Some clauses have the normal present-day order S-V-O, as in *a-certain man had two sons*. But some have the order (Adv)-V-S(-O), as in *Then said the younger to his father*. This order often occurs when the clause begins with an adverbial expression, especially adverbs like *þā* 'then' (and *þær* 'there'). Yet other clauses have the order S-O-V, as in *When he them had all wasted*. This order occurs mostly in subordinate clauses, opened by such conjunctions as *þā* 'when'.

Let us jump to the ME period, skipping several hundred years.

[Text 2: from Middle English]

11. A man hadde twei sones. 12. And the yonger of hem seide to the fadir, "Fadir, yiue me the porcioun of catel that fallith to me." And he departide to hem the catel. 13. And not aftir many daies, whanne alle thingis weren gederid togider, the yonger sone wente forth in pilgrymage in to a fer cuntre; and there he wastide hise goodis in lyuynge lecherously. 14. And aftir that he hadde endid alle thingis, a strong hungre was maad in that cuntre, and he bigan to haue nede. 15. And he wente, and drough hym to oon of the citeseyns of that cuntre. And he sente hym in to his toun, to fede swyn. 16. And he coueitide to fille his

---

of English phonetic alphabets.
11) A macron is a diacritical mark placed above a vowel to indicate a long sound or phonetic value in pronunciation.

wombe of the coddis that the hoggis eeten, and no man yaf hym. 17. And he turnede ayen to hym silf, and seide, "Hou many hirid men in my fadir hous han plente of looues; and Y perische here thorough hungir. ..."

The above passage, the same part of the Bible (the parable of the Prodigal Son), is written in ME. It is from the translation of the Bible by John Wycliffe (1330-1384)[12] or one of his followers in the 1380s. So this is a sample of the 14th century English. It looks more familiar to us than the previous OE text. The English of the 14th century is easier to understand for the contemporary English reader, but still requires a certain amount of philological training.[13] Here we can see that the spellings such as <ð>, <þ>, <Ð>, <æ> and <Æ> are all gone and that the macron showing the vowel length also disappeared. Thus the spellings are not much strange to us. Nevertheless, it is not easily read and understood because the spellings of many words have changed since then and it still contains some words which are not used any more. However, if we go to

---

[12] **John Wycliffe** was born around the year 1330, probably at Wycliffe, near Richmond in North Riding of Yorkshire and died in 1384. He was the first person who translated the entire Bible into English. His name is sometimes written as **Wyclif**.

[13] Philology, derived from the Greek φιλολογία (*philologia*, from the terms φίλος *philos* meaning "loved, beloved, dear, friend" and λόγος *logos* "word, articulation, reason") is a branch of the human sciences dealing with language and literature, specifically a literary canon, combining aspects of grammar, rhetoric, historical linguistics (etymology and language change), interpretation of authors, textual criticism and the critical traditions associated with a given language. ("Philology" In *Wikipedia*. Retrieved July 31, 2008)

the next stage, i.e. the Early ModE period, the situation is much improved.

[Text 3: from Early Modern English]

11. A certaine man had two sonnes: 12. And the yonger of them said to his father, Father, giue me the portion of goods that falleth to me. And he diuided vnto them his liuing. 13. And not many dayes after, the yonger sonne gathered al together, and tooke his iourney into a farre countrey, and there wasted his substance with riotous liuing. 14. And when he had spent all, there arose a mighty famine in that land, and he beganne to be in want. 15. And he went and ioyned himselfe to a citizen of that countrey, and he sent him into his fields to feed swine. 16. And he would faine haue filled his belly with the huskes that the swine did eate: and no man gaue vnto him. 17. And when he came to himselfe, he said, How many hired seruants of my fathers haue bread inough and to spare and I perish with hunger ...

The above passage is from the King James Bible,[14] published in 1611. This stage of English is not much different from PDE, so we have no great difficulty in understanding this passage. Nevertheless, we can find several different points when we compare the above passage with Text 4. For example, the letters <u> and <v> were not used to distinguish vowel from consonant. <V> was always used at the beginning of a word, irrespective of whether it is a vowel or a consonant, and <u> was used elsewhere, as we can see in such words as *v̱nto* (cf. *u̱nto*), *giu̱e / gau̱e* (cf. *giv̱e / gav̱e*),

---

[14] This is an English translation of the Bible from Hebrew and Greek, published in 1611, under the auspices of King James I. It is also called the *Authorized Version*.

diuided (cf. *divided*), *liuing* (cf. *living*) and *seruants* (cf. *servants*). The use of <v> initially and <u> elsewhere was a printer's convention, which in England lasted from after the introduction of printing until about 1630. Before that, i.e. at the time of hand-written manuscripts the two letters were used indiscriminately (Barber 1993: 36). The passage also uses <i> instead of <j>, as in *iourney* (cf. *journey*) and *ioyned* (cf. *joined*). The letter <j> was in fact merely a decorative variant of <i>, so they could be used indiscriminately. The modern vowel-consonant distinction in their use was not established until about 1630. Some words contain an unnecessary word-final <e>, as in *certaine* 'certain', *sonne* 'son', *departide* 'departed', *againe* 'again', *hee* 'he' and *eate* 'eat'. And we can see the now obsolete verb ending -(*e*)*th*, as in *falleth*, which was supplanted by the -(*e*)*s* ending (cf. *falls*).[15] Notwithstanding, we can read and understand this passage without much difficulty. As a matter of fact, this period corresponds to the Shakespeare times and the beginning stage of the 'real' English literature. Therefore, we need to have a good knowledge on the English of this period.

The next passage is written in PDE:[16]

---

[15] The -(*e*)*s* ending was introduced from Old Norse, which was the language of the Vikings and the ancestor of Modern Northern Germanic languages like Danish, Swedish and Norwegian. The replacement of -(*e*)*th* by -(*e*)*s* has been dealt with in numerous studies, notably, e.g. Nevalainen and Raumolin-Brunberg (2003). This change was one long process, beginning in the north in the 10th century and ending in the most resistant forms *hath* and *doth* in Late ModE.

[16] This passage is from Good News Bible.

[Text 4: from Present-day English]

11. And he said, "There was a man who had two sons; 12. and the younger of them said to his father, 'Father, give me the share of property that falls to me.' And he divided his living between them. 13. Not many days later, the younger son gathered all he had and took his journey into a far country, and there he squandered his property in loose living. 14. And when he had spent everything, a great famine arose in that country, and he began to be in want. 15. So he went and joined himself to one of the citizens of that country, who sent him into his fields to feed swine. 16. And he would gladly have fed on the pods that the swine ate; and no one gave him anything. 17. But when he came to himself he said, 'How many of my father's hired servants have bread enough and to spare, but I perish here with hunger! ...

Through the glimpse of the Englishes from four different periods, we can easily notice that English has changed enormously in the past thousand years. "New words have appeared, and some old ones disappeared. Words have changed in meaning. The grammatical endings of words have changed, and many such endings have disappeared from the language. ... There have been changes in word order. ... Pronunciation has changed. Taken all together, these changes add up to a major transformation of the language" (Barber 1993: 38).

In particular, the changes between OE and ME were dramatic and radical, reshaping the English language. We will see in the next chapters that it is mainly due to the extreme changes of the English society at that time. This also means that the history of a language is inalienable to the history of the people who speak the language and to the history of the society in which it is spoken. This is why we should pay attention to the external history of a language as well as its internal history.

2.5. English is Still Changing

We saw that English has undergone a lot of changes over the centuries. English is still changing. By and large, language change is very slow and gradual, so it is not easily noticeable. Nevertheless, we can observe changes occurring even in present-day languages when we compare the present state with the one of a hundred or so ago.

Let us take some examples showing that English is still undergoing changes. Lexical change, i.e. change in words, is the most common and universal in every language. Thus, some words are disappearing and others are entering the new word stock. Old words go and new words come. For example, the words given below are all recent entries to English vocabulary:[17]

- *Mouse potato*: somebody always at computer, i.e. somebody who spends an excessive amount of time sitting at a computer. This word is from *couch potato* meaning a lazy television viewer, i.e. an inactive person who spends too much time sitting watching television.
- *Supersize*: extremely large or enormous. It is also written as *super-size* or *super-sized*. It seems that this word is from the fast food industry,

---

[17] For the newly-appearing English words, consult such websites as www.onelook.com or www.wordspy.com.

e.g. *a supersize(d) hamburger*.

- *Sandwich generation*: a generation of people who give care to their children and their parents at the same time.
- *Text messaging*: sending short text messages from a mobile phone to other mobile phone users using the SMS standard.
- *Drama queen*: a melodramatic person, i.e. somebody who likes to make a drama out of a situation by acting in an emotional way.
- *Soul patch*: a small patch of facial hair just below the lower lip and above the chin. It came to prominence in the 1950s and 1960s and was a style popular with beatniks and jazz artists. Prior to this period it was referred to as a *small beard*.
- *Manga*: Japanese comic books or cartoons, i.e. a Japanese style of comic books or animated cartoons, often very violent or erotic. It is from Japanese (*man* "indiscriminate" + *ga* "picture").
- *Ringtone*: the sound made by a telephone when ringing, especially the customizable tone of a mobile phone.
- *Euro-Sceptic* (Culpeper 1997: 11): a person who is sceptical of increasing the powers of the European Union, and wishes to preserve national sovereignty.
- *Grunge* (Culpeper 1997: 11): a sub-genre of alternative music, originating from Seattle, Washington, which melds punk and metal.

Merriam-Webster has added more than 100 new entries to its 2008 edition of the *Collegiate Dictionary*. A Korean word, *soju*, which is a Korean vodka distilled from rice, was included. Here are more of the new entries, along with the year in which Merriam-Webster first found them used in an English-language publication (AP News by Stephanie Reitz; July 8, 2008):

- *Air quotes* (1989): gesture made by raising and flexing the index and middle fingers of both hands, used to call attention to a spoken word or expression.
- *Dark energy* (1998): hypothetical form of energy that produces a force that opposes gravity and is thought to cause the accelerating expansion of the universe.
- *Dirty bomb* (1956): bomb designed to release radioactive material.
- *Dwarf planet* (1993): celestial body that orbits the sun and has a spherical shape, but is too small to disturb other objects from its orbit.
- *Edamame* (1951): immature green soybeans, usually in the pod.
- *Fanboy* (1919): boy who is an enthusiastic devotee, such as of comics or movies.
- *Infinity pool* (1992): outdoor swimming pool with an edge over which water flows into a trough, but seems to flow into the horizon.
- *Jukebox musical* (1993): musical that features popular songs from the past.
- *Kiteboarding* (1996): the sport of riding on a small surfboard propelled across water by a large kite, to which the rider is harnessed.
- *Malware* (1990): software designed to interfere with a computer's normal functioning.
- *Mental health day* (1971): day that an employee takes off from work to relieve stress or renew vitality.
- *Mondegreen* (1954): word or phrase that results from a mishearing of

something said or sung. From the mishearing in a Scottish ballad of "laid him on the green" as "Lady Mondegreen."

- *Netroots* (2003): grassroots political activists who communicate via the Internet, especially by blogs.
- *Norovirus* (2002): any of a genus of small round single-stranded RNA viruses; specifically, Norwalk virus.
- *Pescatarian* (1993): vegetarian whose diet includes fish.
- *Phytonutrient* (1994): bioactive, plant-derived compound (as resveratrol) associated with positive health effects.
- *Pretexting* (1992): presenting oneself as someone else to obtain private information.
- *Prosecco* (1881): a dry Italian sparkling wine.
- *Racino* (1995): racetrack at which slot machines are available for gamblers.
- *Soju* (1978): a Korean vodka distilled from rice.
- *Subprime* (1995) 1: having or being an interest rate that is higher than a prime rate and is extended especially to low-income borrowers; 2: extending or obtaining a subprime loan.
- *Supercross* (1983): motorcycle race held in a stadium on a dirt track having hairpin turns and high jumps.
- *Texas Hold 'em* (1995): Poker in which each player is dealt two cards face down and all players share five cards dealt face-up.
- *Webinar* (1998): live, online educational presentation during which participating viewers can submit questions and comments.
- *Wing nut* (c. 1900): Slang: one who advocates extreme measures or changes; radical.[18]

Another tendency observed in the development of contemporary English lexicon is the wide use of the so-called '*e*-terms' or 'Netspeak', which reflects the enormous burgeoning of various '*e*-activities' (*e*-mail, *e*-commerce, *e*-business, *e*-training, etc.). The following is the sample list from Svartvik and Leech (2006: 220):

Table 2.1 '*E*-terms'

Coinages of new words	*blog* (< *Web log*), *geek, nerd, netiquette*
Creating new compounds	*download, inbox, mailbomb, voicemail*
Using specialized prefixes such as *e*- ('electronic'), *cyber*-, and *multi*-, and suffixes like -*ware*	*e-mail, e-cash, e-commerce, e-courses, e-training*
	cyberspace, cyber-café, cyber-culture
	multi-tasking, multi-user
	software, courseware, firmware, freeware, spyware
Words converted from one class to another	*bookmark, boot, e-mail, flame, messag(ing), text(ing)*: all from nouns to verbs
New metaphorical uses of existing words	*browse, bug, chat, client, cookie, dump, gateway, hack, link, menu, portal, spam, surf, virus, wizard*
Abbreviations, alphabetism and acronyms	*Gb* (gigabyte), *IP* (Internet protocol), *FAQ* (Frequently asked questions), *ROM* (read-only memory), *MUD* (Multi-User Dimension)

Change is happening in pronunciation, too.[19] For example, according to

---

18) Bauer (2002: 56) also gives many more newly-coined English words like *spam, user-friendly, the net, URL, couch potato, downsizing, DVD, ethnic cleansing, flat white, eco-terrorism, smoke-free, spin doctor, stalker, superbug, tough love, tree-hugging*, etc. If you are not familiar with the meaning of some words, consult any good dictionary of neologisms or the Internet OneLook Dictionary (www.onelook.com).

Stewart (2003), there is a tendency in present-day colloquial English to stress unimportant words (i.e. functional words like prepositions, conjunctions or pronouns, which are not stressed in a normal situation) without any intention to emphasize or bring them into contrastive focus:

(1) a. We are AT the McEwan Centre.
   b. The music OF the choral
   c. They are involved IN the scandal.
(2) The President AND his advisors are discussing the issue.
(3) a. SHE said that the estimated loss was $2 million.
   b. HE was informed after the event. (Stewart 2003: 57)

Morphological and syntactic changes are also observed. There are so many examples showing the still going-on morphological and syntactic changes. According to Mair and Leech (2006: 320), we can make up a list of changes suspected to be going on in present-day standard English, as follows:

① a tendency to regularize irregular morphology
   (e.g. *dreamt* → *dreamed*)

② use of the "mandative" subjunctive, probably inspired by formal US usage (e.g. *We demand that she take part in the meeting.*)

---

19) For other changes in PDE pronunciation, refer to Bauer (1994: 93-130, 2002: 56-57) and Stewart (2003).

③ elimination of *shall* as a future marker in the first person[20]

④ development of new, auxiliary-like uses of certain lexical verbs (e.g. *got to* (> *gotta, gorra*),[21] *want to* (> *wanna*) - *The way you look, you wanna see a doctor soon.*)[22]

⑤ extension of the progressive to new constructions, e.g. modal passive progressive, present perfect passive progressive, and past perfect passive progressive (e.g. *The road would not be being built / has not been being built / had not been being built before the general elections.*)[23]

⑥ increase in the number and types of multi-word verbs (e.g. *have/take/give a ride*, etc.)

⑦ placement of frequency adverbs before auxiliary verbs (even if no emphasis is intended - e.g. *I never have said so.*)

---

20) In the past, the future tense in English was formed with *shall* in the first person (*I shall go, We shall go*) and *will* in the second and third persons (*You will go, Charlie will go, They will go*). In modern English, it is much more common to use *will* for all three persons (*I will go*, etc.), although some people still keep the difference between *shall* and *will*. (*Cambridge International Dictionary of English* 1995: 1308, *shall*)

21) This form was from *have got to* through *got to*.

22) Similarly, *be going to* also underwent changes typical of auxiliaries such as phonological reduction. The three morphemes *go+ing+to* could be reduced into one in the development of *gonna*.

23) For the extension of the progressive to new constructions, see Lee (1999a: Chapter 13, 1999b).

⑧ *do*-support for *have* (e.g. *Have you any money?* and *No, I haven't any money.* → *<u>Do</u> you have any money? (or Have you got any money?)* and *No, I <u>don't</u> have any money. (or No, I haven't got any money.)*)24)

⑨ demise of the inflected form *whom*25)

⑩ increasing use of *less* instead of *fewer* with countable nouns (e.g. *For the time being the <u>less</u> people who know about it at this stage the better* (Follett, J. 1990. *Torus*. London: Methuen, 36-7, quoted from Bauer (2002: 57))26)

⑪ spread of the *s*-genitive to non-human nouns (e.g. *the book's cover*, cf. *of*-genitive)27)

---

24) The main verb *have* in British English used to be treated like an auxiliary Verb, so it moved to the front in the interrogative and was positioned just before *not* or *n't* in the negative, as in *<u>Have</u> you a pen?* or *I <u>haven't</u> any milk*. But American English treats *have* as a main verb, so *do*-support is obligatory in the interrogative and negative, like *<u>Do</u> you have a pen?* or *I <u>don't</u> have any milk*. The middle construction using the supportive verb *got*, like *<u>Have</u> you <u>got</u> a pen?* or *I <u>haven't</u> got any milk*, is found in both varieties, but less in American English than British English.
25) On the Dwindling of *Whom*, see Lee (2009).
26) *More* can be used with both countable and non-countable nouns, as in *The doctors can't cope with any <u>more</u> <u>patients</u>*. vs. *She kept on asking if I wanted <u>more</u> <u>food</u>*. Yet their respective opposites have different forms *fewer* vs. *less*, as in *<u>fewer</u> patients* vs. *<u>less</u> food*. "Probably because you could use *more* in either kind of construction, the feeling has arisen that there should be a single word for the opposite of *more* on all occasions. The words that has been chosen is *less*." (Bauer 2002: 57)
27) An increase in the use of the *s*-genitive, at the expense of the corresponding *of*-phrase, is a trend towards greater density of information (i.e. towards packing

⑫ omission of the definite article in certain environment
   (e.g. (*the*) *renowned Nobel laureate Derak Walcott*)

⑬ "singular" *they*[28] (e.g. *Everyone / Everybody came in their car.*)[29][30]

---

more information into a smaller number of words).

28) For the so-called singular or epicene *they*, see Lee (2006, 2007: Chapter 7). Lee (2006) is concerned with the so-called 'generic' or 'epicene' pronoun *he* and its alternative usages. Especially, an analysis was done to see if there is any change in the attitudes toward this sex-biased English pronominal convention, what alternative usages have been proposed, which ones are actually employed by English native speakers, and what the preference among the alternatives is. The analysis was carried out in two ways; one was to review the descriptions of the topic in English handbooks and grammar books, and the other was to take a test for the actual usages by English native speakers. Through the analysis, it was found that the 'generic' *he* cannot be tolerated any more and should be avoided. The singular *they* was proved to be the best recommended alternative and the *he or she* form was the next preferred alternative. In particular, the use of the singular *they* was found to be influenced by structural factors. For example, it was preferred when the antecedent was an indefinite pronoun, or when it appears in an independent clause from the antecedent.

29) The singular *they* has its own reflexive pronoun *themself*, which occurred since the 1970s (e.g. *Someone has hurt themself. Anyone who wants a car like mine can buy one themself*).

30) English shows a tendency to become a more democratic language. The use of the singular *they* is a representative example, since the main reason for the use is to avoid the sexist generic *he*. The tendency to take an egalitarian position is also found when we try to eliminate sexist words or expressions, like *-man* words (e.g. *man > human being, human, person; businessman > business person, executive, manager; fireman > fire-fighter; foreman > supervisor; juryman > juror; mailman/postman > mail/letter carrier/deliverer; policeman > police officer; salesman > salesperson*, etc.) and other male/female terms (e.g. *housewife > housemaker; steward(ess) > flight attendant; forefathers > ancestors/forebears*. etc.).

⑭ *like, same as* and *immediately* used as conjunctions (e.g. *It looks <u>like</u> I'm going to be in the office until late tonight, I need some time to myself, <u>same as</u> (=like) anybody else (does), <u>Immediately</u> (=As soon as) she'd gone, the boys started to mess about.*)

⑮ a tendency towards analytical comparatives and superlatives (e.g. *politer* → *more polite, cf. synthetic* comparatives and superlatives)[31]

⑯ expansion of usage of the objective case

As another example of morphological change, there is a drift in English personal pronouns towards objective forms in subjective (or nominative) contexts. That is to say, the objective case can be used instead of the expected subjective case, while the subjective case was the only choice formerly. Subject complement positions ((4) and (5)), elliptical constructions without a finite verb (6), clauses of comparison (7), coordinated nominal subjects (8) all show this tendency, as follows:

---

31) It is a rule that monosyllabic adjectives generally add the affix *-er* for the comparative and *-est* for the superlative (synthetic forms), while adjectives with three or more syllables add the word *more* for the comparative and the word *most* for the superlative (analytical or periphrastic forms). But there is usage vacillation between synthetic and analytical comparison for disyllabic adjectives. According to Mair and Leech (2006: 320) and Bauer (1994: 51-61), there has been an increase in the use of analytical comparison for disyllabic adjectives, although there are a few exceptional cases (For example, disyllabic adjectives ending in *-le* take suffixed synthetic comparison only, as in *humbler*, rather than *more humble.).

(4) a. 'That's *her*', I said. (Cary, *The Horse's Mouth*: 369)

　b. 'I knew that would be *us*.'

　　(Bowen, *The House in Paris*: 60)

(5) a. ... I wanted to become *her*.

　　(Lessing, *The Golden Notebook*: 572)

　b. When he was warned, I put myself back to sleep, and instantly I was the old man, the old man had became *me* ...

　　(Lessing, *The Golden Notebook*: 544)

(6) a. 'Tired?' 'Not *me*.' (Sillitoe, *A Start in Life*: 25)

　b. 'Who's to stop it - *us*?' (Lessing, *The Golden Notebook*: 172)

(7) a. 'When you're as old as *me*, you begin to lose your identity.'

　　(Murdoch, *Flight from the Enchanter*: 115)

　b. 'We keep forgetting that George is older than *us* ...'

　　(Lessing, *The Golden Notebook*: 129)

(8) a. 'Mr. Jeavens and *me* are on the same warden-post,' he said.

　　(Powell, *The Soldier's Art*: 157)

　b. 'On top, when Roger and *me* went on - he stayed back.'

　　(Golding, *Lord of the Flies*: 139)

In the previous stage of English, the subjective case form was normal in the above constructions, as in *It is I, You are as old as I, Mr. Jeavens and I are on the same warden-post*.[32] However, the objective case form is expanding its usage, encroaching the subjective territory. There is a well-known early example of the replacement of the subjective form by the objective. The 2nd person pronoun *you* was objective originally, and its subjective form was *ye*. But the objective form *you* supplanted the

---

32) These are still accepted as formal usage.

subjective form *ye* completely in the Early ModE period. So there is no formal distinction in the 2nd person pronoun between subjective and objective. The examples given above indicate that a similar change is still going on in PDE.

We can observe the converse phenomenon to the case mismatch shown in (4)-(8), i.e. the use of the subjective case form in objective context, as follows:

(9) a. They join my friend and *I* for after-dinner drinks.
    (Sue Ashby, *The Observer*, 19 February 1984)
  b. It's difficult for my wife and *I* to find time.
    (Denison 1996: 293 (19a))

Redfern (1994) and Bauer (2002: 58) convincingly argues that *between you and I* should be accepted as good English.[33] Redfern's argument is based on eight years' efforts of collecting oral and written instances of the "wrong" pronoun in coordinate phrases. The following is a few of his examples which were actually heard around him:

---

33) If my observations are correct, native speakers of English - whether British or American, whether well or poorly educated - say *between you and I* and the like unless they have been schoolmastered into using *me* instead of *I*. (Redfern 1994: 188)

... most native speakers of English, unless they have been schooled to do otherwise, use *I* or another subject pronoun after a coordinator in phrases in object position. (Redfern 1994: 192)

(10) a. There is a brother between Mark and *I*.
 b. It was so nice for Nancy and *I* to go off together.
 c. The next step is for Jud, Jack and *I* to talk it over.
 d. ... and it would let you and *I* and other people know where to go to register.
 e. Thank you so much for taking care of Anne and *I* while we were in Clarion.
 f. They denied my wife and *I* an enjoyable visit.
 (Redfern 1994: 187, 188)

The following examples, quoted from Angermeyer and Singler (2003: 171-72, 174) and Johannessen (1998: 15), clearly show that this usage is not "simply illiterate", "substandard" or "inescapably a blunder."[34] It was employed by such celebrities as the US president and the British monarch:[35]

(11) a. if you're tired of being heartbroken when you go home at night and you want a spring in your step and a song in your heart, you give Al Gore and *I* a chance to bring America back. (Bill Clinton, 1992, *New York Times*, July 23, 1992)
 b. This has been a thrilling experience for Ron and *I*. (Tina Brown, former editor of Vanity Fair and the New Yorker, quoted in the

---

[34] For the (un)acceptability or (un)grammaticality of this usage, see *Merriam-Webster's Dictionary of English Usage* (1994), Redfern (1994), Angermeyer and Singler (2003: 171-76) and references cited there.

[35] "My impression of change in perceptions comes from talking to my students, nearly all of whom these days see a construction like *between you and I* as being more formal, and in some sense 'better' than *between you and me*." (Bauer 2002: 58)

New York Times, January 19, 2002)

c. It would not be right for either you or *I* to be where we planned to be on D-Day. (King George VI's reported comment to Winston Churchill)

d. It is a wonderful moment for my husband and *I* after nearly six months away to be met and escorted by ships of the Home Fleet. (Queen Elizabeth II, in 1954)

Furthermore, this usage is not a grammatical innovation introduced in the PDE period, but a historically deep-rooted one, since this phenomenon has "distinguishing ancestry", as follows:[36]

(12) a. Here's none but thee and *I*.
(Shakespeare, *2 Henry* VI; I, ii, 69)

b. It is an argument too deepe to be discussed between you and *I*.
(Delony, *Jacke of Newberie*, 1597)

c. What difference is between the Duke and *I*.
(Webster, *The White Devil*, 1612)

---

36) More examples are found in Angermeyer and Singler (2003: 174) and Jespersen (1909-49, Vol VII: 236-37, 273). Jespersen (1909-49, Vol VII: 236-37, 273) cites some two dozen sentences containing coordinate phrases in which a subject pronoun, usually *I*, occurs instead of the object pronoun which traditional grammar requires. He says that "the combination *between you and I* has been frequent from Elizabethan English to the present day, though *between you and me* may be found. According to Redfern (1994: 191), *The Oxford English Dictionary* (second edition) gives eleven examples of this type, the first of which, dated 1596, is a line from Shakespeare's *Merchant of Venice*: *All debts are cleerd betweene you and I.* (= *All debts are cleared between you and I.*)

Likewise, *whom*, which is objective, is being replaced by the subjective *who*, as follows (cf. ⑨ demise of the inflected form *whom*):

(13) a. *Who* do you love?   cf. *Whom* do you love?
  b. the man *who* I love   cf. the man *whom* I love
(14) a. Who is going to marry *who(m)*?
  b. Who said what to *who(m)*?
(15) a. A: You should give them away. B: To *who(m)*?
  b. A: I met a friend of yours on the bus. B: Oh, *who*?
  (Huddleston and Pullum 2002: 465)

Whom has been optionally replaceable by *who* in many common uses like the construction (13) since the Early ModE period.[37] Such examples as (14)-(15) are acceptable to (at least some) English native speakers without any resistance. These examples show that *whom* itself is disappearing from English.

⑰ an increasing tendency of singular concord with collective nouns

---

37) Look at the following examples from the famous literary masters;

  i. *Who* doth he [time] trot withal? (Shakespeare, *As You Like It* III.ii.304)
  ii. *Who* did that worthy Lord, my brother, single out of the Side-box to sup with him t'other night? (Farquhar, *The Beaux Strategem*, 1707)
  iii. There is a German *who* he recommends for a sober man and very capable. (Anne Hatton, *Letter*, 1695)
  iv. Why, look'ee here! Do you know *who* this belongs to?
    (Dickens, *David Copperfield* 2.277, 1847)

Bauer (1994, 2002) reports other grammatical changes that are still going on. According to him (1994: 61-66), there is an increasing tendency of singular concord with collective nouns (e.g. *industry, press, association, the right,* etc. cf. *The club/party is aware of the problem.*).38)

⑱ the measure noun *amount* used with countable nouns

Similar to the increasing use of *less* instead of *fewer* with countable nouns, mentioned above in ⑩, the measure noun *amount* is regularly used with countable nouns, "especially in speech and especially by younger speakers", as follows:39)

(16) a. There would be just the right *amount* of *people* on the street (Eric van Lustbader, *French Kiss*. London, etc.: Grafton, 1989: 111)
 b. The faceplate came off easily, exposing a circuit board and an amazing *amount* of small *wires*. (Stephen Coonts, *Final Flight*. New York, etc.: Doubleday, 1988: 225)
 c. Digital reception increases the *amount* of *calls* that can be made

---

38) "... although it is not possible to predict with any accuracy whether singular or plural concord will be used on any given occasion, or even how much singular concord will be used in any given text, there appears to be a general trend for singular concord to increase over time." (Bauer 1994: 63). See also Aremo (2005), who examines some uses of the singular collective nouns *congress, council, government, management, parliament* and *senate* in contemporary English.
39) Generally, changes in the grammar of English seem to come from the spoken language, then gradually spread into the written language. This process is called 'colloquialism' (Svartvik and Leech 2006: 207-9) or 'colloquialization' (Mair and Leech 2006: 331-3).

on the cellular network stations, lowering the chance of overloads on the system. (*Contact*, Wellington, New Zealand, 14 Jan 93, p. 10: Cellular phone network spreads)(Bauer 2002: 57)

⑲ some changes observed in relative clauses

Some changes are observed in relative clauses, too (Bauer 1994: 66-83, Mair and Leech 2006: 334-6). To begin with, there is a tendency to use fewer *wh*-relatives with non-human antecedents. That is, instead of such construction as *the Italian restaurant <u>which</u> I mentioned in my letter*, the relative marker *that* or an absence of any relative marker, which is called a zero relative, is preferred. On the other hand, *that* tends to be avoided being used with human antecedents. And zero relatives (e.g. *the Italian restaurant ø I mentioned in my letter*) and preposition stranding (e.g. *the bag ø I put my book <u>in</u>*),[40] which are both typical of less formal styles and spoken forms, are increasing, especially in American English. The most notable change in English relativization is that agreement for human-ness

---

40) For the origin and the cause(s) of preposition stranding in English, see Lee (2005, 2007: Chapter 9). Lee (2005) is an investigation of the direct relationship between morphological richness and the preposition-stranding (im)possibility. The (im)possibility in preposition stranding or in pied-piping of a preposition is directly related to the richness of morphological case. The basic assumption is that, the richer the morphology of a language is, the less a preposition can be stranded. It is because the function of a preposition is assumed to license the morphological case of its object, besides assigning the abstract case. The article convinces us that the loss or weakening of morphological cases is at least a prerequisite and necessary condition for preposition stranding, even if it is not proved be the necessary and sufficient condition for it.

between an antecedent noun and the relative marker may be becoming less fixed, as follows:[41]

(17) a. These men and women ... bore *children* for *which* they had to provide (Ludlum, Robert, *The Apocalypse Watch*. London: HarperCollins 1995: 401)
 b. The First National *customers which* had borrowed most heavily ... were forced under. (Erdman, Paul, *The Panic of '89*. London: Sphere. 1986: 14)
 c. "There are currently 19 Maori *students* doing post-graduate work, of *which* 18 are women," said Kathy. (*VUW Equal Employment Opportunities News*, Number 14, September 1993: 2) (Bauer 2002: 58)

Here we should be careful in drawing the conclusion that all these (new) usages are examples of language change. There is another possibility that these are mere variant forms, being used along with the standard forms and being acceptable to only a certain group of people or a certain language community. In the latter case, the usages shown above might be disappearing without causing real and permanent changes in English. However, we repeat Bauer's (1994: 83) remarks that "at least some of the variation in the use of relatives does indicate change."

---

[41] "This pattern, ... , is of considerable antiquity, *which* being frequent with human antecedents until the late seventeenth century (consider the King James Bible's *Our father, which art in Heaven*) (Romaine 1982: 69). Again, it is not clear whether this pattern has always existed in non-standard forms and is being reintroduced as standard, or whether it has vanished in between times." (Bauer 1994: 78)

2.6. Reasons for the Study of the History of English

Let us ask ourselves why we should study the history of English. We, as speakers of English as a Foreign Language, have a lot of difficulty in learning and using PDE. So it may appear that we do not have extra time and energy to spend for the study of the history of English. Regrettably, the course of the History of the English Language is regarded as one of the most difficult and the least understood subjects among the major courses of the Department of English. The course is "perceived more and more as old-fashioned, traditional and even conservative when looked at side-by-side with new courses being proposed into the curriculum" (Buck 2003: 48). This perception is due to several reasons. The topics dealt with in the course were too specific in its coverage and too remote from the English we use everyday. Furthermore, we do not have suitable textbooks for the course.[42] We, educators of this course, are also responsible for the unpopularity of the History of the English Language course,[43] because we are not equipped with the broad knowledge on all stages and all areas of the development of English which is necessary to make the course an interdisciplinary field.

In spite of these problems and difficulties to overcome, there are several

---

42) For the critical assessment of the textbooks which have been used for the course, see Buck (2003: 46-47).

43) "..., the biggest challenge for us as educators is to attempt to define specifically what we believe are the goals of such a course, what skills or knowledge we want to be able to develop in our students, and how we wish our students to use this knowledge after they leave our classrooms." (Buck 2003: 46-47)

reasons for us to keep on studying the past stages of English, along with the purely academic purposes.[44] To begin with, the present state of English cannot be fully understood without the proper knowledge about its past.[45] To understand how things are, it is often helpful and sometimes necessary to know how they got to be that way, i.e. how they could reach the present state. This is true for languages, too. By investigating the history which is relevant to the present state of English, we can gain insight into PDE and are able to explain and understand the anomalies or irregularities found in PDE, which were mostly once regular patterns.[46] Not a few linguistic historians, including Fisiak (1995) and Rastall (2002), advocate this method of "English in a Historical Perspective". What will you say if you are asked such questions as the following?

① Why does the second person personal pronoun not have the number distinction (i.e. no formal difference between the singular *you* (e.g. *Be careful with that knife or you'll cut yourself*!) vs. the plural *you* (e.g.

---

44) I guess that most readers of this book are advanced students of the Department of English. After graduation they can be an English teacher or a person doing business with English-speaking people. Certainly, a certain amount of the knowledge on the history of English will be very useful and sometimes necessary for those purposes.
45) "The more we learn about where the language has been, how it is structured, how it is used, and how it is changing, the more we will be able to judge its present course and help to plan its future." (Crystal 2002: 296)
46) "It is possible, however, to look at PDE retrospectively in order to account for features of current spelling, phonology, grammar, lexicon, personal names, place names, fixed expressions and texts in relation to historical origins and development." (Rastall 2002: 28)

You could have killed yourselves.), unlike the pairs such as *I* vs. *we* or *he/she/it* vs. *they*?⁴⁷⁾

② Why does *you* have the same case form for the subjective and the objective? (e.g. *You are my beloved students.* vs. *I really love you.*)

③ Why does only the third person singular present form of the verb take an inflectional ending (i.e. -(*e*)*s* ending)?

④ Why does English have highly irregular plural forms of nouns? (e.g. *foot - feet, man - men, mouse - mice, goose - geese, tooth - teeth, woman - women, louse - lice; ox - oxen, child - children, brother-brethren* (cf. *brothers*); *sheep - sheep, deer - deer*; etc)

⑤ Why does English have such chaotic and unruly spellings? Do you know that the pronunciation of *gaol* is [dʒéil]?

⑥ Why does the subject - auxiliary inversion or the subject - main verb inversion occur in the following sentences, even when the sentences are not interrogative?

  — *Never* had I been so angry in all my life.
  — *Only* yesterday could I see him at last.

---

47) "There are special forms or phrases for the second person plural pronoun in varieties of spontaneous spoken English across the world. The forms are different from the second person singular *you*. For example, *youse* (Irish English, Northumberland/Tyneside), *y'all* (Southern US), *aay, yufela*, or phrases like *you ... together* (East Anglia), *all of you, you ones/'uns, you guys, you people*." (Kortmann 2006: 605)

- <u>Down</u> came the rain in torrents.
- <u>In</u> marched the soldiers.

There are so many questions like the ones given above that cannot be properly answered and understood without the knowledge about the past of English. The knowledge about the history of English will help us to understand and to answer these and many similar questions. "Knowledge of the history of English is no nostrum or panacea for curing all our linguistic ills, but it can at least alleviate some of the symptoms" (Pyles and Algeo 1993: 2). This is the first and probably the most important reason why we should study the history of English.

In spite of the need to seek for the explanation of contemporary usage in a historical light, we did not achieve this goal at the courses of the Department of English, since "most English-language courses, nowadays, are either concerned with developing a practical competence or with understanding the synchronic structure of English" (Rastall 2002: 31).[48] This situation is severely observed in the non-native environment, as at Korean universities. We, Korean professors, are forced to take such practical classes like TOEIC, English Composition, English Grammar, etc., as the major courses of the Department of English and, at the same time, are pressed to give up teaching so-called 'academic' subjects like the history of English.

---

48) "Pedagogically, it is better for students of English (native speakers or not) to be encouraged to observe, research and explain (from the direct experience of historical texts and the use of research tools such as historical dictionaries and histories of English) than to attempt to follow progressions of facts remote from their experience, or to concentrate exclusively on synchronic issues of variety, structure and usage." (Rastall 2002: 31)

Of course, it should be admitted that the course was taught too atomistically without the proper connection with contemporary English. So what matters is not the course itself but the teaching method for the course. In any case, for "English in Historical Perspective", the history of English should be taught, at least for the students of English major.

Secondly, "the knowledge of past stages of a language allows us to read and appreciate earlier literature in its original" (Fisiak 1995: 26). It is a greatly worrying situation that the students' interest in the literature or in the humanities has recently been weakening in Korea. However, we, as a student or a professor of the Department of English, need and should study at least the essential parts of English literature. To read English literature is one of the best ways of understanding the way of thinking of the people who use English as their mother tongue. As is often said, a language is the product of the culture of the society in which it is spoken. And literature can be a window through which we can see and taste the culture of that society. English literature has developed over the past several centuries, so the knowledge on the history of English is necessary to understand the original literary works written a long time ago. Consider the following passage from Shakespeare's masterpiece, *Hamlet* (Act I, Scene V, 1-10), probably written between 1599 and 1601:[49]

---

[49] *Hamlet* is a tragedy by William Shakespeare. The play, set in Denmark, recounts how Prince Hamlet exacts revenge on his uncle Claudius, who has murdered Hamlet's father, the King, and then taken the throne and married Hamlet's mother. The play vividly charts the course of real and feigned madness - from overwhelming grief to seething rage - and explores themes of treachery, revenge, incest and moral corruption. ("Hamlet" In *Wikipedia*. Retrieved July 31, 2008)

Enter Ghost *and* Hamlet

Ham. Whither wilt thou lead me? Speak, I'll go no further.

Ghost. Mark me.

Ham. I will.

Ghost. My hour is almost come

When O to sulph'rous and tormenting flames

Must render up myself.

Ham. Alas, poor ghost.

Ghost. Pity me not, but lend thy serious hearing

To what I shall unfold.

Ham. Speak, I am bound to hear.

Ghost. So art thou to revenge when thou shalt hear.

Ham. What?

Ghost. I am thy father's spirit,

Doom'd for a certain term to walk the night, ...

Even this short passage shows not a few lexical and grammatical differences between Early ModE and PDE. For example, ① the second person singular <th-> pronouns (i.e. *thou, thy/thine* and *thee*) are still used here. As early as the late 13th century, the second person plural forms (*ye, you, your*) began to be used with singular meaning in circumstances of politeness or formality. In imitation of the French use of *tu* and *vous*, the English historical plural forms were used in addressing a superior, whether by virtue of social status or age. For this reason, the singular form was regarded as an impolite and sometimes rude form, so people tried to avoid using the singular forms. But the <th-> forms are seen in this passage. ②

We can also see the obsolete present tense verbal ending for the second person (-(e)st > -(s)t > ø), as in *wilt* 'will' and *art* 'are'.50) ③ The imperative construction was different, too: *Pity me not* vs. *Do not pity me*. This reveals that the use of the 'dummy' auxiliary *do* was not obligatory for negation and interrogation at this time. Meanwhile, the positive statement could contain the auxiliary *do* without the meaning of emphasis. To put it bluntly, the use of the auxiliary *do* was completely optional in the Early ModE period. ④ The rather unrestrained deletion of (a) letter(s) in an unaccented syllable is also observed, as in *sulph'rous* (< *sulphurous*) and *Doom'd* (< *Doomed*).51) It is needless to say that the knowledge of these facts are necessary to understand the passage given above. The knowledge about the history of English can help to clarify the literature written in earlier periods.

Thirdly, if we study the history of English, we can be liberated from certain prejudices regarding English grammar. When we study English grammar, we tend to make a black and white decision on the grammaticality. Our concern is mainly about what is grammatical or what is ungrammatical. But there are a lot of phenomena which cannot be ascribed to fully grammatical (100%) or to fully ungrammatical (0%). In many cases, grammar is a matter of naturalness and gradience. Some expressions are more natural in this situation and others are in that context. It is mainly because English is changing. English is not fixed. It fluctuates continually, so the present situation is on the move to the further future change. Thus

---

50) The past tense also had an inflectional ending for the second person singular (-*e*(*st*)).
51) The use of an apostrophe means that there is/are (a) missing letter(s) in the position, as in *I'm* (< *I am*), *We'll* (< *We will*) and *they've* (< *they have*).

grammar is also changing, allowing the older usage and the new one at the same time. So variation occurs in many cases.

If we study the history of England, the English language, its literature and culture together, we can get the better understanding of the English-speaking community.[52]

---

[52] "The man who does not know some history is a man who loses one of the major dimensions of his humanity. History has made man what he is today, and to understand him one must know something of his past." (Bloomfield and Newmark 1963: 19)

The Pre-Old English Period (before 449)

3.1. Ancestor of English: Proto-Indo-European Language

Many languages share common words that are quite similar to each other in its spelling and sound. For example, English *father* resembles German *Vater*,[1] Dutch *vader*, Icelandic *faðir*, and Norwegian/Danish/Swedish *fader*. Some words in other languages, such as Latin *pater*, Spanish *padre*, Portuguese *pai*, Catalan *pare*, French *père*, Greek *patēr*, Sanskrit *pitar-* and Persian *pedar* are less similar to English *father*. The thing to note here is not only that the words look alike, but that there are regular correspondences. For example, some languages have the beginning sound [f], while others have [p] instead of [f]. The following table, from Barber (1993: 63, Table 3.4), shows more examples of the sound correspondence between [f] and [p]:

---

1) The letter <v> in German is sometimes the same sound as English <f>, as in *voll* 'full', *vier* 'four', *verbietan* 'forbid', and many others. However, there are exceptions like *vital* 'vital', *Votum* 'vote', *Vision* 'vision', etc.

Table 3.1 Similarities in Five Ancient Languages

Old English[2]	Gothic	Latin	Greek	Sanskrit
fæder ('father')	*fadar*	*pater*	*pater*	*pitar*
nefa ('nephew')	-	*nepos*	-	*napāt*
feor ('far')	*fairra*	-	*peraā*	*paras*
faran ('go, fare')	*faran*	*(ex-)perior*	*peraō*	*pr-*
full ('full')	*fulls*	*plēnus*	*plērēs*	*plūrna*
fearh ('pig')	-	*porcus*[3]	-	-
feþer[4] ('feather')	-	*penna*	*petron*	*patra-*
fell ('skin')	*fill*	*pellis*	*pella*	-

We can easily recognize that these words are closely related to each other.[5] This related group of words are generally called "cognates". The similarities found among cognates cannot be ascribed to coincidences or to the result of borrowing through contact with speakers of other languages, because the number is numerous and the differences are systematic. The only plausible explanation is that the cognate words developed over varying intervals of time as a result of the gradual divergence of the languages. This is what is meant when we say that historically a language derives from another language, and that particular words derive from earlier words.

---

2) English lost such words as *faran*, *fearh* and *fell*.

3) The etymological origin of the word *pork* 'the flesh of a pig' is dated back to this word. That is, *pork* was from Old French *porc* 'pig', again from Latin *porcus*.

4) OE <þ> is the spelling corresponding to the present-day <th> and has the pronunciation of either [ð] or [θ].

5) When two or more languages have evolved from some earlier single language, we say that they are **related**. "Such correspondences arise when *related* languages are produced by divergent development, because … the changes in pronunciation in any one language or dialect follow regular sound laws." (Barber 1993: 58)

So the important role of cognates is that they reveal the closeness and remoteness between various languages. If we trace the cognates found in languages, we can classify the languages according to the degree of similarity. The similarity is based on systematic and regular sound correspondences between component segments in semantically related cognate words. The related languages that share cognates are said to belong to the same "language family". Every human family has its ancestors and kinsmen. A language is the same; languages also have their ancestors, family members and relatives.

In talking about a language family, we use female metaphor terms, like "mother" and "daughter" languages. And the degree of relationship is expressed as if languages had "offsprings". Languages are developments of older languages in the same sense that people are descendants of their ancestors. Of course, the terms "family", "ancestor", "parent" and other genealogical expressions should not be understood as more than metaphors.

Now we know that language is changing and can develop into quite a different form from its previous stage. Then, what is the ultimate ancestor of English? The explanation that was first proposed about 200 years ago and is now well supported with evidence from many languages is that there was once a language (now no longer spoken) that developed in different ways in the various parts of the world to which its speakers traveled.[6] We

---

6) "The Indo-European family of languages, with its numerous branches and its millions of speakers, has developed, if we are right, out of some single language, which must have been spoken thousands of years ago by some comparatively small body of people in a relatively restricted geographical area. This original language we can call Proto-Indo-European (PIE). The people who spoke it or who spoke languages

give the name Proto-Indo-European (or simply Indo- European) to that prehistoric and now dead language. At the beginning of historical times, this common language spread from Europe in the west to India in the east. Proto-Indo-European was thus the ancestor of most languages of Europe and of many of south Asia. That is, this (reconstructed) language (without leaving any real written data) is the forefather of English and many other languages spoken in Europe and India. Its descendants, which make up the Indo-European language family, include all of the languages spoken in Europe, such as German, French, Dutch, Danish, Russian, Polish, Czech, Bulgarian, Albanian, Armenian, even Gypsy, and many others.

Although we do not know the original Indo-European homeland exactly, we can make a conjecture, partly through the philological examination of the vocabulary of Proto-Indo-European (cf. Pyles and Algeo 1993: 83, Barber 1993: 77-80).[7] The most widely accepted view, developed by an archaeologist Marija Gimbutas, is that the early Indo-Europeans lived northwest of the Caucasus and north of the Caspian Sea as early as the 5th millennium BC.[8] Early in the 4th millennium BC (i.e. roughly between 4,000 BC and 3,500 BC), they began expanding into the Balkans and northern Europe, and thereafter into Iran, Anatolia, and southern Europe. The peoples speaking the Proto-Indo-European language were nomadic or

---

    evolved from it we can for convenience call Indo-Europeans." (Barber 1993: 67)
7) "Arguments have been advanced for several different areas as the Indo-European homeland: Scandinavia and the adjacent parts of northern Germany, the Danube valley, especially the Hungarian plain, Anatolia (now in Turkey), and the steppes of the southern Ukraine, north of the Black Sea." (Barber 1993: 77)
8) "Gimbutas places the original Indo-Europeans ..., north of the Caucasus range and around the lower Volga (north of the Caspian Sea)." (Barber 1993: 78)

semi-nomadic pastoral peoples, as evidenced by the vocabulary of Proto-Indo-European for *ox, cattle* and *sheep*. They formed a loosely linked group of communities with common gods and similar social organization.[9]

Now we know that English is a descendant of an ancient language named Proto-Indo-European which spread all over Europe and some Asian areas. So our next task should be to trace the development of English after the Indo-European stage.

3.2. Language Families within the Indo-European Group

A language takes a different shape from the one of the previous stage and from the one spoken in other regions. Change and regional variation are inevitable for language. Thus a new dialect or a new language appears constantly. The Indo-European language was surely a single language without any variations at first. But it was expanded in its territory where it is spoken, thus developing regional varieties. Regional varieties themselves again form a new family, and then develop new varieties within. The result is the creation of new languages that are more or less similar to each other.

Most comparative linguists, whose main concern is to compare various

---

[9] Proto-Indo-Europeans believed in a "Sky God", who is the Father God. Examples are the Greek *Zeus*, the Latin *Jupiter* (literally meaning 'Sky Father'), the Sanskrit *Dyaus*, the OE *Tīw* (whose name survives in the word *Tuesday*, i.e. *Tīw's day*). So the names of female god, like a *Great Mother Goddess* or an *Earth Goddess*, were not of Indo-European origin, but taken over from a non-Indo-European people. This shows that the Proto-Indo-European society was male-oriented. (cf. Barber 1993: 76-77)

languages and to establish the relationship between them on the basis of the found similarities and differences, agree that the Indo-European language developed into roughly ten or so sub-language families.[10] The following is the family relationships of the various Indo-European languages:

---

[10] It was the work of Sir William Jones, a British scholar living in India, that fired the imagination of European comparative linguists. In 1786 he delivered a paper in which he observed that there was amongst Sanskrit, Greek and Latin 'a stronger affinity than could possibly have been produced by accident.' He suggested that these languages had 'sprung from a common source', and that Celtic and even Germanic might possibly belong to this group.

Table 3.2 The Indo-European Language Family[11]

(Proto-) Indo-European	Western (Centum) languages	① (Proto-) Germanic	West (Old Saxon)[12]	Anglo-Frisian	English
					Frisian[13]
				Netherlandic -German	Low: Dutch
					Flemish[14]
					Afrikaans[15]
					Low German
					high: (Standard) High German
					Yiddish[16]
			North (Old Norse)[17]		Norwegian
					Icelandic
					Faeroese[18]
					Danish
					Swedish
			East		*Gothic*[19]
		② Celtic	Britannic		*Gaulish*[20]
					Cornish[21]
					Welsh
					Breton[22]
			Gaelic		Irish Gaelic
					Scottish (or Scots) Gaelic
					Manx[23]
		③ Italic[24] or Romance[25]	*Latin*		Portuguese
					Spanish
					French
					Italian
					Rumanian
		④ Helenic			
		⑤ *Anatolian*			
		⑥ *Tocharian*			
	Eastern (Satem) languages	⑦ Albanian			
		⑧ Armenian			
		⑨ Balto-Slavic			
		⑩ Indo-Iranian			

---

11) This table contains individual languages of only three language families; Germanic, Celtic and Romance. It is because English has some connection and relationship with these three language families in the main. The other language groups are beyond our interest here.

From the table given above we might work out which branches migrated

12) The earliest recorded form of West Germanic is called **Old Saxon**. Thus Old Saxon is the ancestor language of the modern West Germanic languages, including English. It began to break up into dialects from about the 5th century AD onwards, and developed into the modern West Germanic languages.
13) **Frisian** is the language spoken in the Frisian Islands, which is a chain of islands in the North Sea off the coast of the Netherlands, Germany and Denmark. It is the language most closely related to English.
14) **Flemish** is the term for the dialects of Dutch spoken in Flanders, which is a historical region of northwest Europe including parts of northern France, western Belgium and southwest Netherlands along the North Sea.
15) **Afrikaans** is a language that developed from the 17th-century Dutch and is an official language of South Africa.
16) **Yiddish** is the language of Jews living in Central and Eastern Europe, resulting from a fusion of elements derived principally from medieval German dialects.
17) The earliest recorded form of North Germanic is called **Old Norse**. Thus Old Norse is the ancestor language of the modern North Germanic languages. It began to break up into the dialects from about AD 800 onwards, and developed into the modern Scandinavian languages.
18) **Faeroese** is the language spoken by the inhabitants of the Faeroe Islands, located in the North Atlantic about midway between Iceland and Great Britain. It is highly similar to Icelandic.
19) The italicized language is a dead language, not spoken any more. *Gothic* is the extinct East Germanic language of the Goths.
20) **Gaulish** is the name given to the Celtic language that was spoken in Gaul (now in France) before Latin became dominant there.
21) **Cornish** is the Celtic language spoken in Cornwall. It has been extinct since the late 18th century.
22) **Breton** is the language of the descendants of those people who, roughly at the time of the Germanic invasion, moved to the mainland Europe and settled in the northern France, naming their new home for their old one - Brittany.
23) **Manx** is the extinct Celtic language spoken in the Isle of Man.
24) Accurately speaking, the **Italic** subfamily is not the same with the **Romance** family.

together, in what order different groups broke away, and so on.

The first division was into a Western Group and an Eastern Group. The two groups show a number of differences in phonology, grammar and vocabulary, since there was an early division of the Indo-Europeans into two main areas, perhaps representing migrations in different directions. The Western Group and the Eastern Group are referred to in other way as Centum (or Kentum) languages and Satem languages, respectively.26)

The Italic family includes both the Romance languages and a number of extinct languages of the Italian Peninsula, such as *Umbrian* (an extinct Italic language formerly spoken by the Umbri in the ancient Italian region of Umbria) and Oscan (the language of the Osci). By contrast, only the languages descended from Latin (more precisely, from its different spoken forms, Vulgar Latin) are called Romance languages, so Latin itself is an Italic language but it is not a Romance language. However, the two names are often used indiscriminately.

25) The term *Romance* comes from the Vulgar Latin adverb *romanice*, meaning "in Roman (that is, the Latin vernacular or colloquial Latin)", contrasted with *latine*, meaning "in Latin (Medieval Latin, the conservative version of the language used in writing and formal contexts)". From this adverb the noun *romance* originated, which applied initially to anything written *romanice*, or "in the Roman vernacular". The word *romance* with the modern sense of romance novel or love affair has the same origin. In the medieval literature of Western Europe, serious writing was usually in Latin, while popular tales, often focusing on love, were composed in the vernacular and came to be called "romances". ("Romance Languages" In *Wikipedia*. Retrieved July 31, 2008)

26) Centum and Satem are, respectively, the Latin and Avestan (an ancient Iranian language) words corresponding to *hundred* (Pyles and Algeo 1993: 66). The classification is based on the development, in very ancient times, of Indo-European [k] sound. If the complex story is put in a simple way, the original [k] sound became [s] (or [ʃ]) in Satem languages; for example, Sanskrit (Indic) *śatam*, Lithuanian (Baltic) *šim̃tas*, Old Church Slavic *sŭto*. Indo-Iranian, Balto-Slavic,

Centum languages tend to be spoken in the West and Satem languages in the East.27)

These two main divisions were again divided in the flow of time into ten sub-branches, which again form its own language family; Germanic, Celtic, Romance, Helenic, Anatolian, Tocharian, Albanian, Armenian, Balto-Slavic, Indo-Iranian. Albanian and Armenian are Indo-European but do not fit into any other language, so it constitutes a single-membered family. Anatolian and Tocharian are no longer spoken in any form. What is important here is that English belongs to the Germanic language family.

Take a look at the following word lists, which are from three Germanic languages (including English) and three representative Romance languages. There is an undeniable overall similarity among all the members of both groups (cf. *me* - words). Nevertheless, we observe that the similarities within the subgroups are greater.

Armenian and Albanian are such Satem languages. Meanwhile, the [k] sound remained [k] in the other Indo-European languages, as in Greek (Hellenic) *(he)katon* and Welsh (Celtic) *cant*. These are Centum languages. Later, the [k] sound of the Centum languages shifted again into [h] in the Germanic group, thus English *hundred* and German *hundert*.

27) The apparent exception is Tocharian. It was spoken in Western China, so it is an eastern (to Europe) language. But it was a Centum language (*känt*, meaning 'hundred' in Tocharian).

Table 3.3 Some Cognate Words

Germanic			Romance		
English	German	Swedish	French	Italian	Spanish
<u>w</u>inter	<u>W</u>inter	<u>v</u>inter	h<u>i</u>ver[28]	<u>i</u>nverno	<u>i</u>nverno
<u>f</u>oot	<u>F</u>uß	<u>f</u>ot	<u>p</u>ied[29]	<u>p</u>iede	<u>p</u>ie
<u>t</u>wo	<u>z</u>wei	<u>t</u>vå	<u>d</u>eux[30]	<u>d</u>ue	<u>d</u>os
<u>m</u>e	<u>m</u>ich	<u>m</u>ig	<u>m</u>oi	<u>m</u>e	<u>m</u>e

We see here from the basic quality of the sounds in the same positions within these cognate words that English, German and Swedish form a separate group (or a subfamily, that is, the Germanic language family), while French, Italian and Spanish form another. The former group shares [f] and [t] (or [tz], spelled as <z>), while the latter group has the corresponding sounds of [p] and [d]. Although Germanic and Romance languages were the members of the same parent group Indo-European, they took a different path of development. The result was the forming of different language families.

3.3. Germanic Language Family

3.3.1. Development from Indo-European to Germanic

We have seen that English belongs to the Germanic language family. Thus we need to treat the Germanic group in a more detailed way than any of

---

[28] The word-initial <h> is not pronounced in Romance languages.
[29] Thus we can notice that such words as *pedal* and *pedestrian* are not of Germanic origin but show Romance origin. They are borrowed from Latin or French.
[30] The words like *duo, dual* and *duet* are also of Romance origin.

the other groups. In the course of the spreading of Indo-Europeans, the Germanic tribes settled in the region of the present-day Denmark and its neighboring regions. Some tribes went up to the Scandinavian peninsular, forming the northern Germanic part. During this period, their language, which was a more or less unified form descending directly from their Indo-European ancestor, developed into separate languages. This stage of the language spoken by the Germanic tribes is referred to as Proto-Germanic (or simply Germanic).31) The Proto-Germanic language is a relatively unified language, which is distinctive in many of its sounds, its inflections, its accentual system and its word stock.32) Unfortunately, we

---

31) "Round about the beginning of the Christian era, the speakers of Proto-Germanic still formed a relatively homogeneous cultural and linguistic group, living in the north of Europe." (Barber 1993: 81)
32) Germanic became differentiated from (Proto-)Indo-European principally in several respects (Pyles and Algeo 1993: 84-86, Barber 1993: 87-98):

  i. Germanic has a large number of words that have no known cognates in other Indo-European languages.
  ii. All Indo-European distinctions of tense and aspect were lost in the verb save for the present and the past (or preterite) tenses. Thus Germanic languages have only two tenses of the verb.
  iii. Germanic developed a preterite tense form with a dental suffix, that is, one containing <d> or <t>. Proto-Indo European way of forming past tense was to change the vowel sound of the verb. This change of the vowel sound for grammatical purposes is called "vowel gradation" and the verbs forming past tense in this way are called "strong verbs" (now "irregular verbs)". Meanwhile, the verbs developing a past tense form with a dental suffix are called "weak verbs" (now "regular verbs"). Today strong verbs, which were the original type, are a small minority, and weak verbs are the norm. So all new verbs are made weak, as in *downloaded* and *e-mailed*.

have no written record of the language in this period.33) It is just known that English, German, Dutch and some Scandinavian languages like Danish, Norwegian and Swedish are all descendants of this language.

3.3.2. Development from Germanic to West Germanic

Earlier Germans had probably been confined to a small area of southern Scandinavia and northern Germany, "but round about 300 BC they had

---

iv. All the older forms of Germanic had two ways of declining their adjectives: Strong and Weak declensions.

v. The first syllable was regularly stressed in Germanic languages. The tendency to put the main stress on the first syllable had profound consequences, e.g. the weakening or loss of the inflectional endings.

vi. Some Indo-European vowels underwent Germanic modification. For example, Indo-European [o] was retained in Latin but became [a] in Germanic (compare Lat. *octō* 'eight,' Gothic *ahtau*). Indo-European [ā] became [ō] (Lat. *máter* 'mother', OE *módor*).

vii. There were some consonant changes, which were alternatively called the First Sound Shift (Grimm's Law and Verner's Law). The respective contrasts between Indo-European/Romance [p], [d] and Germanic [f], [t], shown in Table 3.3, are examples of these sound changes. But this will not be explained here in detail. Refer to Pyles and Algeo (1993: 84-91) or Barber (1993: 92-96).

33) Instead of their own records, they are described by Roman authors, e.g. by Tacitus in AD 98. He wrote a book titled *Germani* "Germans". According to this book, the Germans as a tribal society lived in scattered settlements in the woody and marshy country of North West Europe, worshipping the gods like *Woden (god of wisdom and war)*, *Thor (god of thunder)* and *Tiw (god of combat, victory and heroic glory)*. These three gods left their vestiges on the English names of the day of the week, like *Wednesday* (< *Woden's day*), *Thursday* (< *Thor's day*) and *Tuesday* (<*Tiw's day*).

begun to expand in all directions, perhaps because of overpopulation and the poverty of their natural resources" (Barber 1993: 83).34) Because Germanic spread over a large area, it again developed marked dialectal differences leading to a division into North Germanic, West Germanic and East Germanic. The North Germanic languages are Danish, Swedish, Norwegian, Icelandic and Faeroese. The West Germanic languages are (Standard) High German, Low German (Plattdeutsch), Dutch (and the practically identical Flemish), Frisian and English.35) Flemish is the main language of Flanders in northern Belgium and Frisian is spoken in the Frisian Islands in the northern coast of the Netherlands. As a matter of fact, the region is the nearest to England, so Frisian is the closest language to English genealogically.36) Afrikaans is another variant of Dutch and is

---

34) Thus there were several different Germanic-speaking peoples: Goths, Vandals, Franks, Angles, Saxons, Jutes, later Scandinavian Vikings, etc.
35) West Germanic is again divided into smaller subgroups. For example, High German and Low German are distinguished from each other by the changes in the stop sounds that occurred in the High German areas. The changes are termed the Second Sound Shift or the High German Shift, which is summarized as follows (Pyles and Algeo 1993: 92-93):

   i. Proto-Germanic (one direct descendant of which is English) <p> appears in High German as <pf> or, after vowels, as <ff> (*pepper-Pfeffer*).
   ii. Proto-Germanic <t> appears as <z> (having [ts] sound) or, after vowels, as <ss> (*tongue-Zunge; water-Wasser*).
   iii. Proto-Germanic <k> appears after vowels as <ch> (*break-brechen*).
   iv. Proto-Germanic <d> appears as <t> (*dance-tanzen*).

Note that English shares with Low German, Dutch, Flemish and Frisian, rather than High German, because the Angles, Saxons and Jutes, who are the ancestors of the present English people, lived in the low countries in the northern Europe.

spoken in South Africa, which was the former colony of the Netherlands before the British Empire occupied the region. Yiddish is the language of some Jewish people living in Germany. It was strongly influenced by German, so it is classified as one branch of the Germanic languages.

Meanwhile, High and Low Germans are the two variants of the German language, reflecting the geological features of Germany. The southern part of Germany is mainly mountainous, embracing some parts of the Alps. High German is spoken in this high region of the Southern Germany and functions as the modern standard German, whereas Low German is the language of the northern Germany, which is low and forms the mouths of the rivers like the Rhine and the Elbe entering the Atlantic Ocean.

Figuratively speaking, Frisian is the sister language of English, and such languages as German and Dutch are its cousins. Danish, Swedish and Norwegian are its second or third cousin languages.

"The only East Germanic language of which we have any detailed knowledge is Gothic" (Pyles and Algeo 1993: 75), the language of the Goths.[37] Although it is dead at present, it left the earliest records of the Germanic language. We have parts of the New Testament translated into Gothic in the 4th century by Wulfila,[38] bishop of the Visigoths, those

---

36) The closeness between English and Frisian is clearly revealed by some cognate words like *boat/boat, cat/kat, cow/ko, dream/dream, green/grien, house/hus, lamb/lam, mother/mem, ox/okse, sheep/skiep, three/ trije,* etc. (cf. Svartvik and Leech (2006: 19))

37) The **Goths** were East Germanic tribes who, in the 3rd and 4th centuries, harried the Roman Empire. In the 5th and 6th centuries, divided as the Visigoths and the Ostrogoths, they established powerful successor-states of the Roman Empire in the Iberian peninsula and Italy, respectively. ("Goths" In *Wikipedia*. Retrieved July 31, 2008)

Goths who lived north of the Danube. These remains of Gothic provide us with a clear picture of a Germanic language in an early stage of development. However, we do not have any descending language from the early East Germanic.

3.4. Celtic and Romance Language Families

Our primary concern is on the Germanic family because English is a (West) Germanic language. As we will see in the next chapters dealing with its external history, English has contacted many foreign languages, among which several Celtic languages and French merit separate accounts.

Celtic languages were and still are the languages of the Celts living over central and western Europe and in Britain. "The Celts spread over a huge territory in Europe long before the emergence in history of the Germanic peoples. Before the beginning of the Christian era, Celtic languages were spoken over the greater part of central and western Europe" (Pyles and Algeo 1993: 73). They were the original inhabitants of the British Isles before the coming of the Germanic peoples.[39] They are the ancestors of

---

38) **Wulfila** (meaning "little wolf") (c. 310 – 383; or Latin **Ulfilas**), bishop, missionary and bible translator, was a Goth or half-Goth who had spent time inside the Roman Empire. ("Wulfila" In *Wikipedia*. Retrieved July 31, 2008)

39) The **British Isles** are a group of islands off the northwest coast of continental Europe, comprising Great Britain, Ireland and a number of smaller islands. There are two sovereign states located on the islands: **the United Kingdom of Great Britain and Northern Ireland** and **the Republic of Ireland**. The term British Isles is controversial in relation to Ireland where its use is objected to by many people and by the government of the Republic of Ireland. Its use is also avoided in

the present Irish and Scottish peoples.

Celtic languages can be divided into three groups: Gaulish, Britannic (or British Celtic) and Gaelic. Gaulish was spoken in France and northern Italy in the time of the Roman Empire, so it has no direct contact with English and died out during the early centuries of the Christian era. Britannic was the branch of Celtic spoken in most of Britain before the Anglo-Saxon invasion. It survived into modern times in three languages: Cornish, Welsh and Breton, although Cornish and Breton are now dead. Gaelic was the Celtic language of Ireland. It spread to the Isle of Man in the 4th century, and to Scotland in the 5th, thus giving rise to the main branches of Gaelic - Irish Gaelic, Scottish (or Scots) Gaelic and Manx. But the Celtic languages spoken in the British Isles were severely threatened after the Angles, Saxons and Jutes arrived. Thus such Celtic languages as Cornish, Breton and Manx completely disappeared. Only Welsh, Scottish Gaelic and Irish Gaelic are spoken by some speakers of Wales, Scotland and Ireland, respectively. However, the number of the speakers of these languages is decreasing every year, unfortunately.[40]

French also deserves a separate mention because it is one of the languages having exerted a profound influence on the development of English, particularly during the Mediaeval times. French is one of the Romance languages, like Portuguese, Spanish, (Modern) Italian (which is different from Latin, the old language of the Italian people) and Rumanian (the

---

relations between the governments of the Republic of Ireland and the United Kingdom, who generally employ the term *these islands*. ("British Isles" In *Wikipedia*. Retrieved July 31, 2008)

40) See Section 1.4.

language of Rumania).41) These languages are all descendants of Latin. Latin was the language of the Roman Empire, which governed the most part of Europe (except for the Northern Germany and the Scandinavian Countries) for several hundred years. The Romance languages like French have quite different phonological, morphological and syntactic features from those of the Germanic languages.42) Due to the close contact with French, English became to have quite a different form from the other Germanic languages. So PDE is a kind of mixed language, comprising both Germanic and non-Germanic elements (especially, in the word stock).

3.5. Typological Classification of English

Up to now, we have traced the genealogical classification of English on the basis of such correspondences of sound and structure as indicate relationship among various languages. Thus it was found that English is a West Germanic language like German and Dutch. These kinds of findings are the greatest contribution of 19th-century comparative linguists' painstaking investigation of those correspondences.

Meanwhile, other scholars classify languages as isolating, agglutinative, incorporative and inflective. These are exemplified, respectively, by Chinese

---

41) *Rumania(n)* can be spelled as *Romania(n)* or *Roumania(n)* in other way.
42) We should be cautious not to conclude that English and French have some genealogical kinship by noting that an enormous number of English words closely resemble French words of similar meaning: e.g. E. *people, battle, change* vs. F. *peuple, bataille, changer*. All these English words were borrowed from French after the Norman Conquest in 1066, so they do not say anything about the genealogical relationship between the two languages.

(isolating), Korean/Turkish (agglutinative), Eskimo (incorporative) and Latin/English (inflective). The isolating languages are supposed to represent the most primitive type: they are languages in which each idea is expressed by a separate word and in which words tend to be monosyllabic. In the meantime, in such languages as Korean and Turkish, words were made up of parts "stuck together" as it were; hence the term agglutinative. In such languages, the elements that are put together are usually whole syllables having very definite meanings. Setting aside the incorporative language like Eskimo, the final type is inflective, to which all the Indo-European languages belong, including English. However, the distinction between agglutinative and inflective is a little vague and there is considerable overlapping. It is because the inflective languages also use the small particles to indicate various grammatical relations, just like the word endings of the agglutinative languages.

Anyway, all the Indo-European languages are inflective - that is, they all depend on inflections (that is, endings and sometimes vowel changes) to indicate such grammatical functions as case, number, tense, person, mood, aspect, and the like. For example, Sanskrit is notable for its complicated inflectional system, revealing the original inflectional system of Indo-European. German also retains a relatively complicated inflectional system, with its various forms of the noun and the article and its strong adjective declension. But most of the modern Indo-European descendants, including English, have lost much of the inflectional complexity that was once characteristic of them.

3.5.1. Verbal Inflections

Look at the following inflectional system of the present indicative (i.e. not subjunctive or imperative) of the Sanskrit verb corresponding to English 'to bear':

Table 3.4 Indo-European Verbal Inflections for Present Tense[43]

Number	Person	Sanskrit	English
Singular	1st	*bharā-mi*	'I bear'
	2nd	*bhara-si*	'you bear'
	3rd	*bhara-ti*	'he/she bear-s'
Plural	1st	*bharā-mas*	'we/you/they bear'
	2nd	*bhara-tha*	
	3rd	*bhara-nti*	

Here the verbs have six different endings for all persons both in the singular and the plural. However, the OE verbal endings were already quite simplified (into four), as we can see in Table 3.5 given below, and the PDE counterparts are more simplified, adopting just one ending (the third person singular ending, -(e)s):

Table 3.5 English Verbal Inflections for Present Tense

Number	Person	Old English	Present-day English
Singular	1st	*cēp-e*	'I keep'
	2nd	*cēp-est*[44]	'you keep'
	3rd	*cēp-eð*[45][46]	'he/she keep-s'
Plural	1st	*cēp-að*[47]	'we/you/they keep'
	2nd		
	3rd		

---

43) This table is from Pyles and Algeo (1993: 78).

44) We will study later that there was a number distinction for the second person singular personal pronoun in English (*thou/thy/thine/thee* vs. *ye/your/yours/you*). And

3.5.2. Nominal Inflections

It is assumed that there were eight cases for Proto-Indo-European nouns, as follows (Pyles and Algeo 1993: 81):

Table 3.6 Eight Cases for Proto-Indo-European Nouns

Cases	Functions or Meanings	Examples
nominative	subject of a sentence	*They* saw me.
vocative	person addressed	*Officer*, I need help.
accusative	direct object	They saw *me*.
genitive	possessor or source	*Shakespeare's* play
dative	indirect object, recipient	Give *her* a hand.
ablative	what is separated	He abstained *from it*.
locative	place where	Stay away *from the edge of the cliff*.
instrumental	means, instrument	She ate *with chopsticks*.

Indo-European nouns were inflected for eight cases:[48] nominative,

---

the singular form had the *-(e)st* ending on its verb. The distinction disappeared in the Early ModE period.

45) The letters <ð> (called "eth") and <þ> (called "thorn") correspond to <th> in PDE. They were used in OE and then replaced by the diagraph <th> in ME, probably under the influence of French spellings employed by French scribes working in England.

46) The third person singular present verbal ending was *-(e)þ*, which was changed into *-(e)th*, and then disappeared. Instead, new endings *-(e)s* was introduced from the Scandinavian languages.

47) The plural present verbal ending was *-(a)þ*, which was also changed into *-(e)th* in ME, and then completely disappeared.

48) Pronouns and adjectives also inflected for these eight cases.

vocative, accusative, genitive, dative, ablative, locative and instrumental. These eight cases were well preserved in Sanskrit. Yet, Proto-Germanic reduced the number of case-distinctions: for all practical purposes, they had only five or six cases. OE nouns had just four cases (nominative, accusative, genitive and dative) although demonstratives, adjectives and interrogative/relative pronouns had another case, instrumental. Later, accusative and dative cases were collapsed into a single case, i.e. objective. The accusative case was for the (direct) object in general, while the dative was only for the indirect object. So the merged objective case is sometimes called the accusative. Anyway, PDE has three cases only; nominative (or subjective), genitive (or possessive) and accusative (or objective).[49] What is more, nominative and accusative are not formally differentiated in nearly all (pro)nouns. Instead, English uses word order to indicate who (nominative) did what (accusative), and uses prepositions in many cases, like *from it* (ablative), *from the edge of the cliff* (locative) and *with chopsticks* (instrumental), as in Table 3.6. The following table shows the process of nominal case reduction that English has experienced from its Indo-European stage to present-day. All the exemplified words mean 'horse':

---

[49] Case reduction is still going on even in PDE. Although English has three cases, only six word pairs have the formal distinction between subjective and objective; *I/me, we/us, he/him, she/her, they/them* and *who/whom*. However, even these word pairs are losing case distinction. For example, *whom* is rarely used in an informal English, as in *Who did you see?* or *Who did you talk to?* For this matter, refer to Section 2.5.

Table 3.7. Indo-European Noun Inflections[50]

	Indo-European	Sanskrit	Old English	Present-day English
Singular				
Nom.	*ekwos 'horse'	aśvas	eoh 'horse'	horse
Voc.	*ekwe	'horse'		
Acc.	*ekwom	aśva	eoh	horse
Gen.	*ekwosyo	aśvam	ēos	horse's
Dat.	*ekwōy	aśvasya	ēo	
Abl.	*ekwōd	aśvāya		
Loc.	*ekwoy	aśvād		
Ins.	*ekwō	aśve		
		aśvena		
Plural				
N.-V.	*ekwōs	aśvās	ēos	horses
Acc.	*ekwons	aśvān(s)	ēos	horses
Gen.	*ekwōm	aśvānām	ēona	horses'
D.-Ab.	*ekwobh(y)os	aśvebhyas	ēom	
Loc.	*ekwoysu	aśvesu		
Ins.	*ekwōys	aśvais		

---

[50] This table is from Pyles and Algeo (1993: 80).

II.

The History of English: External History

The Old English Period (449-1100)

The recorded history of the English language begins with the arrival and settlement of several Germanic tribes in the British Isles.[1] Before the movement, they lived on the European Continent. They used a branch of West Germanic languages while they were living on the Continent.[2] The language spoken by them in Europe is known as pre-Old English (literally, the language before Old English). It was not a distinct language from the other Germanic languages. However, when it was separated from the Continent after the movement to the British Isles, it became an independent and separate language from its Continental cousins that have developed into such languages as German and Dutch. English took its own way of evolution after that.

---

1) See Footnote 39 of Chapter 3.
2) For the development and classification of Germanic languages, refer to Section 3.3.

4.1. Before the English: Celtic and Roman Britain

Before the English (mainly composed of such Germanic peoples as Angles, Saxons, Jutes, and possibly some Frisians[3]) migrated from the Continent to Britain in the 5th century, the British Isles were already inhabited by non-Germanic peoples. That is, Celtic peoples had been there for a few centuries, experiencing a number of important political and military events.

First of all, Britain was invaded and subsequently occupied by the Roman Empire.[4] Julius Caesar invaded Britain two times, in 55 and 54 BC.[5] But these two attacks did not lead to its political occupation. Caesar

---

[3] Frisians speak a language considered to be closest to English to this day. Look at Table 3.2.

[4] **Rome** was traditionally founded by Romulus in 753 BC. It was ruled first by Etruscans, who were overthrown c. 500 BC. **The Roman Republic** gradually extended its territory and expanded its influence, giving way to the Roman Empire. **The Roman Empire** succeeded the Roman Republic during the time of Augustus, who ruled from 27 BC to AD 14. At its greatest extent it encompassed territories stretching from Britain and Germany to North Africa and the Persian Gulf. After 395 it was split into **the Byzantine Empire** (i.e. **the Eastern Roman Empire**) and **the Western Roman Empire**, which rapidly sank into anarchy under the onslaught of barbarian invaders from the north and east. The last emperor of the West, Romulus Augustulus (born c. 461), was deposed by the Goths in 476, the traditional date for the end of the empire. (*Rome* and *Roman Empire*, *The American Heritage Dictionary of the English Language*, 4th edition, 2000)

[5] **Gaius Julius Caesar** (July 12, 100 BC - March 15, 44 BC) was Roman general, statesman and historian who invaded Britain (55), crushed the army of his political enemy Pompey (48), pursued other enemies to Egypt, where he installed Cleopatra as queen (47), returned to Rome, and was given a mandate by the people to rule as dictator for life (45). On March 15 of the following year he was murdered by a group of republicans led by Cassius and Brutus, who feared he intended to

just wanted to warn the Celts not to have connection with other Celtic peoples in Gaul,[6] who he had just conquered after the 7 year military campaign. Almost a century later, in AD 43, the real occupation occurred by the Emperor Claudius.[7] He made Britain (or Britannia, the land of the Britons)[8] a part of the Roman Empire. Britain remained as the northern border of the Empire until the beginning of the 5th century.

However, the whole part of Britain was not under the Roman Rule. The northern part of the Isle still was the land of the unconquered Celtic tribes, especially the Scots[9] and the Picts.[10] So the border was always in turmoil. In 122 AD the Emperor Hadrian decided to build a long defence wall along the northern border of Roman rule in Britain.[11] The Wall, called Hadrian's

---

establish a monarchy ruled by himself. (*Caesar*, *The American Heritage Dictionary of the English Language*, 4th edition, 2000)

6) **Gaul** (Latin: Gallia) was the name given, in ancient times, to the region of Western Europe comprising present-day northern Italy, France, Belgium, western Switzerland, the parts of the Netherlands and Germany on the west bank of the River Rhine.

7) **Tiberius Claudius Caesar Augustus Germanicus** or **Claudius I** (August 1, 10 BC - October 13, AD 54) was the fourth Roman Emperor, ruling from January 24, AD 41 to his death in AD 54.

8) **Britain** was called **Britannia** in Latin, from which come the modern forms Britain and British. In the meantime, the Romans called Scotland Caledonia and Ireland Hibernia.

9) The **Scots** was originated from Ireland, then moved to the north-western coast of Britain. They are ancestors of the present Scottish people.

10) The **Picts** were politically annihilated in the 9th century for an unclear reason.

11) **Publius Aelius Traianus Hadrianus** (January 24, 76 - July 10, 138), known as **Hadrian** in English, was emperor of Rome from 117 to 138 AD, as well as a Stoic and Epicurean philosopher. Hadrian was the third of the Five Good Emperors. During his visit to Britain (122), he ordered the construction of the so-called Hadrian's Wall (Latin: perhaps *Vallum Aelium*, "the Aelian Wall").

Wall or the Roman Wall, is well preserved in parts until today. It is regarded as one of the great wonders of the world, and was designated a World Heritage Site in 1987. In the late 4th century and the early 5th century, Rome itself was attacked by several Germanic tribes.[12] Thus the Roman troops had to retreat to their homeland to defend themselves. The record says that the last troops departed Britain in 410 from London. With this, the Roman rule in Britain ended after its about 350 year occupation (from 43 to 410).

Such a long political and military occupation inevitably left its traces on the Island. Britain was Romanized. It is therefore not surprising that there are so many Roman remains in modern England. Some of them were discovered in the very heart of London. The Romans are famous for their civilized life, with well-constructed roads[13] and towns and cities. The houses and villas had all the luxuries like heating, water supply, floor mosaics and painted walls. Baths, large villas, temples and theaters give

---

[12] In particular, the Vandals were notorious in their brutality. The following words are all from the name of this tribe;

vandal: a person who intentionally damages property belonging to other people.
(e.g. *Vandals* smashed windows and overturned cars in the downtown shopping district.)
vandalism: the deliberate damaging of things, especially public property.
(e.g. Cutting down the old forest was the act of *vandalism*.)
vandalize: to intentionally damage property belonging to other people.
(e.g. The walls had been horribly *vandalized* with spray paint.)

[13] "The Latin word for the Roman road was *via strata* 'paved road', which is the origin of English *street*, German *Strasse* and Italian *strada*." (Svartvik and Leech 2006: 17)

evidence to a rather high standard living and well developed cultural life. There is a small city named Bath in Britain. It was Britain's first spa resort constructed by the Romans.14)

The language spoken by the Romans, i.e. Latin, also left its trace on the Island. The most conspicuous and permanent trace is place names. The towns or cities ending in *-chester* or *-castor* 'city' (L. *castra* 'camp') were the places for the military camps of Roman troops. The Roman army first built their fortress and the residential facility within it when they occupied some region. The towns or cities with *-chester* or *-castor* in its name have a connection with this Roman military camp. *Chester*, *Winchester*, *Manchester*, *Colchester*, *Silchester*, *Woodchester*, *Chesterton*, *Chesterford*, *Chesterfield* and *Lancastor*, *Doncastor*, *Casterton* are such examples. There are more examples of Latin borrowing in this period.

Despite the long occupation by the Romans, the British Celts continued to speak their own languages, though many of them, particularly those in the towns and cities who wanted to be "social climbers", learned to speak and write the language of their Roman rulers. The Celts were not a single national or ethnic group, and spoke a group of Celtic languages. These languages now survive as modern Celtic languages such as Welsh, Scottish Gaelic and Irish Gaelic.15) "Indeed the number of Celtic words taken into English in the whole of its history has been very small" (Barber 1993: 101).16) There are a few British place names and river names which are

---

14) The name of this city appears in the Tale of the Wife of Bath in Chaucer's *Canterbury Tales*. We should pronounce it as [baːθ] not as [bæːθ] according to British pronunciation.

15) For the development and classification of Celtic languages, refer to Section 3.4.

partly or completely of Celtic origin; *Kent* (C. *canto-* 'rim, border'), *Avon* (cf. *Stratford-upon-Avon*), *Dover* (C. *Dobrā* 'water') and *London* (C. *Londo* 'wild, bold'). And the element *-cumb* 'a deep, narrow valley', as in *Duncombe* and *Holcombe*, is also of Celtic origin.

4.2. The Early Old English Period (c. 450-900)

4.2.1. The Germanic Conquest

The invasion and settlement by the Romans in AD 43 lasted about 350 years, but the Roman culture and language (i.e. Latin) were quickly overlaid with those of the northern European settlers who followed. After the Roman troops were withdrawn from Britain in the early 5th century, the Picts and Scots from the north and west savagely attacked the unprotected British Celts (also called Britons).[17] The British Celts were also Celtic peoples, like the Picts and Scots, but they were Romanized and lived together with the Romans without any military and political resistance. They had completely depended on the Roman troops for their defence and safety. So they could not repel the attacks by the Picts and Scots after the withdrawal of the Roman legions. They had to defend

---

16) The reason is clear. Celtics were the languages of the defeated peoples, having no prestige compared with that of the conquerors.
17) The word **Briton** is ambiguous. Historically, the **Britons** were the indigenous peoples that inhabited the island of Britain. They were Celtic people, but their language and culture was largely replaced by invading Anglo-Saxons. The word now means the citizens of the United Kingdom in general. These **contemporary Britons** are descended mainly from the varied ethnic stocks.

themselves.

In this situation they sought helpers from out of the British Isles. At that time several Germanic tribes such as Angles, Saxons, Jutes, Frisians and probably other more, moved and settled along the coastal areas of the Northwestern Europe. When Rome could or would help no more, the wretched "Romano-Celts" called these Germanic tribes to help them "from the parts beyond the sea." It was ironical for the people of Celtic blood to call Germanic tribes against other Celtic peoples. As a result of their appeal, shiploads of Germanic warrior-adventurers, led by two Saxon warriors, Hengist and Horsa, began to arrive and ultimately occupied Britain, expelling the original owners to the western and northern barren mountainous areas.[18] "By about 700, the Anglo-Saxons had occupied most of England (the exceptions being Cornwall and an area in the North-West) and also a considerable part of southern Scotland" (Barber 1993: 100). This is the so-called Germanic Invasion or the Germanic Conquest. And it is the beginning of the English people and the English language.

Although we do not have lots of historical records on this incident, one reliable document is available. It is a book written in 731, almost three centuries after the event. It was originally written in Latin and its title is *Historia Ecclesiastica Gentis Anglorum*, translated into English as *The Ecclesiastical History of the English People*.[19] Its author is Venerable Bede,

---

[18] "Anglo-Saxons and their cousins the Frisians were famous as deep-sea sailors and pirates." (Barber 1993: 60)

[19] The **Historia Ecclesiastica Gentis Anglorum** (in English: **The Ecclesiastical History of the English People**) is a work in Latin by the Venerable Bede on the history of the Church in England and of England generally; its main focus is on the conflict between Roman and Celtic Christianity. It is considered to be one of the

who was a monk-scholar in the Jarrow monastery in the northern England. He describes the incident as follows (Book 1, Chapter 15, from http://www.fordham.edu/halsall/basis/bede-book1.html):

CHAPTER XV

THE ANGLES, BEING INVITED INTO BRITAIN, AT FIRST OBLIGED THE ENEMY TO RETIRE TO A DISTANCE; BUT NOT LONG AFTER, JOINING IN LEAGUE WITH THEM, TURNED THEIR WEAPONS UPON THEIR CONFEDERATES. [A.D. 450-456.]

In the year of our Lord 449, ... the nation of the Angles, or Saxons, being invited by the aforesaid king, arrived in Britain with three long ships, and had a place assigned them to reside in by the same king, in the eastern part of the island, that they might thus appear to be fighting for their country, whilst their real intentions were to enslave it. Accordingly they engaged with the enemy, who were come from the north to give battle, and obtained the victory; which, being known at home in their own country, as also the fertility of the country, and the cowardice of the Britons, a more considerable fleet was quickly sent over, bringing a still greater number of men, which, being added to the former, made up an invincible army. The newcomers received of the Britons a place to inhabit, upon condition that they should wage war against their enemies for the peace and security of the country, whilst the Britons agreed to furnish them with pay. **Those who came over were of**

---

most important original references on Anglo-Saxon history. It is believed to have been completed in 731, when Bede was approximately 60 years old. ("*Historia Ecclesiastica Gentis Anglorum*" In *Wikipedia*. Retrieved July 31, 2008)

the three most powerful nations of Germany the Saxons, Angles, and Jutes (emphasis added).[20] From the Jutes are descended the people of Kent, and of the Isle of Wight, and those also in the province of the West Saxons who are to this day called Jutes, seated opposite to the Isle of Wight. From the Saxons, that is, the country which is now called Old Saxony, came the East Saxons, the South Saxons, and the West Saxons. From the Angles, that is, the country which is called Anglia, and which is said, from that time, to remain desert to this day, between the provinces of the Jutes and the Saxons, are descended the East Angles, the Midland Angles, Mercians, all the race of the Northumbrians, that is, of those nations that dwell on the north side of the river Humber, and the other nations of the English. **The two first commanders are said to have been Hengist and Horsa** (emphasis added). Of whom Horsa, being afterwards slain in battle by the Britons, was buried in the eastern parts of Kent, where a monument, bearing his name, is still in existence ...

Another source for this event and for the (early) OE period is *The Anglo-Saxon Chronicle*,[21] which is a history book recording the important

---

20) "In a later chapter of his History (V: ch. 9), Bede adds that Frisians and other tribes were also involved in the migration, and there is further contemporary evidence for a Frisian presence, but recent scholarship denies that Frisians were part of the invading force." (Robinson 1994: 2869)

21) The **Anglo-Saxon Chronicle** is a collection of annals narrating the history of the Anglo-Saxons and their settlement in Britain. The chronicle has entries spanning AD 1 to 1154. Much of the information in these documents consists of rumors of events that happened elsewhere and so may be unreliable. However, some periods and places, the chronicle is the only substantial surviving source of information.

event(s) of every year from the date for Caesar's invasions of Britain to 1154. According to these two sources, the Britons appealed to Rome for help against the Picts and Scots. But Rome dispatched only a single legion, which was organized with about 6,000 soldiers. It was only temporarily effectual. The decision made by the desperate Britons was to call the more ferocious Germanic tribes from the Continent to expel the Picts and Scots. However, it was a fatal mistake to them.

The date that Bede gives for the first landing of these peoples is 449. With it the OE period begins. These Germanic sea raiders in short order expelled the Pictish and Scottish aggressors. Then, "with a complete lack of any sense of international morality and no fear, they very unidealistically proceeded to subjugate and ultimately to dispossess the Britons whom they had come ostensibly to help. Word of the cowardice of the Britons and the fertility of the island reached Continental kinsmen and friends, and in the course of the next hundred years or so more and more of these peoples arrived to seek their fortunes in a new land" (Pyles and Algeo 1993: 96). As for the Britons, who made a wrong fatal decision, their plight was hopeless. Many fled to the western mountainous areas such as Wales and Cornwall, some crossed to Ireland, others were ultimately assimilated to the English by marriage or otherwise. Many, we may be sure, lost their lives in the long-drawn-out fighting. The famous legendary King Arthur is believed to have been a Celtic leader fighting against the Germanic invaders in this period of turmoil.[22]

---

22) **King Arthur** was a fabled British leader and a prominent figure in Britain's legendary history. He is said in many medieval tales and chronicles to have taken the mantle of rulership over Britain and defended his land against Saxon invaders

The invading newcomers came from the great North German plain and from the southern part of the Jutland peninsula (modern Schleswig-Holstein of Denmark). Their Continental homes are guessed as in the following map:

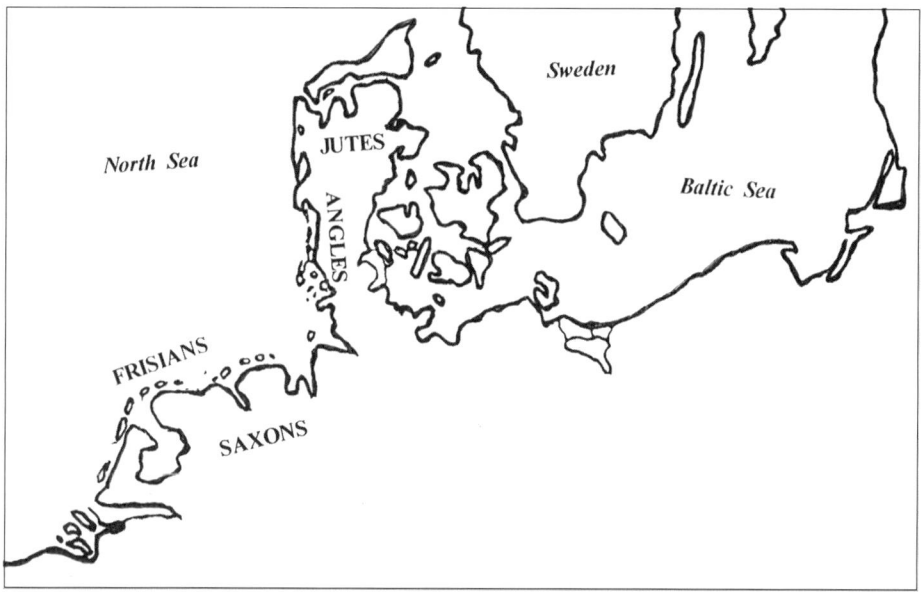

Figure 4.1 The Home of the English

4.2.2. *England* and *English*

With the Germanic Conquest Britain became to be understood as England. *Britain* means the land of the Britons, the original occupants of the British

---

following the withdrawal of Rome. Arthur's story includes considerable elements of legend and folklore, and his very existence is debated and has become a point of fierce controversy among modern historians. ("King Arthurt" In *Wikipedia*. Retrieved July 31, 2008)

Isles, whereas *England* means the land of the Angles. Among the various Germanic tribes, Saxons were the most influential tribe on the Continent before coming to Britain, so they were called Saxons all together. However, the Angles occupied the wide middle area of Britain and became the representative Germanic tribe in Britain. *English*, meaning the language of the Angles, was also from this people. The language spoken by the Germanic tribes in Britain was not called *English* (OE *Englisc*)[23] from the beginning. But the descendants of Germanic peoples a century and a half later were already beginning to think of themselves and their speech as *English*.[24] The name of a single tribe was thus to be adopted as the names of a nation and of a national language.

The original OE spelling for *Angles* was something like *Ængles*. The letter <Æ> (and its corresponding small letter <æ>) is the combination of <A> and <E> (<a> and <e> for the small letter).[25] When the letter disappeared, <A> or <E> had to be used instead for the old <Æ>. So sometimes <A> is used as in *Anglo-Saxon*, and sometimes <E> was used as in *England* (from OE *Ænglaland, the land of the Ængles*) and *English* (from OE *Ænglisc*,[26] *the language of the Ængles*).

---

23) In OE <sc>, instead of <sh>, was used to indicate the sound [ʃ]; for example, *scīr* 'shire,' and *fisc* 'fish.'

24) "The word *Engle* 'the Angles' came to be applied to all the Germanic settlers in Britain, and the related adjective *Englisc* was similarly applied to all these peoples and their language, not just to the Angles. Political union came slowly, however." (Barber 1993: 103)

25) See Footnote 7 of Chapter 2.

26) The suffix *-ish* means a language, as in *Spanish*, *Danish*, *Swedish*, *Flemish* and *Polish*.

4.2.3. The English in Britain: Anglo-Saxon Heptarchy

In the early days after the Germanic Conquest there was a medley of petty kingdoms in Britain. By a process of conquest and amalgamation, however, these small kingdoms were eventually reduced to seven, sometimes called the (Anglo-Saxon) Heptarchy;[27] Northumbria,[28] Mercia, East Anglia, Essex, Wessex, Sussex and Kent.[29] The locations of the seven kingdoms

---

27) **Heptarchy** (Greek: ἑπτά + ἀρχή *seven* + *realm*) is a collective name applied to the Anglo-Saxon ancient kingdoms of south, east and central Great Britain during late antiquity and the early Middle Ages which eventually unified into England. At this time the areas now known as Scotland and Wales were also divided into several smaller political units. ("Heparchy" In *Wikipedia*. Retrieved July 31, 2008)

28) **Northumbria** (*Nort(h)-Humb(e)r-ia*) means 'the land to the north of the Humber', a river (actually, a large tidal waterway) on the east coast of northern England. It was an Anglo-Saxon kingdom of northern England formed in the 7th century by the union of the two earlier kingdoms, **Bernicia** and **Deira**, Angle kingdoms originally established c. AD 500. Much of Northumbria fell to invading Danes in the 9th century and was annexed to Wessex in 954. Note that the suffix *-ia* means the land, territory or country, as in *India*, *Austria*, *Australia*, *Georgia* (*Georg(e)* 'farmer' *-ia*), *Bolivia*, *Bohemia*, etc.

29) The names of these kingdoms are still found in the provincial place names in modern Britain. All these names are also found in the university names, such as *the University of Northumbria* (http://northumbria.ac.uk), *the University of East Anglia* (http://www1.uea.ac.uk/cm/Home), *the University of Essex* (http://www.essex.ac.uk), *the University of Sussex* (http://www.sussex.ac.uk) and *the University of Kent* (http://www.kent.ac.uk/). But there is no university named *the University of Mercia* or *the University of Wessex*. Instead of *the University of Wessex*, there is *the University of Winchester* (http://www.winchester.ac.uk) in southern England. Winchester was the capital city of the kingdom of Wessex in the OE period.

are as in the following map:

Figure 4.2 Locations of Anglo-Saxon Heptarchy

These kingdoms rivaled each other. Sometimes one kingdom was more dominant and spread its power over the borders. But others also could gain its supremacy in time. At first, Kent became the chief center of culture and wealth. Especially, King Æthelberht (c. 560-616) could claim the hegemony over all the other kingdoms south of the Humber.[30] The early supremacy of Kent is quite clearly related to the fact that Kent accepted Christianity directly from Rome with the arrival of St. Augustine's missionary in 597 AD.[31]

The Early OE period (c. 450 - 900) is roughly equal to the period of Three Kingdoms (Baekje; BC 18 - AD 660, Koguryu; BC 37 - AD 668, and Shilla; BC 57 - AD 938) and the Kingdom of Unified Shilla (668-938) in Korean history. During this period, the three kingdoms also competed each other, trying to dominate the others. In general, the kingdom which accepted Buddhism before the other kingdoms could gain its supremacy in this period. It is because Buddhism in the Orient had more meanings and functions beyond religion. The same is true with Christianity in the West.

Later in the 7th century, the supremacy was passed from Kent to Northumbria. Northumbria also accepted Christianity, not from Rome but from Ireland this time. Ireland became a Christian country much earlier than Britain, so they sent missionary to the northern part of Britain for the propagation of their devoted religion. They set up a monastery on the isle of Iona, which is located between Ireland and Scotland. Then they moved to the northern Britain. With the help of these Irish monks and priests, Northumbria could hold several great monasteries functioning as the center

---

[30] **Æthelberht** (also **Æthelbert, Aethelberht, Aethelbert,** or **Ethelbert**) (c. 560 - February 24, 616) was King of Kent from about 580 or 590 until his death. In his *Ecclesiastical History of the English People*, the monk Bede lists Æthelberht as the third king to hold *imperium* over other Anglo-Saxon kingdoms. He was the first English king to convert to Christianity. ("Æthelberht" In *Wikipedia*. Retrieved July 31, 2008)

[31] The transmission of Christianity to Britain is explained in more detail in Section 4.2.5.

of learning, at Lindisfarne, Jarrow, Wearmouth and Whitby. Jarrow was the Venerable Bede's monastery, where he wrote a book on the early history of his people in relation to his religion, i.e. *Historia Ecclesiastica Gentis Anglorum* (*The Ecclesiastical History of the English People*). However, the cultural dominance of Northumbria did not last long because they were attacked by Viking invaders from Denmark and from Scandinavian countries such as Norway and Sweden.[32] With these attacks, most of the famous monasteries were burnt down to the ground. So the supremacy passed again to Mercia in the 8th century, which was located adjacently to the south of Northumbria. But finally the ultimate supremacy was gained by Wessex, the most southern kingdom of Britain. Its location was advantageous in defending themselves from the northern Viking invaders. In particular, Wessex had a brilliant line of kings beginning with Egbert (or Ecgberht),[33] who overthrew the Mercian king in 825, and culminating in his grandson, Alfred the Great (871-899).[34] Alfred is noted for his

---

32) **Viking** refers to a member of the Norse (Scandinavian) seafaring traders, warriors and pirates who raided and colonized wide areas of Europe from the late 8th to the 11th century. These Norsemen used their famed longships to travel as far east as Constantinople and the Volga River in Russia, and as far west as Newfoundland. This period of Viking expansion is commonly referred to as the Viking Age of Scandinavian History. ("Viking" In *Wikipedia*. Retrieved July 31, 2008)

33) **Egbert** (also spelt **Ecgberht**, 802-839) was King of Wessex from 802 until 839. *The Anglo-Saxon Chronicle* described Egbert as a *bretwalda*, or "Ruler of Britain". When Egbert died in 839, **Ethelwulf** succeeded him. The southeastern kingdoms were finally absorbed into the kingdom of Wessex after Æthelwulf's death in 858. And **Alfred** was the first to use the title *Rex Anglorum* (*King of the English*).

34) Wessex had a brilliant line of kings beginning with Egbert (Ecgberht, 802-839), then Ethelwulf (Æþelwulf, 839-855), Ethelbald (Æþelbald, 855-860), Ethelbert

defence of the kingdom against the Danish Vikings, becoming the only monarch to be awarded the epithet "the Great" in the British history. As a learned man, Alfred encouraged education and improved the kingdom's law system. Under his rule, Wessex became politically and culturally the leading kingdom of England, paving the way for the future political unification of the country.35) Finally, in the late 9th century, the kings of Wessex took the title *Rex Anglorum* (*King of England*). In this vein, the dialect spoken in Wessex (i.e. West Saxon) was OE, and Wessex itself was understood as the English nation of the OE period.

Table 4.1 The Rough Supremacy among the Kingdoms in the Old English Period

6th century	7th century	8th century	9th century
Kent	Northumbria	Mercia	Wessex

4.2.4. Old English Dialects

OE was not a completely uniform language mainly because the English people themselves were not originated from a single tribe. The Germanic tribes who came to establish themselves in Britain commanded different dialects on the European Continent. These dialects are distinguished from one another by features of pronunciation, grammar and vocabulary.

(Æþelberht, 860-866), Ethelred (Æþelred, 866-871), culminating in Alfred (Ælfred, 871-899). Ethelbald, Ethelbert, Ethelred and Alfred are Ethelwulf's four sons and so they are all bothers.

35) "If it had not been for Alfred, the history of the English language might have taken quite a different turn - the standard language of Great Britain might actually have been a Scandinavian tongue." (Svartvik and Leech 2006: 23)

Furthermore, their locations after the movement were a little different from each other. We can distinguish four dialects in OE times; Kentish, the speech of the Jutes who settled in Kent; West Saxon, spoken in the region south of the Thames exclusive of Kent (i.e. Wessex and Sussex); Mercian, spoken from the Thames to the Humber exclusive of Wales (i.e. Mercia, East Anglia and Essex); and Northumbrian, spoken north of the Humber. The localization of each dialect is as follows:

Figure 4.3 The Dialects of Old English

Mercian and Northumbrian have certain characteristics in common linguistically that distinguish them from West Saxon and Kentish.36) Thus they are sometimes grouped together as Anglian (the language of the Angles), since those who spoke these north-of-the-Thames dialects were predominantly Angles. We can see from the following table the linguistic closeness of Mercian and Northumbrian:

Table 4.2 Differences in Spellings and Pronunciations between the OE Dialects (slight revision of Hogg (1992: 432))

Modern Word	West Saxon	Northumbrian	Mercian	Kentish
broke	bræcon	brēcon	brēcon	brēcon
old	eald	ald	ald	eald
land	land	lond	lond	land
light	·	lēht	lēht	·
seat	setol	seatol	seotul	setol
evil	yfel	yfel	yfel	efel
yet	gīet	gēt	gēt	gēt

Other dialects presumably existed, but we possess no written remains of them. The OE facts of composing tribes, their kingdoms, and the dialects are summarized as in the following table:

---

36) Look at Table 4.3 to see the closeness between Mercian and Northumbrian.

Table 4.3 Composing Tribes, their Kingdoms
and the Dialects of the Old English Period

3 Tribes	7 Kingdoms	4 Dialects[37]	
Angles	Northumbria	Northumbrian	Anglian > English
	Mercia	Mercian	
	East Anglia		
	Essex		
Saxons	Wessex	West Saxon (Standard in OE)	
	Sussex		
Jutes	Kent	Kentish	

Although the standard form of PDE is in large part a descendant of Mercian speech (the dialect of the central England), the standard dialect of OE was West Saxon. During the time of Alfred and for a long time thereafter, Winchester, the capital of Wessex and therefore in a sense of all England, was the center of English culture, thanks to the encouragement given by Alfred himself to learning. There is an extensive collection of texts written in West Saxon. With the ascendancy of the West Saxon kingdoms (Wessex and Sussex), the West Saxon dialect attained something of the position of a literary standard at the time. When a standard English once more began to arise in the ME period, however, it was on the basis of the Midland, especially the East Midland dialect. The East Midland dialect of the ME period was the descendant of OE Merican dialect.[38]

---

[37] The names of languages frequently take the suffix -(a)n (e.g. *Korean, Mongolian, Frisian, German, Norwegian, Romanian, Bulgarian*, etc.) or - *ish* (OE *-sc*, e.g. *Danish, Spanish, Swedish, Flemish, Polish*, etc.).

[38] We have seen that the name of *English* is indebted to the Angles, who were the speakers of the Mercian dialect. So we can guess the central role played by the

Though London was an important and thriving commercial city even in OE times, it did not acquire its cultural and political importance until later. It is thus in West Saxon that most of the extant OE records were written. The records of Anglian and Kentish are scant.

4.2.5. Christianization of Britain

As was already mentioned above, Christianity played a very important cultural and political role in the OE period. "We know little about the Anglo-Saxons until after their conversion to Christianity,[39] which introduced them to writing" (Barber 1993: 106). It came to Britain from two different directions: straight from Rome to Kent and from the Irish-Scottish monastery of Iona to the northwest.

When Gregory became Pope (Pope Gregory I the Great) in 590,[40] he sent a band of missionaries comprising St. Augustine[41] and forty monks

---

Angles and by the Mercian (i.e. Midland) dialect in the formation of the standard English.

39) "There is a 'dark age' between the arrival of the Anglo-Saxons and the first OE manuscripts." (Crystal 2002: 171)

40) **Saint Gregory I the Great** or **Pope Saint Gregory I** (c. 540 - March 12, 604) was pope from September 3, 590 until his death. He is also known as **Gregorius Dialogus (Gregory the Dialogist)** in Eastern Orthodoxy because of the Dialogues he wrote. He was the first of the Popes from a monastic background. Gregory is a Doctor of the Church and one of the four great Latin Fathers of the Church (the others being Ambrose, Augustine and Jerome). Of all popes, Gregory I had the most influence on the early medieval church. ("Pope Gregory I" In *Wikipedia*. Retrieved July 31, 2008)

41) **St. Augustine** mentioned here (birth unknown - 604) should not be confused with

to Kent in 596 in order to convert the Kentish king Æthelberht. The kingdom of Kent is the nearest to the Continent. Gregory probably chose Kent as the start of the missionary efforts because Æthelberht was married to a Christian Frankish princess and Kent was close to the already Christian kingdoms in Gaul. At first, the missionaries turned back before reaching Kent, but Gregory urged them to return, and in 597 Augustine landed on the Isle of Thanet and went to Æthelberht's main town of Canterbury (literally *Kent's city* or *Kent's town*). Æthelberht allowed the missionaries to preach freely, and later was converted to Christianity himself. He gave land to Augustine to build his cathedral, and also gave land to the missionaries to found a monastery outside the walls of Canterbury. Four years later, in 601, Augustine was consecrated first Archbishop of Canterbury, and went on to convert numbers of the king's followers. Ultimately, there was a church in England.[42] This made Kent the most influential kingdom of the time in Britain. Since then Canterbury has remained the ecclesiastical capital of England.

Meanwhile, Irish missionaries crossed the sea from Iona to the northern Britain and found a monastery at Lindisfarne and then several others. Through their efforts, many people converted to Christianity in Northumbria and Mercia. In the course of the 7th century the new faith

---

the African-born bishop of Hippo of the same name who wrote *The City of God* (probably more well-known St. Augustine (354 - 430)) more than a century earlier. **Augustine of Canterbury** was a Benedictine monk and the first Archbishop of Canterbury. He is considered the "Apostle to the English" and a founder of the English Church.

42) We can see a magnificent cathedral in Canterbury, which shows its role as the mecca of early Christianity in Britain.

spread rapidly and by the end of that century England had become the most important part of Christendom.

Christianity was the official religion of the Roman Empire, the most powerful and culturally prestigious empire in the human history. So the transmission of Christianity meant the import of the highest culture of the time in Europe. For this reason, the Christianization of Britain also had important consequences for the development of culture and scholarship in the country. Many schools were established within churches throughout England and scholarly monasteries, too, in Canterbury, Lindisfarne, Jarrow, Wearmouth and Whitby. The establishment of academic institutions brought knowledge of Greek and Latin and, with it, it became possible to access to the high Roman civilization. In particular, missionaries brought the language of the Roman Empire, Latin, and its writing system, the Roman alphabet[43] together.[44] They also brought with them the parchment,[45] the

---

[43] The word **alphabet** itself comes to ME from the Late Latin **Alphabetum**, which in turn originates from the Ancient Greek **Alphabetos**, from *alpha* and *beta*, the first two letters of the Greek alphabet.

[44] The Roman Alphabet is the most widely used alphabetic writing system in the world today. It evolved from the western variety of the **Greek alphabet** and was initially developed by the ancient Romans in Classical Antiquity to write the Latin language.

[45] **Parchment** is a thin material made from calfskin, sheepskin or goatskin. Its most common use is as the pages of a book, codex or manuscript. It is distinct from **leather** in that parchment is not tanned, but stretched, scraped and dried under tension, creating a stiff white, yellowish or translucent animal skin. The finer qualities of parchment are called **vellum.** It is very reactive with changes in relative humidity and is not waterproof. ("Parchment" In *Wikipedia*. Retrieved July 31, 2008)

writing material to leave priceless records of history and literature. Germanic peoples used their own writing system called Runes (or the Runic Alphabets) before accepting the Roman Alphabet.[46] In other words, the first alphabet or script used by the Germanic peoples were Runes, which, over time, developed several variant types. But the Runes were used only for short inscriptions (i.e. mainly for epigraphic purpose), not for texts of any length. They are not adequate in writing on parchment because they are mostly angular in their forms, along with the vertical and slanting strokes. The Anglo-Saxon Runes are as follows:

---

46) The **Runic alphabets** were used in northern Europe, in Scandinavia, present-day Germany and the British Isles. The alphabets are a set of related alphabets using letters (known as *runes*), formerly used to write Germanic languages before and shortly after the Christianization of Scandinavia and the British Isles. The Scandinavian variants are known as *Futhark* (or *Fuþark*, derived from their first six letters: *F, U, Þ, A, R* and *K*); the Anglo-Saxon variant as *Futhork* (or *Fuþorc*, due to sound changes undergone in OE by the same six letters). The common runic alphabet used throughout the area (i.e. *Futhark*) consisted of twenty-four letters, but the version found in Britain (i.e. *Futhork*) used extra letters to cope with the range of sounds found only in OE. At its most developed form, it consisted of thirty-one, sometimes thirty-three letters, as Table 4.4 shows. ("Runic Alphabet" In *Wikipedia*. Retrieved July 31, 2008)

Table 4.4 Anglo-Saxon Runes (Fuhorc, Futhork)

	Rune	Name	Transliteration	Modern Spelling or Sound
1	ᚠ	feoh	"wealth"	f [f], [v]
2	ᚢ	ur	"aurochs"	u
3	ᚦ	þorn	"thorn"	ð [θ], [ð]
4	ᚩ	ós	"[a] god"	ó
5	ᚱ	rad	"ride"	r
6	ᚳ	cen	"torch"	c [k]
7	ᚷ	gyfu	"gift"	ȝ [g], [j]
8	ᚹ	wynn	"joy"	w [w]
9	ᚻ	hægl	"hail (precipitation)"	h
10	ᚾ	nyd	"need, distress"	n
11	ᛁ	is	"ice"	i
12	ᛄ	ger	"year, harvest"	j
13	ᛇ	eoh	"yew"	eo
14	ᛈ	peorð	unknown	p
15	ᛉ	eolh	"elk-sedge"	x
16	ᛋ	sigel	"Sun"	s [s], [z]
17	ᛏ	Tiw	"Tiw"	t
18	ᛒ	beorc	"birch"	b
19	ᛖ	eh	"horse"	e
20	ᛗ	mann	"man"	m
21	ᛚ	lagu	"lake"	l
22	ᛝ	ing	"Ing (a hero)"	ŋ
23	ᛟ	éðel	"estate"	œ
24	ᛞ	dæg	"day"	d
25	ᚪ	ac	"oak"	a
26	ᚫ	æsc	"ash-tree"	æ
27	ᚣ	yr	"bow"	y
28	ᛡ	ior	"eel"	ia, io
29	ᛠ	ear	"grave"	ea
30	ᛢ	cweorð	unknown	kw
31	ᛣ	calc	"chalice"	k
32	ᛥ	stan	"stone"	st
33	ᚸ	gar	"spear"	g

The runic letters were only suitable to make an inscription on hard materials such as stones or animal bones, so they were easily replaced by the new alphabets imported from Rome through Christianity.

The adoption of Christianity also influenced the English vocabulary, too. The diverse Latin vocabulary was imported to English in a great deal under the influence of Christianity.[47] New ideas should be expressed by the imported words, mainly from Latin; *apostle* (OE *apostle*), *pope* (OE *pāpa*), *monk* (OE *munuc*), *abbot* (OE *abbot*), *mass* (OE *mæsse*), *verse* (OE *fers*),[48] *school* (OE *scōl*) and *teacher* (OE *mægester* > *master*).

4.3. The Late Old English Period (900-1100)[49]

4.3.1. The Viking Invasion of the British Isles

The Late OE period was the times of chaos caused by the Scandinavian invasions of England.[50] These invasions, beginning in the later years of the 8th century, exerted a profound influence on all walks of life of the English people and at the same time on the English language, too.[51] These

---

47) "Altogether, there have been recorded some 400 Latin words in Old English introduced as a result of the spread of Christianity." (Svartvik and Leech 2006: 21)

48) Here, *verse* means the unit of the Bible (one of the series of short parts into which the writing of the holy book is divided, e.g. *Gospel of Matthews*, Chapter 11, Verses 11-13), not the poems.

49) This section is mostly based on Pyles and Algeo (1993: 99-101).

50) "There were at least three phases of Viking activities, stretching over some 250 years: sporadic raids, permanent colonization and political supremacy." (Svartvik and Leech 2006: 23)

51) "The harrying of Europe by the Scandinavian Vikings, which took place between about 750 and 1050, was the last phase of the expansion of the early Germanic peoples." (Barber 1993: 127)

Scandinavian invaders are generally called the Vikings.[52] They were also Germanic peoples like Anglo-Saxons and they consisted of Swedes, Danes and Norwegians. They spoke the common language called Old Norse, from which Swedish, Danish and Norwegian are descended. They did not have a faith for Christianity when they came to Britain. That is, they were pagans. Instead, they believed in traditional Germanic gods such as *Thor* and *Woden* (also known as *Odin*).[53]

The Scandinavian invaders could approach Britain from two directions; from the north and the south. The northern route was mainly followed by the Norwegians, while the southern approach was taken mainly by the Danes. The earliest attacks, according to *The Anglo-Saxon Chronicle*, took place in 787 from the north by the Norwegians. The pagan Viking raiders sacked, looted and pillaged various churches and monasteries, including Lindisfarne and Jarrow. Due to these attacks on the northern Britain, the

---

52) **Viking** is from Old Norse *víkingr*, perhaps meaning 'creek-dweller', and hence 'pirate'. The corresponding OE word is *wīcing* 'pirate'. They were called by many different names, including 'heathens', 'pagans', 'Northmen' or 'Danes'. Due to their skill and daring as sailors and navigators, they were able to reach North America ('Vinland') long before Columbus, perhaps earlier than the year 1000.

53) *Woden* was the supreme god of Germanic and Norse mythology, like *Zeus* or *Jupiter* in the Greek and Roman mythology. *Thor* in Old Norse (*Thunor* in OE), like *Jupiter*, was lord of the sky. The names of the days of the week, such as Wednesday (from OE Wodnesdæg 'Woden's day') and Thursday (from OE Thunresdæg 'Thor's day') were from the names of these gods. In fact, the days of the week are all the names of Roman or Germanic gods: *Sunnandæg,* Sunday; *Monandæg,* Monday; *Tiwesdæg,* Tuesday (*Tiw*, like *Mars*, was the Germanic god of war); *Frigedæg,* Friday (*Frig*, like *Venus*, was the Germanic goddess of love); and *Sæternesdæg,* Saturday (*Saturn*, the Roman god of agriculture and harvest).

kingdoms of Northumbria and Mercia became to lose their political and cultural supremacy, yielding their hegemony to the southern kingdoms like Wessex. During the first half of the 9th century other more or less disorganized but disastrous raids, this time led by the Danes from the south, took place. Then, in 865 a great and expertly organized army landed in East Anglia and defeated the counterattacks by the East Anglians. During the next fifteen years the Vikings came very near to conquering the whole of England. In 870 the Vikings finally attacked Wessex, the most southern and the last surviving kingdom in Britain. At that time, Wessex was ruled by Ethelred (Æþelræd, 837-871, king of Wessex from 866-871)[54] with the able assistance of his brother Alfred. Alfred succeeded his brother Ethelred's throne in the following year (i.e. in 871) due to his brother's death at the battlefield. After years of discouragement, very few victories, and many crushing defeats, Alfred in 878 won a signal victory at Edington (Chippenham in Modern England) over Guthrum, who was the Danish king ruling East Anglia. They signed a kind of peace treaty at Wedmore and the Danes departed from Wessex. Thus the territory under Guthrum's rule was restricted to the northern Britain including East Anglia. This region was

---

54) King **Ethelred I** (OE: Æþelræd) (c. 840 - April 23, 871) was the fourth son of **Ethelwulf** of Wessex. He succeeded his brother, **Ethelbert**, as King of Wessex and Kent in 865. Ethelred I was not able to control the increasing Danish raids which devastated England. On January 4, 871 at the Battle of Reading, Ethelred suffered a crushing defeat, although he did hand the Danes a Pyrrhic victory. Soon after, however, Ethelred was able to re-form his army in time to win a stunning victory at Ashdown. However, he suffered another defeat on January 22 at the Battle of Basing and was killed at the Battle of Merton on April 23, 871. ("Ethelred" In *Wikipedia*. Retrieved July 31, 2008)

still subject to the laws of the Danes, so it became known as the Danelaw.[55] And Guthrum himself was baptized, having Alfred his godfather when the sacrament was later administered. With this victory Wessex could be the dominant kingdom in Britain. Alfred's sons and grandsons were able to consolidate England and this royal dynasty eventually came to rule all of the Anglo-Saxon England (in 927). The other kingdoms of Anglo-Saxons were nearly collapsed with the Viking attacks.

4.3.2. The Viking Conquest of the British Isles

However, the troubles with the Danes were by no means over.[56] In the Late OE period, specifically in the later years of the 10th century, trouble started again. This time the attacks were from the north and the south jointly. The troubles began with the arrival of a fleet of warriors led by Olaf Tryggvason,[57] king of Norway, who was in a few years to be joined by

---

55) The **Danelaw**, as recorded in *The Anglo-Saxon Chronicle*, is a historical name given to a part of Great Britain in which the laws of the Danes held predominance over those of the Anglo-Saxons. The part of Great Britain which was part of the Danelaw is now northern and eastern England. ("Danelaw" In *Wikipedia*. Retrieved July 31, 2008)
56) The Vikings were generally called the Danes (OE *Dene*) by the English, though there were Norwegians and later Swedes among them.
57) **Olaf Tryggvason** (960s - 1000) was King of Norway from 995 to 1000. He played an important part in the conversion of the Vikings to Christianity. He is said to have built the first church in Norway (in 995). We should notice in passing that the Vikings were not always "barbaric". They were sophisticated, technologically advanced peoples, proficient sailors, ship and town builders. ("Olaf Tryggvason" In *Wikipedia*. Retrieved July 31, 2008)

Danish King Sweyn Forkbeard.[58] For more than twenty years there were repeated attacks, most of them crushing defeats for the English. The famous OE poem *The Battle of Maldon* describes the glorious but unsuccessful stand made by the men of Essex under the valiant Byrhtnoth in 991. However, the attacks by the Vikings were not met with such vigorous resistance any more.

Finally in 1016 the English king Ethelred II (Æðelræd, 979-1016) was killed by the Vikings.[59] And the Danish king Canute, son of Sweyn Forkbeard came to the English throne. Ultimately, Britain became a part of the 'Viking Empire'. But the Danish rule was not barbarous any more. In fact, Canute is known as a wise king (called Canute the Great) for both the Danish and English peoples.[60] Furthermore, the Danish rule did not last for a long time.

---

58) **Sweyn Forkbeard** (c. 960 - February 3, 1014) was King of Denmark and England, as well as parts of Norway. He was a Viking leader and the father of **Canute (or Cnut) the Great**. On his father Harald Bluetooth's death in late 986 or early 987, he became King of Denmark. After a long effort at conquest, he became King of England. For the last months of his life, he was the Danish sovereign of the 'Viking Empire'. ("Sweyn Forkbeard" In *Wikipedia*. Retrieved July 31, 2008)

59) This king is a different person from Alfred's brother with the same name of the late 9th century. **Ethelred II** (c. 968 - April 23, 1016) is also known as **Ethelred the Unready** (OE Æþelræd Unræd). The majority of his reign (991 - 1016) was marked by a defensive war against Viking invaders.

60) **Canute the Great**, or **Canute I**, also known as **Cnut** in *The Anglo-Saxon Chronicles* (died November 12, 1035) was a Viking king of England, Denmark, Norway and parts of Sweden. He was in diplomatic, even amicable relations with the Holy Roman Emperors and the Germanic kings. His reign - nearly two decades long - was over a northern empire spread across Scandinavia and the British Isles, and saw the Danish sovereignty at its height. ("Canute the Great" In *Wikipedia*. Retrieved July 31, 2008)

The line of Alfred was restored in 1042, with the accession of Edward the Confessor.[61] He was the son of the English king Ethelred II. He fled to Normandy after his father's death, but he restored the English throne after the death of Canute. Strangely, the Vikings radically weakened and disappeared to the back curtain of the European history in the 11th century.

4.3.3. Scandinavian Influences on English

"Despite the enmity and the bloodshed, there was a feeling among the English that when all was said and done the Northmen belonged to the same 'family' as themselves, a feeling that their ancestors could never have experienced regarding the British Celts" (Pyles and Algeo 1993: 103). The Vikings are Germanic like the Anglo-Saxons, while the Celts are not.

Whereas the earlier raids had been dictated largely by the desire to pillage and to loot, the 10th and early 11th century invaders from the north seem to have been much more interested in colonization and establishment in Britain, seeking new homes instead of their homeland of the harsh winter. This was successfully accomplished. The Danes settled down peaceably enough in time, living side by side with the English. Scandinavians were good colonizers, willing to assimilate themselves to their new homes. "England still remained England; the conquerors sank quietly into the mass of those around them; and Woden yielded without a struggle to Christ."[62]

---

61) **Edward the Confessor** (c. 1003/1004 - 4 January 1066), son of Ethelred the Unready, was the last Anglo-Saxon king of England, ruling from 1042 until his death.
62) This is a statement of John Richard Green, cited by Jespersen (1954: 58) and by Pyles and Algeo (1993: 101).

As has been pointed out, those whom the English called Danes were not all from Denmark. Linguistically, however, this fact is of little significance, for the various Scandinavian tongues were in those days little differentiated from one another. So their languages are called Old Norse collectively. Furthermore, they were sufficiently like OE as to make communication possible between the English and the Scandinavians. The languages are all branches of Germanic language family. The English were perfectly aware of their racial as well as their linguistic kinship with the Scandinavians, many of whom had become their neighbors. The most famous OE poem *Beowulf* is exclusively concerned with the events of Scandinavian legend and history. Due to the intimate linguistic relationship between OE and Old Norse, the two languages exerted influences on each other.[63] OE and Old Norse had a whole host of frequently used words in common, among others, *man, wife, mother, folk, house, thing, winter, summer, will, can, come, hear, see, think, ride, over, under, mine* and *thine*.[64] The contact with Old Norse had a tremendous impact on the development of English as evidenced by a large number of Scandinavian elements in the English language.[65] These elements include loanwords, place names, personal names and grammatical (both morphological and syntactic) modification. Loanwords of Scandinavian origin are associated with the sea, law, and a variety of everyday objects, activities, qualities, etc. Examples are *bank,*

---

[63] "Old English and Old Norse were still reasonably similar, and Englishmen and Danes could probably understand each other, and pick up each other's language, without too much difficulty." (Barber 1993: 130)

[64] These words are cited from Jespersen (1954: 60).

[65] "English triumphed, but not before a great deal of Scandinavian had got mixed with it." (Barber 1993: 130)

bull, egg, fellow, gap, law, loan, toot, sister,[66] *skill, skirt, steak, window, ill, low, weak, wrong, call, get, give, take*,[67] *want*, etc. Scandinavian influence on English place names may be illustrated by the names ending in Scandinavian elements like *-by* (farm(stead), town, village; from Norwegian), such as *Grims<u>by</u>, Der<u>by</u>, Rug<u>by</u>* and *Whit<u>by</u>*, *-thorp(e)* (farm(stead), town, village; from Danish), such as *Al<u>thorp</u>* and *Lin<u>thorpe</u>*, *-thwaite* (woodland clearing, meadow), such as *Mickle<u>thwaite</u>, Brai<u>thwaite</u>* and *Lang<u>thwaite</u>*, and *-toft* (building-site, plot of land, ground), such as *Eas<u>toft</u>, Lang<u>toft</u>* and *Nor<u>toft</u>*.[68] Some personal names also reflect the Scandinavian influence, such as *Harald, Eric, Orm, Rainald* and *Ulf*. Especially, the suffix *-son* was from Scandinavia, such as *John<u>son</u>* (John's son), *Richard<u>son</u>, Johann<u>son</u>*, etc.

Some grammatical words are also from Scandinavian, for instance, the conjunctions *though, till* and *until*. The third person plural pronouns, i.e. the <th-> forms, such as *they, their* and *them*, are of Scandinavian origin.[69] Thus we can see that, although the total number of Scandinavian loans is in fact rather small, many of them are words in very frequent use.

---

66) The scandinavian form *sister* (ON *systir*) has won out the OE form *sweostor*.
67) This word is not found in OE, which uses the verb *niman* 'to take'.
68) According to Crystal (2002: 175), "there are over 1,500 place names of Scandinavian origin in England, especially in Yorkshire and Lincolnshire."
69) OE forms were *hī(e)* 'they', *him/he(o)m* 'them' and *hi(e)ra/he(o)ra* 'their'. The form *hem* meaning 'them' still survives as *'em* [əm] in PDE. The initial [h] is regularly lost in unstressed words, as in *Give 'em what they want*.

4.4. Old English Literature

OE is also English, and PDE has its root on OE. Nevertheless, we seldom read OE literary works in its original because it is very difficult to read them without special training. Furthermore, the true literary works are not abound. The written records of this period are mainly in the form of charters, wills and other official records, rather than literary works.[70]

The OE literature is primarily characterized by poetry. As in other cultures, prose literature appears much later than the verse. The most important work of OE poetry is undoubtedly *Beowulf*.[71] The poem of 3183 lines was composed some time in the 8th or 9th century by an unknown poet. The poem is a folk epic in the form of a narrative of the young Scandinavian warrior Beowulf, fighting and destroying monsters, and finally dying as a hero.[72] Apart from *Beowulf*, the Germanic tradition is reflected

---

70) According to Robinson (1994: 2870), approximately three million words of OE are preserved in some two thousand extant texts.
71) **Beowulf** is an OE heroic epic poem of anonymous authorship. This work of Anglo-Saxon literature dates to between the 8th and the 11th century, the only surviving manuscript dating to c. 1010. At 3183 lines, it is notable for its length. It has risen to national epic status in England. In the poem, Beowulf, a hero of the Geats, battles three antagonists: Grendel, who is attacking the Danish mead-hall called Heorot and its inhabitants; Grendel's mother; and, later in life after returning to Geatland (modern southern Sweden) and becoming a king, an unnamed dragon. He is mortally wounded in the final battle, and after his death he is buried in a barrow in Geatland by his retainers. ("Beowulf" In *Wikipedia*. Retrieved July 31, 2008)
72) Tolkien's *Lord of the Rings* is a similar adventurous story. **John Ronald Reuel Tolkien** (1892 - 1973) was an English philologist, writer and university professor,

in such shorter poems as *The Wanderer*, *The Seafarer*, *Deor* and *Widsith*.

It is frequently supposed that the OE period was somehow gray, dull and crude. But it is not true. As was already mentioned, due to the early conversion to Christianity at the end of the 6th century (in 597), England became a veritable beehive of scholarly activity. The famous monasteries at Canterbury, Wearmouth, Lindisfarne, Jarrow and York were great centers of learning. The culture of the northern England in the 7th and 8th centuries was to spread over the entire country, despite the decline that it suffered as a result of the hammering onslaughts of the Danes. Luckily, because of the tremendous energy and ability of Alfred the Great, it was not lost. He inspired translation of Latin works into English. For instance, Bede's *Ecclesiastical History of the English People* and Pope Gregory's *Pastoral Care* were translated into English from Latin under his order.[73] And Ælfric,[74] the most representative writer and scholar of the late 10th and early 11th century, left

---

who is best known as the author of *The Hobbit* and *The Lord of the Rings*. He was an Oxford professor of Anglo-Saxon language (1925 to 1945) and English language and literature (1945 to 1959).

73) In this vein, Alfred the Great is comparable to Sejong the Great, one of the most respected figures in Korean History. They both are scholars themselves. They were greatly worried about the illiteracy of their people, having a deep sympathy towards their people. Alfred tried to translate as many Latin documents as possible into English for the lay people to access to them, while Sejong rather invented a new writing system (i.e. Hanguel, literally the Great Letters) for his people to read and write without the knowledge on difficult Chinese characters.

74) Ælfric of Eynsham (c. 955 - c. 1010) was an English abbot, as well as a consummate, prolific writer in OE of hagiography, homilies, biblical commentaries and other genres. He mainly thought of himself as a humble teacher, responsible for the souls in his care. ("Ælfric" In *Wikipedia*. Retrieved July 31, 2008)

many documents about Christianity, such as *Homilies* and *Lives of Saints*. His works compose the main prose documents of this period and function as the primary data for the study of OE.

Chapter 05

The Middle English Period (1100-1500)

The ME period began with a political event that occurred in 1066. The event was the Norman Conquest. However, the division of the historical stages of English is rather arbitrary. So the dates for the beginning and the end of ME are different among scholars. Some mention 1066, the year of the Norman Conquest itself, as the beginning of ME,[1] while others say that the year should be around 1100. This book adopts the 1100 theory, because it must have taken some years for the English language to be influenced by the French-speaking Normans after the Conquest.

The ME period is transitional from OE to Early ModE. Through this period English became quite a different language deviating from its original Germanic shape, mainly due to the influence of French. French is not a Germanic language. The changes that occurred during this transitional or middle period may be noted in every aspect of the language: in sounds,

---

[1] For example, Smith (1994: 2487) says, "The English of the period between the Norman Conquest of 1066 AD and the arrival of printing in England in 1476 is generally referred to as Middle English."

in the meanings of words and in the nature of the word stock. The influences by French made English a kind of mixed language, having both Germanic and Romance characteristics together. A lot of original Germanic words simply disappeared or were replaced by the corresponding French ones. And many new words were also borrowed from French (and some words from Latin).[2] And new spellings and pronunciations were introduced.[3] Because there were such extensive changes in pronunciation, particularly of unaccented inflectional endings,[4] grammar too was profoundly altered.[5] Thus at the end of this period, the English language became a language that is structurally far more like PDE.

---

[2] "While English was thus left without a standard literary dialect, the prestige languages in England were Latin and French. Latin was the language of the church, of scholarship and of international communication: after the Conquest it was also important in administration, but here it gradually gave way to French." (Barber 1993: 140)

"Judging by the documents which have survived, it seems that French was the language of government, law, administration and the church, with Latin also used as a medium of education and worship." (Crystal 2002: 191)

[3] For example, the spellings such as <j, q, v> are all imported from French.

[4] In Germanic languages, the word stress falls in the word-initial position, whereas in Romance languages like French, it falls to the word-final position. With the mixture of these two characteristics, the stress patterns of English words are largely unpredictable, as in *ínteresting* (stress on the 1st syllable), *infléction* (on the 2nd syllable) and *employée* (on the 3rd syllable).

[5] During the ME period the inflectional system of grammatical endings was reduced and simplified. At the end of the period, very much as in today's English, the grammatical relationships of a sentence are mainly indicated by prepositions and a fixed word order.

5.1. The Early Middle English Period (1100-1300)

5.1.1. The Norman Conquest

Towards the close of the OE period, "the great catastrophe of the Norman Conquest befell the English people - a catastrophe more far-reaching in its effects on English culture than the earlier harassment by the Scandinavians" (Pyles and Algeo 1993: 137). This event had a greater effect on the English language, too, than any other in the course of its history.

Edward the Confessor, the last king in the direct male line of descent from Alfred the Great, died in 1066 without leaving his own child.[6] This immediately caused a controversy about his successor: Who will be the next king? The final winner was Harold (King Harold II), son of the powerful earl Godwin.[7] There was no rival of royal blood in Britain. But such a rival was across the sea. The man was William, the duke of Normandy, a northern province of France. William was a distant relative to Edward the Confessor and felt that he had a better claim to the English

---

6) **St. Edward the Confessor** (*c.* 1004 - 1066), son of Ethelred the Unready, was the penultimate Anglo-Saxon King of England and the last of the House of Wessex, ruling from 1042 until his death. Although Edward got married, he is said to have lived a kind of unmarried life like priests. The result was that he died without issue. He was canonized in 1161 and is considered a saint by the Roman Catholic Church. From the reign of Henry II of England to 1348 he was considered the patron saint of England, and he has remained the patron saint of the Royal Family.

7) **Godwin** (sometimes known as **Godwin of Wessex**) (c. 1001 - April 15, 1053), was one of the most powerful lords in England under the Danish king Canute the Great and his successors. Canute made him the first Earl of Wessex. Godwin was the father of wife of Edward the Confessor. ("Godwin" In *Wikipedia*. Retrieved July 31, 2008)

throne than Harold for a number of reasons. So almost immediately his possession of the crown, Harold was challenged by William. In 1066 William crossed the English Channel to claim the English crown through a military means.[8] He defeated the English under the unfortunate King Harold at the battle of Hastings in 1066.[9] According to a traditional story, Harold was killed by an arrow that pierced his eye, and his two brothers were also killed in the battlefield. The English were defeated, deprived of the effective royal leadership. Finally William was crowned as king of England, getting the nickname the Conqueror. So William the Conqueror opened the Norman dynasty (1066-1154).[10]

Like the earlier harassments by the Vikings in the Late OE period, the Norman Conquest was carried out by Northmen (or Norsemen).[11] The

---

[8] Fortunately for Anglo-American culture and civilization, this was the last invasion of England.

[9] The **Battle of Hastings** was the decisive Norman victory in the Norman Conquest of England. The location was a hill approximately 6 miles north of Hastings, on which was later built an abbey, and the town of Battle in the modern county of East Sussex. The battle took place on October 14, 1066, between the Normans of Duke William of Normandy ("William the Conqueror") and the Saxon army led by King Harold II. Harold was killed, traditionally by an arrow in the eye. And, though there was some later resistance, this moment is seen as the point at which William gains control of England. ("Battle of Hastings" In *Wikipedia*. Retrieved July 31, 2008)

[10] The **Norman dynasty** is a series of four monarchs (William I 1066 - 1087 known as William the Conqueror, William II 1087 – 1100 William I's second surviving son, Henry I 1100 - 1135 William I's fifth son, Stephen 1135 – 1154 William I's grandson), who ruled England from the time of the Norman Conquest in 1066, until 1154.

[11] **Norsemen** means 'people from the North' and was applied primarily to people from southern and central Scandinavia. *Norsemen* is used to refer to the group of people

ancestors of William the Conqueror were Vikings, and they invaded France, roughly at the same time when they were making troubles for Alfred the Great and sacking the British Isles (i.e. about in the late 9th and the early 10th century). William's Viking ancestors had invaded and settled at a northern coast of France which is not-very-remote from their original homes. This region that they settled and governed was to be called *Normandy* (from *Normandia*, literally meaning 'the land of the Norseman/Northman'). This region was ruled by a duke of Viking blood. The first duke of Normandy was Rollo (Hrólf),[12] a Danish chieftain. He became the duke, accepting the king of France (King Charles the Simple) as his overlord. William the Conqueror was the 7th duke of Normandy at the time of the Conquest. In fact, he was not eligible for the dukedom because he was a bastard son of the duke, Robert the Devil[13] and a daughter of a mean tanner in the market. So he took such pains in the early part of his life to be a duke of Normandy. He was accused of poisoning his half brother, the legitimate successor to the duke of Normandy.

---

as a whole who speak one of the North Germanic languages as their native language. (**Norse**, in particular, refers to the Old Norse language belonging to the North Germanic branch of Indo-European languages, especially Danish, Icelandic, Swedish and Norwegian in their earlier forms.) ("Norsemen" In *Wikipedia*. Retrieved July 31, 2008)

12) **Rollo** (c. 860 - c. 932) was the founder and first ruler of the Viking principality in what soon became known as Normandy. He is also in some sources known as **Robert of Normandy**, using his baptismal name. The name Rollo is a Frankish-Latin name probably taken from Scandinavian name **Hrólf**. ("Rollo" In *Wikipedia*. Retrieved July 31, 2008)

13) **Robert the Devil** (June 22, 1000 - 3 July 1035) was the 6th Duke of Normandy from 1027 until his death. He was the father of William the Conqueror.

In the several generations intervening between (the 1st) Duke Rollo and (the 7th) Duke William, the Normans had become French culturally and linguistically.14) Thus their language was French. As a matter of fact, the invaders of 1066 spoke Norman French, a northern dialect of the language different from Central French spoken in Paris. In England this Norman French developed characteristics of its own. From the 13th century onward, Norman French developed in England into what modern scholars call Anglo-Norman and it began to be used for both official and literary purposes.

5.1.2. The Linguistic Influence of the Conquest

The Norman Conquest appears to be irrelevant to the language. But actually it had a profound effect on English. The reason is quite simple. William, who became the English king through the Conquest, and his subjects accompanying him during and after the campaign were all French speakers without any knowledge about English. The impact of the Norman Conquest on the English language, like that made by the earlier Norse-speaking Viking invaders of the OE period, was to a large extent confined to the word stock, though ME also shows some instances of spelling, pronunciation and grammatical influences.

Ultimately, a huge body of French words became part of the English vocabulary.15) "As the new vocabulary arrived, there were many cases where

---

14) "People sometimes talk as though the Norman Conquest were the coming of a higher civilization to the backward and barbaric Anglo-Saxons. This, however, is a misapprehension ..." (Barber 1993: 134)
15) For the more detailed list of the words imported from French (and Latin) in this

it duplicated a word that existed already in English from Anglo-Saxon times. In such cases, there were two main outcomes. Either one word would supplant the other; or both would co-exist in the language, but with slightly different meanings" (Crystal 2002: 193). A lot of OE words were replaced by French equivalents; *leod > people, wlitig > beautiful, stow > place, herian > praise*, etc. There are cases where both OE and French words often both survived with slightly different meanings, because the native English word was not always abandoned when a French word was introduced. The followings are some examples:

Table 5.1. Some French-English Doublets[16]

French (Romance)	English (Germanic)
judgement	*doom*
judge	*deem*
aroma/odor/scent/perfume/fragrance	*stench (OE) / smell, stink (ME)*
cordial	*hearty*

period, refer to Pyles and Algeo(1993: 295-99), Crystal(2002: 192-95), and Baugh and Cable(163-73).

16) The richness of English in synonyms is largely due to this happy mingling of Latin, French, (Greek) and native elements. It has been said that English has a three-level synonym; popular - literary - learned. Such a level distinction between synonyms can be exemplified in the following word sets.

Popular (from English)	Literary (from French)	Learned (from Latin)
rise	*mount*	*ascend*
ask	*question*	*interrogate*
goodness	*virtue*	*probity*
fast	*firm*	*secure*
fire	*flame*	*conflagration*
fear	*terror*	*trepidation*
holy	*sacred*	*consecrated*
time	*age*	*epoch*
kingly	*royal*	*regal*

mansion	house
desire	wish
power	might
demand	ask
avoid	shun
boil	seethe
aid, assist	help
commence	begin, start
conceal	hide
encounter	meet
infant	child
liberty	freedom
marriage	wedding
fraternal	brotherly

Generally speaking, the Romance word is more formal or abstract than the Germanic, which is more homely and direct.[17]

After the Conquest, French was associated with higher social status, while English was the language of the masses and the people of low social ranks. Anybody whose native tongue was English and who wanted to get on in the world had to learn French. Take an example that shows the differences of social import of the two languages. Such words as *ox*, *sheep*, *pig* (older term: *swine*), *deer* and *calf* were the native Germanic terms both for the animals and for their meat, too.[18] But French words such as *beef*

---

17) "A person who falls into the water has far better chances of being rescued by shouting *Help! Help!* rather than *Aid! Aid!* or *Assistance! Assistance!* And we feel more at ease after getting a hearty welcome than after being granted a cordial reception." (Svartvik and Leech 2006: 38)

18) This means that *cow* meant '소' and '소고기' at the same time before the introduction of the French word *beef*. The French word *beef* also meant both '소' and '소고기' in French. But the meaning of '소' disappeared from *beef* after its

(Modern French, *bœuf*), *mutton* (Modern French, *mouton*),[19] *pork* (Modern French, *porc*), *venison* (Modern French, *venaison*) and *veal* (Modern French, *veau*) became to be used for the flesh of these animals after the Conquest because the meat was mostly eaten by the French-speaking higher classes. The lower classes of mainly English blood lived on a diet of grains and pulses. This clearly shows the high prestige of the French language and French-speaking people. A similar dichotomy of the low English and the privileged French can be seen in the fact that rank words such as *master* and *servant*, and some cuisine words such as *bottle, dinner, supper, banquet, cream, fruit, lemon, salad, sauce, sausage and soup* are all of French origin. And the words of culinary processes, like *boil, broil, fry, roast* and *stew*, are all from French, too, which shows that French cuisine was as highly prized in medieval England, as it is today.

The core family relationships - *mother, father, sister* (from the scandinavian form *systir*, replacing the OE form *sweostor*), *brother, son, daughter* - all kept their Germanic names. However, non-nuclear family relationships expressing more complex social relations were eventually designated by French names; *uncle, aunt, cousin, nephew* and *niece*. *Grandmother, grandfather, grandson, granddaughter*, etc. are all hybrid forms.[20]

---

  introduction into English. The English took care of the animals, while the French consumed the meat.

19) **Mutton** is the flesh of fully grown sheep, while **lamb** is the flesh of a young sheep used as meat. A lamb also means a young sheep itself, especially one that is not yet weaned.

20) A **hybrid word** is a word which etymologically has one part derived from one language and another part derived from a different language. Here, *-mother, -father,*

The French (and Latin) tincture of English vocabulary, which began in this ME times, has been maintained or even intensified in ModE. In fact, the French influence on the English language was such that it cannot be fully dealt with in this introductory book. At all events, English acquired a new appearance throughout the ME period, due to the influence of French.[21]

5.2. The Late Middle English Period (1300-1500)

5.2.1. The Changing Conditions

For a long time after the Norman Conquest, French was the language of the governing classes in England. French continued to be used as a means of everyday communication among members of the upper classes beyond the year 1200. However, shortly after 1200, conditions gradually changed. There were social and political changes advantageous to the resurrection of English as the language for the whole English people again. Actually, English did not die out even under the tremendous oppression imposed by the political and cultural power of the French language.[22]

The first and most important event for this effect was the loss of

---

-son and *-daughter* are all original English, while *grand-* (meaning 'great, large, big, high, loafy') is from French.

21) "In the Early Middle English period about 90 percent of the English vocabulary was Germanic but, at the end of the period, it was about 75 percent." (Svartvik and Leech 2006: 37) But Romance words (i.e. words of French and Latin origin) actually outnumber Germanic words in the PDE vocabulary.

22) One reason for the survival of English is that English was still spoken by the majority, although they are 'lowe men'. (Barber 1993: 136)

Normandy in 1204 by King John, a descendant of William the Conqueror. At this time, the English king of Norman origin was the duke of Normandy at the same time, because they originated from Normandy since William the Conqueror. It means that England had the territorial and so personnel and cultural links to France and the European Continent. This link could give the sufficient motivation for the continued use of French in England. This close link was broken after the loss of Normandy. King John, seeing the beautiful Isabel of Angoulême, fell in violently love with her, and married her in great haste in 1200.[23] The problem was that she was a fiancee of Hugh of the Lusignans, a powerful and ambitious French noble family. Furthermore, John, anticipating the attacks from the Lusignans, took the initiative attacks against them. To solve the conflict, they appealed to their common overlord, the king of France, Philip Augustus. He summoned John to appear before his court at Paris to be judged by his peer nobles. English king was a subject of French king, because he was the duke of Normandy, Normandy was a part of France, so its governor, duke of Normandy, was subject to the French crown. But John refused to go to France, saying that as king of England he was not subject to the jurisdiction of the French court. Philip said that as duke of Normandy he was subject to French jurisdiction. Consequently, on the day of the trial the English king did not appear. Philip invaded Normandy and occupied Rouen, the main city of Normandy, and Normandy was lost to English crown and English people. The English nobility lost their estates in France, and the antagonism grew between the two countries.

---

23) This part, describing the loss of Normandy, is based on Baugh and Cable (1993: 124-125).

After the loss of Normandy, in the year 1215, King John signed a legal charter called Magna Carta. It was written in Latin and is known by its Latin name. Its English translation is Great Charter. Magna Carta required King John to proclaim certain rights of freemen, to respect certain legal procedures, and to accept that his will could be bound by the law. Magna Carta was a kind of the first constitutional law in the English speaking world and established the foundation of the democracy.

Anyway, the loss of a territory was wholly advantageous to the English language, because the ties with Normandy were severed and the ex-Norman nobility gradually became English. It became an opportunity for English king, nobles and even common people to look upon England as their concern and to think over their own political and economic ends, which were not the same as those of France. The context for the natural use of French disappeared.

Even after the loss of Normandy, however, the connection to the Continent was not cut completely. The trade and personnel exchanges continued. Through these connections, the conflict of interests and antagonism were aroused between the two countries. And such a severe antagonism finally resulted in a big war. The war lasted more than hundred years, from 1337 to 1453, although there were occasional long breaks. This military confrontation is generally called the Hundred Years' War.[24] At first,

---

24) The **Hundred Years' War** was a conflict between France and England, lasting 116 years from 1337 to 1453. It was fought primarily over claims by the English kings to the French throne and was punctuated by several brief and two lengthy periods of peace before it finally ended in the expulsion of the English from France, with the exception of the Calais Pale. Thus, the war was in fact a series of conflicts

England emerged more victorious, but the final victory was given to France, due to the heroic exploits of Joan of Arc (Her French name is Jeanne d'Arc).25) In spite of the defeat of the war, the English people gained a lot through this war. They could strengthen their patriotism and nationalism and could get the confidence among them. Those whose ancestors were Normans eventually came to think of themselves as English. In particular, they had another chance to get a loving concern for their language, English, instead of French, the language of the enemy. National feeling was beginning to arise in England, so the war gave the death blow to the already moribund use of French in England.

---

and is commonly divided into three or four phases: the Edwardian War (1337 - 1360), the Caroline War (1369 - 1389), the Lancastrian War (1415 - 1429), and the slow decline of English fortunes after the appearance of Joan of Arc (1429 - 1453). The term "Hundred Years' War" was a later historical term invented by historians to describe the series of events. The war owes its historical significance to a number of factors. Though primarily a dynastic conflict, the war gave impetus to ideas of both French and English nationality. Militarily, it saw the introduction of new weapons and tactics, which eroded the older system of feudal armies dominated by heavy cavalry. The first standing armies in Western Europe since the time of the Western Roman Empire were introduced for the war, thus changing the role of the peasantry. For all this, as well as for its long duration, it is often viewed as one of the most significant conflicts in the history of medieval warfare. ("Hundred Years' War" In *Wikipedia*. Retrieved July 31, 2008)

25) **Joan of Arc**, or **Jeanne d'Arc** in French, (c. 1412 - May 30, 1431) was a 15th century saint and national heroine of France. She led the French army to several important victories and led king Charles VII to his coronation. She was captured by the English and tried by an ecclesiastical court led by Bishop Pierre Cauchon, an English partisan; the court convicted her of heresy and she was burned at the stake by the English when she was nineteen years old. ("Joan of Arc" In *Wikipedia*. Retrieved July 31, 2008)

Besides the changes of political conditions, there were also socio- economic developments advantageous to the revival of the English language in England. The process of urbanization began and the conditions of the working classes changed for the better. As a result, a new strong middle class emerged in England, whose language has always been English. Furthermore, because of the spread of the so-called Black Death (1348-50), which caused a 30 to 40 percent decrease of the population of England, the social status of the survived working classes was raised and their labor was valued more. Moreover, the plague probably eradicated many of the educated teachers who could instruct in French and Latin, thereby paving the way for the rise of English in schools. The strengthening of these working classes and new middle classes also affected the prestige of their language, English.

5.2.2. The Decline of French in England

We said that the link connecting England to France was cut due to the loss of Normandy in the early 13th century and that this was a main occasion for the rising prestige of English. Conversely, the use of French declined since then. In the 13th century English began to be used next to French in some important state documents.[26] The decline of French was easily noticed at the end of the 13th century and at the beginning of the 14th century by the artificial efforts to maintain the language. It was not learned as the native language of the English people any more. It became a foreign language that should be taught at homes and in schools. The decline of

---

26) "It is this (i.e. the 13th, the author's addition) century that sees the tipping of the balance away from French and back to English." (Barber 1993: 141)

French in England was also influenced by the fact that the French spoken in England was a regional dialect with the low cultural prestige (i.e. Anglo-Norman) in comparison with the French of Paris, which was the standard French.

Throughout the 14th century, English was used on the occasions of important pronouncements. In 1362 the Chancellor[27] opened Parliament with a speech in English, and by 1388 English was gaining on Latin as the language of the town councils and guilds. Private letters began to be written in English by 1420 and are the rule by 1450. After 1485 Parliament published statutes and petitions in English and French, and by 1489 French was completely eradicated as the language of Parliament. The final resurrection of English as the language of the whole English people, expelling French from England completely, was accomplished roughly by the middle of the 15th century. At this time, English emerged as the victorious language in both its spoken and written use for the whole English people.[28]

5.3. Middle English Dialects

In the last chapter we saw that English was not uniform from the beginning, partly because several (probably 3 or 4) different Germanic tribes, commanding a little different varieties of a language, came to the British Isles and their

---

[27] The **Lord Chancellor** is the second highest non-royal subject in precedence (after the Archbishop of Canterbury). He is head of the Ministry of Justice (i.e. head of the English judiciary) and de facto speaker of the House of Lords.

[28] According to Crystal (2002: 191), the survival of English, in spite of the strong French influence, is due to the fact that "evidently English in the 11th century was too well established for it to be supplanted by another language."

locations were also different even after the establishment in Britain. The situation did not change in ME. That is, the uniform or standardized form of English was not established in ME, either. In ME times, the use of English (especially, in terms of writing) was greatly limited, as we saw in the above. However, in comparison with OE, where documentary evidence in the form of surviving texts is scant, wealthier texts have come down to us from the ME period. The diversity of ME dialects is easily identified through the examination of these existing documents of that time. These written materials document widespread variation, particularly in the Early ME period, unrivaled in any other period of the language before or since. The main reason for this variety in the texts in the Early ME period is that there was no standard way of writing or pronouncing the language, so scribes spelled in the way that reflected their own dialect, in contrast to the West Saxon of the Late OE period. Furthermore, English was used mainly by the low classes of the English people, who had a limited access to writing. We detect the development of a standard form of English in the Late ME period, being used in texts from diverse regions of the country.

Traditionally, we distinguish four or five major dialects of ME, all of which are defined in relation to OE dialects, as we can see in the following table:

Table 5.2 Dialects of OE and ME

Old English Dialects	Middle English Dialects	
Northumbrian	Northern	
Mercian	East Midland	Midland
	West Midland	(> Standard English)
West Saxon	Southern	
Kentish	Kentish (or South-eastern)	

The main dialect divisions of ME broadly correspond to those found in OE, but different names have been given to some of the dialects. Kentish (or South-eastern dialect) remains the same, but West Saxon is now referred to as "Southern", and Northumbrian as "Northern". Also, the Mercian dialect is named as "Midland". The Midland area is traditionally split into "East Midland" and "West Midland", since it was spoken in a large area and we can find some linguistic differences within the area.[29]

There are several reasons that we should study the dialects of English spoken in the British Isles. First, the dialect divisions of OE and ME are still roughly valid. In other words, the English spoken in the British Isles are not uniform even in PDE. The regional varieties of English found today have deep historical roots. Secondly, these dialect divisions influenced the American English. For example, New England (the northeastern part of the

---

[29] Then, how do we distinguish the dialects linguistically? According to Crystal (2002: 203), the evidence lied in the distinctive vocabulary, grammar and spellings of the manuscript texts (and probably in pronunciation, too). For example, the spelling of several verb endings changed from area and to area:

- The *-ing* ending (as in *run<u>ing</u>*) appears as *-and*(e) in Northern English; as *-end*(e) in parts of the East Midlands; as *-ind*(e) in parts of the West Midlands; and as *-ing* elsewhere.
- The *-eth* ending (as in *go<u>eth</u>*) appears as *-es* in Northern English and the northern part of Midland dialects - a form that ultimately became standard.
- The verb ending used in the present tense with such forms as *we* and *they* also varied: it was *-es* in Northern English and the northern part of the East Midland; *-eth* in Southern, Kentish and the southern part of the East Midland; and *-en* elsewhere. But none of these endings survived in modern English.

And refer to Barber (1993: 138-140) for the more linguistic differences between the ME dialects.

US) was largely settled by immigrants from the south of England, so today the speech of New England sounds more like southern British speech than do other North American varieties. The Englishes spoken in the various parts of the world have been derived from the two main sources, British and American Englishes. So the proper understanding of the Englishes widely spoken in the world should start from the historical study about the English dialects. The approximate boundaries of the main dialects of ME can be shown as follows:

Figure 5.1 Middle English Dialects

5.4. The Rise of Standard English

Out of this variety of local dialects there emerged toward the end of the 14th century a written language that in the course of the 15th century won general recognition and has since become the recognized standard at least in writing (partly, in speech, too). It is noticeable that the new standard language which arose in the late Middle Ages was not descended from the West Saxon literary language. It was in fact based on the East Midland dialect of ME, particularly the dialect of the metropolis, London. The East Midland dialect descended from the Mercian dialect of OE. In the latter part of the 15th century the London standard had been accepted, at least in writing, in most parts of the country. There are several causes for this result.[30]

In the first place, the English of this region occupied a middle position between the extreme divergences of the north and south. It shared some of the characteristics of both neighbors, so it represented a kind of compromise.

Secondly, the East Midland district was the largest and most populous of the major dialect areas. The land was a wealthy agricultural area, more valuable than the hilly country to the north and west. With this advantage the area was the most populous and prosperous. In political affairs this region was the most powerful and influential because of the presence of London, the capital of England. London was at the time the political and commercial center of England and the center for the social and intellectual activities of the country. Take an example. "The presence of the Court in London was a compelling attraction for those who wished for social prestige or career opportunities" (Crystal 2002: 205).

A third factor was the presence of the universities, Oxford and Cambridge, in this region. In the 14th century the monasteries were playing a less important role in the dissemination of learning than they had once played, while the two universities had developed into the main social and

---

[30] The causes are explained in Baugh and Cable (1993: 187-189) and Barber 1993: 144-145), on which this section is based.

political center and the main seats of learning.

The influence of Chaucer (c. 1343 - 1400) can be a fourth factor.[31] He was the author of *The Canterbury Tales*,[32] one of the greatest English literary works, and other poetic works. Chaucer was a court poet, and his usage may reflect the speech of the court, which is located in London of the East Midland area. So he must have lent support in a general way to the adoption of his dialect as standard English. Although he was bilingual and was influenced by French as well as Italian literature, he wrote all his works in English. He is now known as 'the father of English literature'.

The fifth factor was the introduction of the printing skill. In 1476 the printing skill using movable metal types, which was invented by Gutenberg (c. 1398 - 1468) in Germany in around 1450,[33] was introduced into

---

31) **Geoffrey Chaucer** (c. 1343 - October 25, 1400?) was an English author, poet, philosopher, bureaucrat, courtier and diplomat. Although he wrote many works, he is best remembered for his unfinished frame narrative *The Canterbury Tales*. Sometimes called the father of English literature, Chaucer is credited by some scholars as being the first author to demonstrate the artistic legitimacy of the vernacular English language, rather than French or Latin. ("Geoffrey Chaucer" In *Wikipedia*. Retrieved July 31, 2008)

32) **The Canterbury Tales** is a collection of stories written by Geoffrey Chaucer in the 14th century (two of them in prose, the rest in verse). The tales, some of which are originals and others not, are contained inside a frame tale and told by a collection of pilgrims on a pilgrimage from Southwark to Canterbury to visit the shrine of Saint Thomas Becket at Canterbury Cathedral. ("*The Canterbury Tales*" In *Wikipedia*. Retrieved July 31, 2008)

33) In fact, the metal printing skill was invented for the first time in our country (by the Goryeo Dynasty) in the 13th century (in 1234), two centuries earlier than Gutenberg. But it is not well-known and not being internationally recognized. Movable type is the system of printing and typography using movable pieces of

England by William Caxton.34) In ME there were numerous different spellings recorded for the same word, partly reflecting different dialectal pronunciations. For example, the word *might* was also spelled *maht, mihte, micht, mist, michte, mithe, myhte*. The word *such* also had several different spellings like *sich, sech, soch, swich,* and *swilk*. So Caxton had to make a decision which spelling to adopt in the translated books that issued from his press. Ultimately, he chose to use the speech of the London area, because he set up his printing press in Westminster. So London was the center of book publishing in England from the beginning. This also resulted in the wide currency of London English and its rapid adoption across the country, marking the end of the ME period and the beginning of ModE.

Conclusively speaking, the history of standard English is almost a history of London English. Although there is some controversy, London English is still revered as standard English.

---

metal type, made by casting from matrices struck by letterpunches. Movable type allowed for much more flexible processes than hand copying or block printing. Around 1040, the first known movable type system was created in China by Bi Sheng out of porcelain. It is claimed by some Korean scholars that metal movable type was first invented in Korea during the Goryeo Dynasty (around 1230). Neither movable type system was widely used, however, one reason being the enormous Chinese character set. ("Moveable Type Printing" In *Wikipedia*. Retrieved July 31, 2008)

34) **William Caxton** (c. 1422 - 1492) was an English merchant, diplomat, writer and printer. He was the first English person to work as a printer and the first person to introduce a printing press into England. He was also the first English retailer of books (his London contemporaries were all Dutch, German or French). ("William Caxton" In *Wikipedia*. Retrieved July 31, 2008)

5.5. Middle English Literature

During the ME times French was the language which most people of upper classes used, so the books they read and wrote were also in French. And a lot of continental French literature was directly imported and enjoyed. So the English literature of this time is poor. Furthermore, the most extant documents of this period are exclusively religious or admonitory, because the religious body was the only patron for English writing. Probably they may have wanted to get an access to the common lay people for the propagation of Christianity. *The Ancrene Riwle*[35] and *The Ormulum*[36] will be such examples. Non-religious but still well-known works are Layamon's *Brut* (c. 1205),[37] a translation of Wace about the British history, and the

---

35) **The Ancrene Riwle** (also **Ancrene Wisse**, the *Guide for Anchoresses*) is a monastic rule (or manual) for anchoresses, written in the early 13th century. (*"Ancrene Riwle"* In *Wikipedia*. Retrieved July 31, 2008)

36) **The Ormulum** is a 12th-century work of Biblical exegesis, written in early Middle English verse by a monk named Orm (or Ormin). Because of the unique phonetic orthography adopted by the author, the work preserves many details of English pronunciation at a time when the language was in flux after the Norman Conquest; consequently, despite its lack of literary merit, it is invaluable to philologists in tracing the development of English. Orm was concerned that priests were unable to speak the vernacular properly, and so he developed an idiosyncratic spelling system to tell his readers how to pronounce every vowel, and he composed his work using a strict poetic meter that ensured that readers would know which syllables were stressed. Modern scholars can use these two features to reconstruct Middle English just as Orm spoke it. (*"Ormulum"* In *Wikipedia*. Retrieved July 31, 2008)

37) **The Brut** (c. 1190) is a Middle English poem compiled and recast by the English priest Layamon. It is named for Britain's mythical founder, Brutus of Troy. The *Brut* is 16,095 lines long and narrates the history of Britain. It is largely based

astonishing debate between *The Owl and Nightingale* (c. 1195), a long poem in which two birds exchange recrimination in the liveliest fashion. There were surely a body of popular literature at this time that circulated orally among the people. But it is beyond our understanding and interest in this book.

The real literary work which deserves our concern is Chaucer's *Canterbury Tales*. Significantly, the general prologue is a matchless portrait of his contemporary medieval society. The composition of this poem (in about 1387) coincides with the general adoption of English by all social classes of English people. Chaucer composed other poetic works such as *Troilus and Criseyde*,[38] a long narrative poem about the unhappy love. William Langland, author of *Piers Plowman* (1362-1387)[39] and John Wycliffe (d. 1384),[40] translator of the Bible and author of a large and

---

on the Anglo-Norman *Roman de Brut* by Wace, which is in turn inspired by Geoffrey of Monmouth's *Historia Regum Britanniae*, though it is longer than both and includes an enlarged section on the life and exploits of King Arthur. ("Brut" In *Wikipedia*. Retrieved July 31, 2008)

38) **Troilus and Criseyde** is Geoffrey Chaucer's poem telling the tragic love story of Troilus, a Trojan prince, and Criseyde. Many Chaucer scholars regard this as his best work, even including the better known but incomplete *Canterbury Tales*. *Troilus and Criseyde* is an example of a courtly romance. ("*Troilus and Criseyde*" In *Wikipedia*. Retrieved July 31, 2008)

39) **Piers Plowman** (written c. 1360 - 1399) is the title of a Middle English allegorical narrative by William Langland. The poem - part theological allegory, part social satire - concerns the narrator's intense quest for the true Christian life, which is told from the point of view of the medieval Catholic mind. ("*Piers Plowman*" In *Wikipedia*. Retrieved July 31, 2008)

40) **John Wycliffe** (also **Wyclif**, **Wycliff**, or **Wickliffe**) (c. 1320 - 1384) was an English theologian and early proponent of reform in the Roman Catholic Church during the 14th century. He is credited as the first person to give a complete translation

influential body of controversial religious prose, are another well-known writers of this time. At the end of the ME times, English literature again reached one of the highest standards in Europe, overcoming the 'dark' side. It could open a new era, anticipating the great period of Shakespeare in the 16th century.

of the Bible into English. ("John Wycliffe" In *Wikipedia*. Retrieved July 31, 2008)

Chapter 06

The Modern English Period (1500-1800)

6.1. The Early Modern English Period (1500-1650)

6.1.1. Developments Opening the Modern Society[1]

We have said that particular events can be marking points for the developmental stages of languages. The Norman Conquest was a representative example, which is understood as the dividing mark between OE and ME. Then what is/are the event(s) dividing ME and ModE? For the ModE period, the beginning of which is conveniently placed at 1500, several new conditions come into play together. These new conditions caused England and European countries to develop into modern societies. At this time, in particular, England was raised to the position of one of the major powers both in Europe and the contemporary world and could get the important momentum to be an Empire (the British Empire) later,

---

1) Section 6.1.1 is greatly indebted to Fisiak (1995: 89-91).

governing roughly one-fourth of the world in her heyday.

This period in England's history roughly overlaps the stage in the evolution of English which is conventionally labelled as Early ModE. Some of the developments in the language of that time are visibly associated with various extralinguistic factors. The most important will be briefly reviewed below.

The opening of a new period in the history of England started with a new dynasty. In 1485 the English throne went to the Tudors,[2] the dynasty which would reign England until 1603. Queen Elizabeth I was from this royal house and its last monarch. She was childless and, on her death in 1603, her crown passed to the King of Scotland, James VI (James Stuart, in England known as James I). The Tudors and the early Stuarts (1603-49),[3] contributed to the expansion of England's interests and the strengthening

---

2) **The Tudor dynasty** or **House of Tudor** was a series of five monarchs who ruled England and Ireland from 1485 until 1603 (Henry VII (1485-1509) > Henry VIII (1509-1547) > Edward IV (1547-1553) > Mary I (1553-1558) > Elizabeth I (1558-1603)). Three of them, (Henry VII, Henry VIII and Elizabeth I) played important roles in transforming England from a comparatively weak European backwater into a powerful Renaissance state that in the coming centuries would dominate much of the world, and Henry VIII and Elizabeth I remain among the most famous English monarchs of all time.

3) **The House of Stuart** or **Stewart** was a royal house of the Kingdom of Scotland, later also of the Kingdom of England and the Kingdom of Ireland, and finally of the Kingdom of Great Britain. The House of Stuart ruled the Kingdom of Scotland for 336 years, between 1371 and 1707. At Elizabeth's death, James Stuart ascended the thrones of the Kingdom of England and the Kingdom of Ireland. From 1603, the Stuarts styled themselves "Kings/Queens of Great Britain". The Stuarts were followed by the House of Hanover. ("House of Stuart" In *Wikipedia*. Retrieved July 31, 2008)

of her international position, despite serious internal problems finally leading to internal wars and a revolution (1642-60, the English Civil War). The victory of the English over the Spanish Armada during the reign of Elizabeth I (exactly, in 1588) opened the seas and roads to the expansion and spread of the English language to overseas territories. Hardly twenty years had passed when Captain John Smith founded Jamestown[4] (in 1607)[5] and the colonization of North America began.

Another significant event was the Protestant Reformation,[6] which took place in England during the reign of Henry VIII (1509-47). He established a separate church from the Roman Catholic Church, i.e. the Church of England. The severing of relations with Rome, the closing of monasteries, and the establishing of the king as the head of the Church of England led to a reduction of the importance of Latin both in church and schools. It further enhanced the growth of patriotism among the ordinary people, thus raising the value of everything English, including the language itself. The Reformation, by introducing English into the church, also opened the way to the translation of the Bible into English, which obviously contributed to

---

[4] The name of this town was derived from the English king of that time, James I.

[5] The first permanent English settlement in North America was established at Jamestown in the Virginia Colony on May 14, 1607.

[6] **The Protestant Reformation** was a movement in the 16th century to reform the Catholic Church in Western Europe. Many western Christians were troubled by what they saw as false doctrines and malpractices within the Church, particularly involving the teaching and sale of indulgences. Another major contention was the practice of buying and selling church positions (*simony*) and what was seen at the time as considerable corruption within the Church's hierarchy. This corruption was seen by many at the time as systemic, even reaching the position of the Pope. ("Protestant Reformation" In *Wikipedia*. Retrieved July 31, 2008)

the improvement of the status of English. The translations contributed largely to the expansion of English vocabulary. Seven major versions of the Bible were produced from 1536 to the so-called *Authorized Version* (or *King James Bible*):[7] *The Tyndale New Testament* (1536), *The Coverdale Bible* (1537), *The Great Bible* (1539), *The Geneva Bible* (1560), *The Bishop's Bible* (1568), *The Donai Bible* (1610) and *The Authorized Version* or *King James Bible* (1611). "The translation of the Bible into English and the changeover from Latin to English in church services raised the prestige of English" (Barber 1993: 176).

Another factor was the arrival of the Renaissance (meaning literally 'rebirth' in French) from the Continent.[8] This cultural movement brought

---

7) **The King James** or **Authorized Version of the Bible** is an English translation of the Christian Bible first published in 1611. When this Bible was translated into English, the king of England was James I, so his name was used. Furthermore, this translation was officially permitted by the king. Before that, the translation of the Bible into the vernacular languages from Latin was severely prohibited in other European countries as well as in England. Although it is often referred to as *The King James Version*, particularly in the United States, the only active part King James took in the translation was lifting the death penalty attached to translating the Bible and setting some guidelines for the translation process, such as prohibiting partisan scholarship and footnotes. It is more commonly known as *The Authorized Version* in the United Kingdom. This Bible has had a profound effect on English literature. The works of famous authors such as John Milton, Herman Melville, John Dryden and William Wordsworth are deeply inspired by it.

8) **English Renaissance** is a relatively recent term used to describe a cultural and artistic movement in England dating from the early 16th century to the early 17th century. It is associated with the pan-European Renaissance that originated in northern Italy in the 14th century. This era in English cultural history is sometimes referred to as **the age of Shakespeare** or **the Elizabethan era**, taking the name of the English

with it the revival of interest in human beings and their life. Together with this came the rediscovery and revitalization of the classical learning in Greek and Latin. Also, the fields of science, medicine and the arts were rapidly developed. The interest in ancient writings led to the translation of the works of Thucydides, Herodotus, Caesar, Tacitus, Plato, Aristotle, Cicero, Seneca, Homer, Virgil, Ovid, Horace, and many others.

Nationalism, enhanced in this period, led to conscious efforts to create a vernacular literature. English, the vernacular language of the English people, was no longer disdained as inferior to Latin. So this period produced a lot of innovative literary works which have found a permanent place both in English and world literature.[9] The names of Christopher Marlowe (1564-93),[10] William Shakespeare (1564-1616),[11] Robert Greene (1558-92),[12] Ben Jonson (1572/3 -1637),[13] John Lyly (?1554-1606),[14] Sir

---

Renaissance's most famous author and most important monarch, respectively. ("English Renaissance" In *Wikipedia*. Retrieved July 31, 2008)

[9] For the Modern English literature, see Section 6.3.

[10] **Christopher "Kit" Marlowe** (baptised 26 February 1564 - 30 May 1593) was an English dramatist, poet and translator of the Elizabethan era. The foremost Elizabethan tragedian next to William Shakespeare, he is known for his magnificent blank verse, his overreaching protagonists, and his own mysterious and untimely death. ("Christopher Marlowe" In *Wikipedia*. Retrieved July 31, 2008)

[11] **William Shakespeare** (baptised 26 April 1564 - 23 April 1616) was an English poet and playwright, widely regarded as the greatest writer in the English language and the world's preeminent dramatist. He is often called England's national poet and the "Bard of Avon" (or simply "The Bard"). His surviving works consist of 38 plays, 154 sonnets, two long narrative poems, and several other poems. His plays have been translated into every major living language and are performed more often than those of any other playwright. ("William Shakespeare" In *Wikipedia*. Retrieved July 31, 2008)

Thomas Wyatt (1503-42),[15] Edmund Spenser,[16] Sir Philip Sidney (1554-86),[17] among others, give best evidence to the weight of the vernacular literary achievements of the time and the development of English vocabulary. "The great age of Elizabethan literature resulted in an unprecedented breadth and inventiveness in the use of the English language" (Crystal 2002: 221).

The impact of the Renaissance on England would not have been so great

---

12) **Robert Greene** (July 11 1558 - September 3, 1592) was an English author and well-known personality. He became perhaps the first professional author in England, publishing autobiography, plays, romances, and in other genres. ("Robert Greene" In *Wikipedia*. Retrieved July 31, 2008)

13) **Ben(jamin) Jonson** (c. 11 June 1572 - 6 August 1637) was an English Renaissance dramatist, poet and actor. A contemporary of William Shakespeare, he is best known for his satirical plays, particularly *Volpone* and *The Alchemist*. ("Benjamin Jonson" In *Wikipedia*. Retrieved July 31, 2008)

14) **John Lyly (Lilly or Lylie)** (c. 1553 or 1554 - November 1606) was an English writer, best known for his books *Euphues, The Anatomy of Wit* and *Euphues and His England*. ("John Lyly" In *Wikipedia*. Retrieved July 31, 2008)

15) **Sir Thomas Wyatt** (1503 - October 11, 1542) was a 16th century English lyrical poet.

16) **Edmund Spenser** (c. 1552 - January 13, 1599) was an important English poet and Poet Laureate best known for *The Faerie Queene*, an epic poem celebrating, through fantastical allegory, the Tudor dynasty and Elizabeth I. ("Edmund Spencer" In *Wikipedia*. Retrieved July 31, 2008)

17) **Sir Philip Sidney** (November 30, 1554 - October 17, 1586) became one of the Elizabethan Age's most prominent figures. Famous in his day in England as a poet, courtier and soldier, he remains known as the author of *Astrophil and Stella* (1581, pub. 1591), *The Defence of Poetry* (or *An Apology for Poetry*, 1581, pub. 1595) and *The Countess of Pembroke's Arcadia* (1580, pub. 1590). ("Philip Sidney" In *Wikipedia*. Retrieved July 31, 2008)

if it had not been for the spread of popular education. This created a relatively large market for books which were printed on an ever increasing scale. As said in the last chapter, the printing skill, which was introduced into England in 1476 by William Caxton, made possible the mass production of books. According to Baugh and Cable (1993: 195), 35,000 books were printed before 1500 across Europe, mainly in Latin, but over 20,000 titles (not copies!) had appeared by 1640 in England only. Before the introduction of printing, all books were hand-written by well-trained scribes. Thus books were greatly valuable things and only a few could get an access to them and to learning itself. Knowledge was the belongings to some people of upper classes. The printing of books in a large scale changed this situation completely. Now anyone could read books, in particular, the Bible.[18] The impact of the spread of the written word on such a large scale contributed to the further spread of the written standard throughout the country. Of all the events that have affected English during the modern period, the introduction of printing can be said to be the most important because it fostered literacy in English and also encouraged the Renaissance.

An economic factor was also important. The beginning of the Tudor reign witnessed the growing wealth of a new middle class. The standard of living of these urban population improved as a whole. They were the practical men, such as skilled craftsmen, instrument makers, explorers, navigators, soldiers, often from the citizen or yeoman classes.[19] These new

---

[18] The translation and printing of the Bible in a large scale was one of the major forces driving the Reformation.

[19] **Yeoman** is a term used to indicate a variety of positions or social classes. In the 15th century, a yeoman was also a farmer of middling social status who owned

social and occupational groups often bought the estates of the nobility. They had little or no Latin. Instead, they were eager to read and to learn, and wanted books in English (cf. Barber (1993: 176)).

6.1.2. The Victory of English against the Prestigious Latin[20]

Although quite a body of literature had been written in English by the end of the 15th century and the language was also used in the numerous formal and official occasions, the English language did not have enough prestige to be used in all fields of knowledge. Latin, which was the language of the powerful and glorious Roman Empire and of the Roman Catholicism, was traditionally regarded as a perfect language.[21] For this reason, scholars and writers preferred to use Latin in handling all shades of thought and all scholarly concepts. To achieve full recognition by the late 16th century and final victory in the early 17th century, the English language would have to struggle against the criticisms of its various inadequacies.

Three reasons may be thought for the use of Latin on such a large scale. The first factor was the position of Latin in education. For example, at the

---

his own land and often farmed it himself. ("Yeoman" In *Wikipedia*. Retrieved July 31, 2008)

20) This section is based on Fisiak (1995: 92-93).

21) In this period the influence of French was not felt so strongly as in the ME times. "The late Middle Ages had seen the triumph of the English language over French in England, and the establishment once more of a standard form of written English. This does not mean, however, that English was now entirely without a rival: Latin still had great prestige as the language of international learning, and it was a long time before English replaced it in all fields." (Barber 1993: 175)

grammar-school level, English was of little significance. Instead, Latin, grammar, composition, geography, philosophy and history were major subjects. In the universities, Latin was the medium of instruction.

As the second factor, the role of Latin in scholarship also contributed to its continued use. Latin was unquestionably the language of scholarship in western Europe and remained in this position until 1650 and even later. The role and importance of Latin in the western society is comparable to that of (written) Chinese in the eastern Asia.

The third reason for the persistent use of Latin was the vested interest of people brought up in the Latin tradition to guard the continuous use of Latin. English was criticized by adherents to the Latin tradition for being 'vulgar', 'barbarous', 'short of words', 'inelegant', 'immature', 'unstable', 'changing', etc., unlike classical Greek and Latin, which were 'fixed' as dead languages. In the meantime, the use of Latin loanwords was taken by some people to be a sign of education or of social superiority. Even people who supported the use of English were often not confident in the face of this common criticism. This critical attitude was strong until 1575-1580.

However, the critical attitude suddenly disappeared, and nearly everybody began to praise English as eloquent. In the 1580's, which was the period of Elizabeth I's reign and the age of Shakespeare, the criticism of English virtually disappeared. The rise in prestige of English and its final recognition in this period was due to several factors.

First of all, patriotism and nationalism were aroused in the 15th century and were still a strong force a century later among the English people. The English people could get confidence in their nation and in their language because of the rising status of England with a great leader like Elizabeth

I. These feelings were instrumental in evoking a pride in their national language and encouraging its use to prove that English was no worse than any other tongue used in Europe, Latin included.

The second factor was the spread of education, which created quite a market for books. Not all educated people mastered Latin to the extent. The third factor was the Protestant Reformation which encouraged religious controversies on matters of faith and dogma. Since the disputants wanted to appeal to more people, English had to be used. Furthermore, the Protestants had translated the Bible into English, and, for that reason as well, the prestige of English went up.

The fourth factor was the efforts to refine English, made by the vernacular writers at the time. The names of the representative writers of this period were already given in Section 6.1.1. English was refined and organized by the efforts of such writers, including Shakespeare.

Ultimately, the English language won its struggle against Latin, proving to be as good as Latin. Although Latin did not disappear entirely, there is no doubt that it was used later not because English was inferior in any sense but for other reasons. All the factors contributing to the rise of prestige of English and its final recognition created a new situation for the further development of the English language.

6.1.3. Expansion of English Vocabulary to Cope with New Demand

The exclusive use of French and Latin in many areas throughout the Middle Ages deprived the English language of the opportunity to make up new words in order to adequately express ideas and thoughts. This problem became clear when many works had to be translated from Latin and Greek in the 16th and early 17th century due to the influence of the Renaissance. The translators faced numerous situations where Latin or Greek works could not be rendered in English properly. Writers could not find suitable English equivalents corresponding to Latin or Greek words. There were three natural ways to cope with this situation; (1) direct borrowing of Latin or Greek words, (2) coining new words through native word-formation processes, and (3) the adaptation of already existing English words.

Since the Early ModE period was the times of world-wide exploration, over 10,000 words were came into English from over fifty languages, including several American Indian languages and the languages of Africa and Asia as well as Latin and Greek.[22] To begin with, the Latin words that entered English during this period are the following (from Fisiak (1995: 101)[23]): *allusion, accent, commensurable, capsule, denunciation, dexterity, disability, drama, excursion, expectation, transept, elegy, fiction, invisibility, jurisprudence, phrase, transalpine, abject, agile, appropriate, expensive, external, habitual, hereditary, insane, jocular, malignant, alienate, assassinate, benefit, consolidate, disregard, eradicate, exist, extinguish, harass, mediate,* etc. A number of words borrowed from Latin were actually Greek words which found their way earlier into Latin and then, via Latin,

---

[22] The example words quoted in this section are mostly from Fisiak (1995: 101-3) and Crystal (2002: 210-13).

[23] "The Latin loans in Old and Middle English are a mere trickle, but in Early Modern English the trickle becomes a river, and by 1600 it is a deluge." (Barber 1993: 178)

came finally into English. Some of the examples are *anachronism, atmosphere, antithesis, autograph, chaos, chronology, climax, crisis, dogma, enthusiasm, parasite, pathetic, scheme, skeleton, system*, etc. (from Fisiak (1995: 101)). Greek words borrowed directly into English include *acme, anonymous, catastrophe, criterion, ephemeral, heterodox, lexicon, ostracize, polemic, thermometer, tonic*, etc.

A significant number of words were borrowed into English from other European languages, such as Italian, Spanish, Dutch and French. Due to travel in France by Englishmen, as well as the prestige of French literature, a lot of French words were imported, like *alloy, anatomy, baluster, bigot, bizarre, bombast, bayonet, counterpoint, comrade, docility, defail, duel, entrance, entrap, equip, essay, explore, genteel, judge, invoice, mustache, naturalize, probability, progress, shock, surpass, vogue, volunteer*, etc.

The exploration and colonization of North and South America resulted in the importation of new words from indigenous languages (frequently via Spanish), e.g. *potato* (from Haitian *batata* via Spanish *patata*), *tobacco, calque, ananas* (later replaced in English by *pineapple*), *hammock, hurricane, cannibal* (all from the Caribbean language via Spanish), *chocolate, tomato* (from Aztec), *wigwam, tomahawk, squaw, wampum* (from North American Indian languages), etc.

There were criticisms against excessive adoptions of loanwords, particularly from Latin. A number of outstanding scholars and writers, who are called Purists, carried on a vigorous campaign against loanwords. They called such 'hard' loanwords 'inkhorn' terms, and condemned them for their obscurity and for the way they interfered with the development of native English vocabulary. Despite purist attacks, however, the process of borrowing went on and the opposition to importing foreign words into English was directed only against excessive borrowing. That is, it is nearly impossible to build a complete block against foreign lexical elements if we continue the cultural exchanges with foreign countries.

Although the enrichment of English vocabulary was achieved in large measure with loanwords, the vocabulary expansion was also enhanced by various word-formation processes (e.g. affixation,[24] compounding[25] and conversion[26]) using the native word stock or combining both the native and foreign elements. Many new derivatives and compounds were introduced into English in the 16th and 17th centuries, notably by leading poets and writers. "The following are examples of suffixes: *straightness, delightfulness, frequenter, investment, relentless, laughable, anatomically, anathemize*; of prefixes: *unforgettable, uncivilized, bedaub, disabuse, forename, nonsense, underground, submarine*; and of compound: *heaven-sent, chap-fallen, Frenchwoman, commander-in-chief.* In addition, increasing use was made of the process of 'conversion' - turning one word class into another without adding a prefix or suffix"[27] (Crystal 2002: 213; cf. Barber (1993: 183)).

---

[24] **Affixation** means of the use of affixes, i.e. prefixes and suffixes, as in *unhappy, misunderstand* or *happiness, referee*, etc. This process is termed as **derivation** in other way, and the words which are formed through this process are called **derivatives**.

[25] **Compounding** is the combination of two or more than two free morphemes, as in *pickpocket, headstrong, mother-of-the-pearl*, etc. Such words are called **compounds**.

[26] **Grammatical/Lexical conversion** or **Functional shift** is the using of one part of speech as another. For example, from the noun *parent* are derived the verb *to parent* and its gerundial noun *parenting* 'performing the functions of a parent' as in *The midwife is very knowledgeable about parenting.*

[27] So conversion is sometimes called 'zero derivation', too. "Three types were especially common: the formation of verbs from nouns (*to bayonet, to gossip, to invoice*); the

Writers also added another source of enrichment, i.e. reviving words no longer in use. Some writers of this period, such as Edmund Spenser, attempted to revive obsolete English words and to make use of little-known words from English dialects (Crystal 2002: 210); e.g. *algate* 'always', *sicker* 'certainly' and *yblent* 'confused'. "Some (notably the scholar John Cheke) used English equivalents for classical terms whenever he could", especially in translating the Bible (Crystal 2002: 210): e.g. *byword* for *parable*, *hundreder* for *centurion*, *crossed* for *crucified*, and *gainrising* for *resurrection*. Another purist, Ralph Lever, invented such words as *endsay* for *conclusion*, *foresays* for *premisses*, *saywhat* for *definition*, *witcraft* for *logic*, and *yeasay* for *affirmation* (cf. Barber (1993: 178)). Other examples of such revival are *forby* 'past, near', *astound* 'to astonish and bewilder', *doom* (n. 1. inevitable destruction or ruin. 2. fate, especially a tragic or ruinous one. 3. a decision or judgment. 4. Judgment Day. 5. a statute or ordinance; v. 1. to condemn to ruination or death. 2. to destine to an unhappy end.), *blameful* 'deserving of blame', 'blameworthy', and many others. However, most of the revived words did not survive much longer.

6.1.4. The Appearance of English Dictionaries

The English language did not have a dictionary until the beginning of the 17th century. In the Middle Ages, difficult words were explained in English in marginal or interlinear notes in individual writings. Sometimes separate lists, not always arranged alphabetically, were appended at the end of texts.

---

formation of nouns from adjectives (*an ancient* 'an old man', *a brisk* 'a fop'); and the formation of nouns from verbs (*an invite*, *a laugh*)." (Barber 1993: 183)

Before the development of dictionaries there were bilingual word-lists, prepared as an aid for the student, and then bilingual vocabularies appeared, which closely resembled modern alphabetical dictionaries. The first dictionary published in England was a small Latin-English dictionary by Sir Thomas Elyot in 1538. Until the end of the 16th century, however, a monolingual dictionary of the English language (i.e. English-English dictionary) was not needed seriously. Such a need began to be felt when thousands of new words were entering the language from the second half of the 16th century. Especially, the new and learned words that ordinary people did not understand should be explained properly by the help of dictionary-like books. Another need for the dictionary was from the feeling of uneasiness at the time that English was changing too fast. To fix the language and to give order to the language, a guide, like the dictionary, was strongly needed.[28]

The first monolingual dictionary of English was published by Robert Cawdrey in 1604. Its title was *Table Alphabeticall* (*Alphabetical Table*). This was a kind of 'dictionary of hard words', containing about 2,500 hard unusual English words borrowed from Greek, Latin, French and other languages. The next English dictionary was John Bullokar's *English Expositor* (1616), which contained more than 4,000 entries. Bullokar's dictionary was soon followed by Henry Cockeram's *English Dictionarie* (1623). Cockeram's dictionary as well as Bullokar's were reprinted several

---

[28] During the same time, there were a lot of proposals to establish an English Academy that would take care of the language in a similar way. However, we know that language could not be kept static, so the efforts to fix the language did not succeed.

times. They were, however, still too small and should be expanded by other authors in the years to come.

We should mention two later dictionaries in this section dealing with English dictionaries: *Samuel Johnson's Dictionary* (1755) and *The Oxford English Dictionary* (*OED*).[29] In 1755,[30] over a seven-year work of compilation, Dr Samuel Johnson completed his dictionary that contains the definitions of 42,773 words.[31] His dictionary is notable because "it illustrates the uses of the words from the best authors since the time of the Elizabethans" (Crystal 1997a: 74). And it became very popular "because of his meticulous research; his depth and breadth of definitions and his careful use of description" (op. cit.). The dictionary conferred stability on the English language. In particular, his spelling choices of the English words in the dictionary were generally accepted and so found in modern practice.[32]

---

29) Another dictionary worthy of mention here is Noah Webster's *American Dictionary of the English Language*, published 1828, but it will be mentioned in Chapter 8 dealing with the American English.

30) As we have seen above, Johnson's was not the first dictionary of the (English-)English language, despite common assumptions. In the preceding 150 years there had been about twenty more English dictionaries.

31) **Samuel Johnson** (September 18, 1709 - December 13, 1784), who was regularly referred to simply as **Dr Johnson**, is among England's best known literary figures. Dr Johnson was an essayist, poet, biographer, lexicographer and a critic of English Literature. Also considered to be a great wit and prose stylist, he was well known for his *aphorisms*. As the single most quoted English writer after Shakespeare, Dr Johnson has been described as being among the most outstanding figures of 18th-century England. ("Samuel Johnson" In *Wikipedia*. Retrieved July 31, 2008)

32) It was one of the aims of his publishing the dictionary, which are shown in the Preface of the Dictionary. See Section 6.2.2.

The most monumental dictionary of the English language and probably of all languages is *The Oxford English Dictionary,* published by the Oxford University Press.[33] The Philological Society of Great Britain, realizing that the existing dictionaries of English at the time were inadequate, appointed a committee to compile a 'New English Dictionary' in 1857. The task of the committee, consisting of Herbert Coleridge, Dean Trench and F. J. Furnivall, was to collect the words that did not appear in any dictionary in order to publish a supplement to them. But it soon turned out that a supplement would not be satisfactory. So in 1879 the Society decided to make a complete 'New English Dictionary' recording the history of all English words in terms of its forms, spellings, uses and meanings from the Anglo-Saxon times (i.e. since c. 1000). Each meaning and use was to be illustrated by quotations from a wide range of original English texts.[34]

The first editor was Herbert Coleridge, who unfortunately died prematurely at the age of thirty-one in 1861 and was replaced by F. J. Furnivall. In

---

[33] This book does not have a separate section for the PDE period, so *The OED* should be mentioned in this section.

[34] *The OED*'s policy was attempting the recording of a word's most-known usages and variants in *all* varieties of English past and present, world-wide; per the 1933 Preface:

> The aim of this Dictionary is to present in alphabetical series the words that have formed the English vocabulary from the time of the earliest records [ca. AD 740] down to the present day, with all the relevant facts concerning their form, sense-history, pronunciation and etymology. It embraces not only the standard language of literature and conversation, whether current at the moment, or obsolete, or archaic, but also the main technical vocabulary, and a large measure of dialectal usage and slang.
>
> ("*Oxford English Dictionary*" In *Wikipedia*. Retrieved July 31, 2008)

1879 the Society reached an agreement with the Oxford University Press for the publication of the dictionary and appointed James A. H. Murray to be its editor.[35] In 1895 the title *The Oxford English Dictionary* was added to the original *A New English Dictionary on Historical Principles* (*NED*). The dictionary was produced in the form of fascicles. The first fascicle, covering part of the letter <A> was produced in 1884 and the final one in 1928, over the 44 years. It was published in 12 volumes as the First Edition, comprising 15,487 pages. The dictionary's latest, complete print edition (Second Edition, 1989) was in 20 volumes,[36] comprising 291,500 entries in 21,730 pages.[37]

---

35) In 1888 Henry Bradley became a co-editor. In 1901 William A. Craigie become a third editor and, finally, in 1914 C. T. Onions was appointed the fourth editor.

36) Once the text of the dictionary was digitized and online, it was also available to be published on CD-ROM. The text of the First Edition was made available in 1988. Afterward, three versions of the Second Edition were issued. Version 1 (1992) was identical in content to the printed Second Edition, and the CD itself was not copy-protected. Version 2 (1999) had some additions to the corpus, and updated software with improved searching features, but it had clumsy copy-protection that made it difficult to use and would even cause the program to deny use to OUP staff in the midst of demonstrating the product. Version 3 was released in 2002 with additional words and software improvements, though its copy-protection remained as unforgiving as that of the earlier version. The current and only edition of the OED on CD is available for purchase from the Oxford University Press, Version 3.1.1 (2007). ("*Oxford English Dictionary*, *Electronic Versions*" In *Wikipedia*. Retrieved July 31, 2008)

37) It is known that its Third Edition is now being prepared by the Oxford University Press.

The planned Third Edition, or OED3, is intended as a nearly complete overhaul of the work. Each word is being examined and revised to improve the accuracy

6.1.5. Early English Grammars and Spelling Reforms[38]

Roughly at the same time of the appearance of the first English dictionary, the first attempts to write on the rules of the English usages began to be made. The importance of the regularization of spellings of English words (i.e. orthography) began to be stressed at the same time, too, because the prestige of English was growing. English was the subject of instruction at schools, yet it had no book of rules (i.e. grammar books) on which students and teachers could depend. Even at around 1550, there was no English grammar book, nor was there a dictionary of the English language, as mentioned in the previous section.

Soon afterwards the first grammar of English was published. It was written by William Bullokar in 1586. The title was *Bref Grammar of English* (*A Brief Grammar of English*), but unfortunately it has not survived until today. In the same year, however, Bullokar published another grammar book, *Pamphlet for Grammar*, which was a short version of his

---

of the definitions, derivations, pronunciations, and historical quotations - a task requiring the efforts of a staff consisting of more than 300 scholars, researchers, readers and consultants, and projected to cost about $55 million. The end result is expected to double the overall length of the text. The style of the dictionary will also change slightly. The original text was more literary, in that most of the quotations were taken from novels, plays and other literary sources. The new edition, however, will reference all manner of printed resources, such as cookbooks, wills, technical manuals, specialist journals and rock lyrics. The pace of inclusion of new words has been increased to the rate of about 4,000 a year. The estimated date of completion is 2037. ("*Oxford English Dictionary*, Third Edition" In *Wikipedia*. Retrieved July 31, 2008)

38) This section is based on Fisiak (1995: 103-7).

earlier *Bref Grammar of English*. Bullokar's grammar books relied heavily on Latin grammars of the period as models. Another grammar of English published before the turn of the century was written by Paul Greaves under the title *Grammatica Anglicana* (1594).

In the first half of the 17th century five English grammars appeared, including Alexander Gil's *Logonomia Anglica* (1619), Charles Butler's *English Grammar* (1633) and Ben Jonson's *English Grammar* (1640). They are limited to the analysis of letters, syllables and words. Most of the grammars are preoccupied with morphology.[39] Only some of them have a section devoted to syntax.[40]

In the next century, several influential grammar books appeared, including Robert Lowth's *Short Introduction to English Grammar* (1762) and Lindley Murray's *English Grammar* (1794).

The grammarians contributed also towards the standardization of English spelling. There were some people who were mainly concerned with regularization of orthography and advocated changes in chaotic spelling practices of the time. These people are called orthoepists. Due to the efforts of these people, English spellings could be much more regularized although the radical changes proposed by some orthoepists have never been successful.

"The earliest spelling reformers were Sir John Cheke[41] and Sir Thomas

---

39) Morphology is a branch of linguistics that studies the structure of words.
40) **Syntax** is a branch of linguistics that studies the principles and rules for constructing sentences. In addition to referring to the discipline, the term syntax is also used to refer directly to the rules and principles that govern the sentence structure of any individual language, as in "the syntax of Middle English".
41) **Sir John Cheke** (16 June 1514 - 13 September 1557) was an English classical scholar and statesman, notable as the first Regius Professor of Greek at Cambridge

Smith.[42] They tried to make the English spelling phonetic, which means that all letters should be pronounced. Cheke proposed, among other things, to dispense with silent letters, to double vowel symbols in order to indicate length (e.g. *taak* for *take*, *maad* for *made*, etc.), and to use <y> for /θ/ and /ð/" (Fisiak 1995: 105).

John Hart was another 16th-century orthoepist. "According to Hart, the orthography of English is corrupt and suffers from four defects: diminution (too few symbols to represent the existing sounds), superfluity (the use of more letters than there are sounds in a given word, (i.e. silent letters like <b> in *doubt*), usurpation (the use of a wrong symbol or the use of the same letter for the different sound, like <g> in *gentle* [dʒéntl] and *give* [giv]), and misplacing (putting the letters in the wrong order, e.g. *fable* should be spelled *fabel* because its pronunciation is [féibəl]). To remedy the corruptions of English orthography of these kinds, Hart proposed a number of changes. Among other things, he introduced a writing system in which one letter stands for one sound, diphthongs are rendered by diagraphs (e.g. *seid* for *side*), <j> represents /dʒ/, and others" (Fisiak 1995: 105-6). However, his proposals were not accepted by the public and failed to influence the development of English spelling in any significant manner.

"A more conservative approach towards spelling reform was represented by Richard Mulcaster, a schoolmaster. Mulcaster was against any radical reform. He only wanted to correct details in English orthography. Consistent

---

University.

[42] **Sir Thomas Smith** (December 23, 1513 - August 12, 1577), was an English scholar and diplomat. He and his friend, Sir John Cheke, were the great classical scholars of the time in England.

usage based on tradition was his credo. According to him, English spelling was on the whole sufficient and required only minor amendments. He dispensed with letters which had no functions (e.g. <t> in *putt* 'put'), regularized the use of final <-e> to indicate length in preceding vowels (e.g. *hope* vs. *hop, cane* vs. *can, shame* vs. *sham*), etc.[43] Mulcaster's work was very popular and contributed to the regularization of spelling. It is interesting to note that his spelling is close to that of Present-day English" (Fisiak 1995: 106). In spite of many reformers' efforts and their some successes, the interest in the reform of English spelling began to decline towards the end of the first half of the 17th century.

English spelling still has some problems, in that its pronunciations are not predictable in most cases. In other words, the spellings of PDE are not fully regularized. The artificial efforts to reform English spellings, mainly driven by some people of social influence, could not be greatly successful and be widely accepted by the public.

6.2. The Late Modern English Period (1650-1800)

6.2.1. Respect for Order, Reason and Regulation

After the long chaotic period of the English Revolution (1640-60)[44] English

---

[43] The exception to this is the words ending in <-ve> such as *give, live, have*. Here the vowel is not long. The final <-e> was added just because no English word ends in <-v>. The only words ending in just <-v> are the clipped words like *gov* (<*government*), *lav* (<*lavatory*) and *Viv* (<*Vivian*).

[44] The term **English Revolution** refers to the period of the **English Civil War** and **Commonwealth** period, 1640-1660, in which Parliament challenged King Charles

people longed for a new period of peace. So new social forces gained importance and a new political order was introduced. The remaining feudalism of the Middle Ages was dissolved and a "true" modern society began.

When Cromwell died,[45] he, his government and the puritan ethics that they advocated[46] had become so unpopular that the English people asked the son of the executed King Charles I to return to England and to become their king, later King Charles II.[47] However, the conflict between King and Parliament soon started again. The monarchs from the Stuarts, i.e. Charles II and his son James II, tried to revive absolutism again and they failed. In 1688 James II, who wanted to be a monarch of absolute power, lost all the support from his subjects and his people and fled to Ireland. Instead, William of Orange, ruler of the Netherlands, and his Stuart wife Mary were invited to become English king and queen.[48] With those events a new

---

I's authority, engaged in civil conflict against his forces, and executed him in 1649. This was followed by a ten-year experiment in republicanism, the "Commonwealth", before monarchy was restored - in the shape of Charles's son, Charles II, in 1660. ("English Revolution" In *Wikipedia*. Retrieved July 31, 2008)

[45] **Oliver Cromwell** (25 April 1599 - 3 September 1658) was an English military and political leader best known for his involvement in making England into a republican Commonwealth and for his later role as Lord Protector of England, Scotland and Ireland. He was one of the commanders of the New Model Army which defeated the royalists in the English Civil War. After the execution of King Charles I in 1649, Cromwell dominated the short-lived Commonwealth of England, conquered Ireland and Scotland, and ruled as Lord Protector from 1653 until his death in 1658. ("Oliver Cromwell" In *Wikipedia*. Retrieved July 31, 2008)

[46] For example, theaters and other forms of amusement were banned during the Commonwealth period.

[47] This event is called the **Restoration** (1660).

period of peace and stability began and lasted throughout the 18th century. This peaceful period laid the more even way for the later British Empire.

Politically, the 18th century was stable, since monarch and Parliament got on quite well together. This new orderly political structure caused changes in the other areas of English life. "The general tendency, for a multitude of reasons, was towards esteem for rules and regularity; towards a desire to discipline the media of expression, whether these were artistic, literary or linguistic" (Fisiak 1995: 116). Because the society was stable, it was reflected in every cultural life. Everything of reason was respected. Grammarians also assumed the task of regularizing the structure of the English language. They tried to "fix" the English language, since they thought that changes cause chaos and "corruption". To be able to refine language and to fix its proper version, one needed rules which would help to eliminate defects. What was taken for "correctness" at the time was Latin grammar. That is, the model for the fixing and regularizing of English was Latin (grammar). It was regarded as "perfect" at the time.[49]

"The end of the 17th and the beginning of the 18th century also witnessed the rise of experimental sciences and the rationalist trend in philosophy" (Fisiak 1995: 117). These two factors were also of positive influence to the tendency calling for the standardization, fixing and refinement of English.

---

48) This event is called the **Glorious Revolution** because it was bloodless.
49) However, it is well conceived nowadays that the expressions like "fix", "corruption" and "perfect" are not proper in describing language matters.

6.2.2. Prescriptive Grammar and the Attempt to Fix the English Language

As was already said, the most important features of the Late ModE period were rule, order and regularity. People tried to make everything around them orderly and rule-governed. Language is not an exception. In the opinion of several outstanding writers, educators and philosophers of the time, English was in desperate need of a few operations which would shape it into proper form. Although English had been refined and polished through a numerous writers and authors since the Late ME period, it was not sufficient. By the end of the 17th century there was a widespread of feeling of unease about the direction in which English was moving. There was a totally unfounded belief that English had so many defects, disadvantages and corruptions. At the time nobody realized that change is an inevitable fate of every language. Only a dead language, like Latin, could stay without undergoing change. Furthermore, it cannot be said that a "stable" or "fixed" language is more superior or perfect. Nevertheless, the grammarians and people of influence in this field argued that English should receive proper operations to be a more "valuable" language. "The operations may be described in brief as the establishing of a standard of correctness, the refining of English (i.e. removal of defects, disadvantages and corruptions) and the "fixing" of it in a permanent form to avoid the potential changes or modifications which can ultimately lead to corruption" (Fisiak 1995: 117-8).

To establish a new standard of English, the grammarians of this period tried to set up rules. They specifically tried to write a dictionary recording the correct use of lexical items and a grammar listing rules concerning the use of constructions. In writing a dictionary and a grammar, the model was of course Latin. In being compared with Latin grammar, English grammar naturally showed different aspects and these differences were conceived as something corrupt and unorderly. So they should be revised according to Latin grammar. For example, the followings are topics of hot debate at the time (Fisiak 1995: 133):

① The distinction between *lie* and *lay*
② The condemnation of the expressions *had rather* and *had better*
③ Rejection of *whose* as possessive for *which*
④ The condemnation of *between you and I*, *it is me*, and *who is it for?*
⑤ Discouragement of the use of prepositions at the end of a sentence (e.g. *Who did you talk to?*)
⑥ The use of *between* for two and *among* for several people or things[50]
⑦ The use of *you were* for singular (until then *you was* was current and defended even by some grammarians, e.g. Noah Webster)
⑧ The use of comparative where two things are involved, e.g. *the taller of the two*, not *the tallest*

---

50) The preposition *between* can be used when more than two things are referred to if it "relates the position of an object to a definite or exclusive set of discrete objects, whereas *among* relates to nondiscrete objects" (Quirk *et al.* 1985: 680). Thus:

   i. The house stands *between* two farms.
   ii. The house stands *among* farms.
   iii. Switzerland lies *between* France, Germany, Austria, and Italy.
   iv. *Switzerland lies *among* France, Germany, Austria, and Italy.

⑨ The condemnation of the double negative ("Two negatives in English destroy one another, or are equivalent to an affirmative.")[51]
⑩ The condemnation of the split infinitive, e.g. *to <u>completely</u> follow*, etc.
⑪ The proscription of contractions like *'em* for *them*
⑫ Obligatory agreement between pronouns and their antecedents[52]

Of these 12 proposals, a few have been accepted, while others have not. For example, only 1, 7, 8 and partly 9 are now accepted. Crystal (1997a: 194) also gives a similar list of the issues of the prescriptive grammar of the 18th century and later:

① *I* should not be used in *between you and <u>I</u>*. The pronoun should be *me* after a preposition, as in *Give it to <u>me</u>*.
② Split infinitives should not be used.
③ *Only* should be next to the word to which it relates. People should not say *I <u>only</u> saw Jane* when they mean *I saw <u>only</u> Jane*.

---

51) The standard English does not permit the double or multiple negation, while it was possible until the Early ModE period even in the standard prestige English. But some English dialects, including African American Vernacular English (the so-called Black English), still commands the double or multiple negation. The following are such examples:
   i. I ai*n't* got *no* money.
   ii. I told you, I do*n't* believe there's *no* God.
52) Consider such sentences as the following (Huddleston and Pullum 2002: 1470-71):
   i. I went to <u>the corner shop</u> but *he* wouldn't sell me any stamps.
   ii. <u>Tom</u>'s getting married at the weekend. *She*'s already three month's pregnant.
   iii. We've just joined <u>the local squash club</u> but *they* won't let school kids play on Saturday and Sunday afternoons.

Chapter 6 | The Modern English Period (1500-1800)

④ *None* should never be followed by a plural verb. It should be *None was left on the table*, not *None were left on the table*.
⑤ *Different(ly)* should be followed by *from* and not by *to* or *than*.
⑥ A sentence should not end with a preposition. We should say *That was the clerk to who(m) I gave the money*, and not *That was the clerk who(m) I gave the money to*.
⑦ People should say *I shall / you will / he will* when they are referring to future time, not *I will / you shall / he shall*.
⑧ *Hopefully* should not be used at the beginning of a sentence as in *Hopefully, Mary will win the race*.
⑨ *Whom* should be used, not *who*, in such sentences as *That is the man whom you saw*. The pronoun is the object of the verb *saw*, and should be in the objective case.
⑩ Double negatives should be avoided, as in *They haven't done nothing*.

These attitudes are known as prescriptivism,[53] which is "the view that one variety of language has an inherently higher value than others and ought to be the norm for the whole of the speech community" (Crystal 1997a: 194).

---

[53] In linguistics, **prescription** is the laying down or *prescribing* of normative rules for the use of a language, or the making of recommendations for effective language usage. It may be (or appear to be) resistant to language change. Prescription is typically contrasted with **description**, which observes and records how language is used in practice. Unlike prescription, descriptive linguistics avoids value judgments and makes no recommendations. In the 18th century, the emphasis was on prescription, while, nowadays, the emphasis is more on description. Prescription and description are often seen as opposites, in the sense that one declares **how language should be** while the other declares **how language is**. But they can also be complementary, and usually exist in dynamic tension.

All the writers of this period opposed the idea of innovation. They accepted a change in language as a sign of corruption and evil.[54] Scholars thought that changes in English should be arrested if the language was to avoid its further decay. Accordingly, attempts should be made to stabilize and purify it from unnecessary modifications. It was widely believed that a society of authority, e.g. the so-called English Academy, should be established to oversee the purity of the English language and to decide about correct usage. In particular, Jonathan Swift,[55] the author of *Gulliver's Travels*, worked very hard to establish the English Academy. In a well-known letter sent to the Earl of Oxford and Lord of Treasurer of England, which is titled *A Proposal for Correcting, Improving and Ascertaining the English Tongue* (1712), he strongly proposes the necessity of establishing an academy which will purify English from "evil corruptions", on the model of the Italian Academy (*Accademia dei Lincei*, founded in 1582) and the French Academy (*l'Académie Française*, founded in 1635).[56] He says in the letter as follows:

---

54) As we have seen through this textbook, change is an inevitable feature of language. So the efforts to fix English, after refining and correcting it according to Latin, could not be a success.

55) **Jonathan Swift** (1667 - 1745) was an Irish cleric, satirist, essayist, political pamphleteer and poet, famous for works like *Gulliver's Travels*. Swift is probably the foremost prose satirist in the English language, although he is less well known for his poetry. He wrote an essay titled *A Proposal for Correcting, Improving and Ascertaining the English Tongue*. ("Jonathan Swift" In *Wikipedia*. Retrieved July 31, 2008)

56) "The first Academy was founded in Italy in 1582, and by 1612 it had produced a dictionary, which as seen as the first step on the road to 'purifying' the Italian language. A French Academy followed in 1635, and its dictionary appeared in 1694." (Crystal 2002: 223)

My Lord; I do here, in the Name of all the Learned and Polite Persons of the Nation,[57] complain to Your Lordship, as *First Minister*, that our Language is extremely **imperfect**:[58] that its daily Improvements are by no means in proportion to its daily **Corruptions**; that the Pretenders to **polish and refine** it, have chiefly multiplied Abuses and Absurdities; and, that in many Instances, it offends against every Part of Grammar ... (Bolton 1966: 108)

In order to **reform our Language**, I conceive, My Lord, that a free judicious Choice should be made of such Persons, as are generally allowed to be best qualified for such a Work, without any regard quality, Party, or Profession. ... The persons who are to under take this Work, will have the Example of the French before them, to imitate where these have preceeded right, and to avoid their Mistakes ... (Bolton 1966: 116)

But this plan was not fulfilled and no significant attempt to establish an academy was made later in the 18th century. The efforts to rectify and fix English were also made by other men of letters at the time. For example, Samuel Johnson, who published in 1712 the first real voluminous English-English dictionary containing a lot of quotations from the various sources,[59] advocates the effort to fix the English language, although he admits that the complete success is impossible. He says in the Preface of his famous dictionary as follows:

---

57) Here he uses the capital letter for the first letter of all nouns as in German.
58) Emphasis was added.
59) See Section 6.1.4.

When I took the first survey of my undertaking, I found our speech **copious without order**, and **energetick without rules**: whenever I turned my view, there was **perplexity to be disentangled**, and **confusion to be regulated**; choice was to be made out of boundless variety, **without any established principle of selection**; adulterations were to be detected, without a settled test of purity; and modes of expression to be rejected or received, without the suffrages of any writers of classical reputation or acknowledged authority. (Bolton 1966: 130)

It is curious from the standpoint of our present experience that the minds of the time could not grasp the essence of language from a historical perspective, i.e. its constant growth, decay and change.[60] Therefore, the efforts to correct English and to fix it in the form of that time was doomed to be a failure. Furthermore, the rules of Latin grammar could not be the standard of proper usage of English. Latin grammar enforced usage and terminology alien to English. According to Crystal (1997a: 192), the so-called traditional grammar, which developed in the middle of the 18th century under the strong influence of prescriptivism, had two hallmarks which caused the negative reaction when people talk about the subject of grammar. "Traditional grammars insisted that only certain styles of English

---

60) Realizing that language cannot be kept static, Johnson says in the same source quoted above (Bolton 1966: 130) that "If the changes that we fear be thus irresistible, what remains but to acquiesce with silence, as in the other insurmountable distresses of humanity? It remains that we retard what we cannot repel, that we palliate what we cannot cure. Life may be lengthened by care, though death cannot be ultimately defeated: tongues, like governments, have a natural tendency to degeneration."

were worth studying - in particular, the more formal language used by the best orators and writers." That is, they focussed on the written language only as their object of research. The more important point is that "Traditional English grammars also treated their subject in a highly abstruse way, describing grammatical patterns through the use of an analytical apparatus which derived from Latin grammar." But the efforts of the 18th and the early 19th century prescriptivists started from the love for their language and contributed to the logical and scientific study of English in any way, paving the way for the true linguistic research of the language in the later centuries.

6.3. Modern English Literature[61]

As we have chosen to define it, the ModE period scans three hundred years or so (from 1500 to 1800). We have seen how, in that time, the status of the English language was raised as the proper medium or vehicle for learning, science, administration and literary activity. At the start of the period English was just beginning to be used for such purposes, by the middle of the period it was being expanded and improved, and by the end of the period the need was felt to fix it in its state of perfection and to regulate it.

The upgraded status and fortunes of the English language are reflected in literature produced throughout the ModE period. For the first century or so of this period was marked by the Renaissance. It was the rebirth of

---

[61] The full treatment of the ModE literary achievements is beyond this introduction. A short survey is given for the general review.

culture and scholarship and interest was turned to classical scholarship, particularly the works of Caesar, Homer, Ovid, Plutarch, Plato and Virgil. Their works were translated into English at this time. Influential religious works, such as those of John Calvin[62] and Martin Luther,[63] were also studied in English translation. Both these activities provided English with important sources of loanwords. The Renaissance was a period of strong Italian influence, flowing through to France, Spain, and then England. The influence of Petrarch on Shakespeare, especially on his sonnets, is well documented.[64] The novel of Boccaccio also influenced English style for many years.[65]

The court of Elizabeth I (1558-1603) inspired or witnessed many great works, including the lyrics of Sir Philip Sidney, Edmund Spenser and

---

62) **John Calvin** (July 10, 1509 - May 27, 1564) was a French Protestant theologian during the Protestant Reformation and was a central developer of the system of Christian theology called Calvinism or Reformed theology. ("John Calvin" In *Wikipedia*. Retrieved July 31, 2008)

63) **Martin Luther** (November 10, 1483 - February 18, 1546) was a German monk, theologian, university professor and church reformer whose ideas inspired the Protestant Reformation and changed the course of Western civilization. ("Martin Luther" In *Wikipedia*. Retrieved July 31, 2008)

64) **Francesco Petrarca (Petrarch)** (1304 - 74) was an Italian scholar, poet and early humanist. Petrarch is often popularly called the "father of humanism". Petrarch is credited for perfecting the sonnet, making it one of the most popular art forms to date. ("Petrarch" In *Wikipedia*. Retrieved July 31, 2008)

65) **Giovanni Boccaccio** (1313 - 75) was an Italian author and poet, a friend and correspondent of Petrarch, an important Renaissance humanist in his own right and author of a number of notable works including *On Famous Women*, the *Decameron* and his poetry in the vernacular. ("Boccaccio" In *Wikipedia*. Retrieved July 31, 2008)

William Shakespeare (*The Sonnets*), and the plays and pageants best represented by the works of Christopher Marlowe (*Tamburlaine the Great, The Jew of Malta, Dr. Faustus*) and again, of course, Shakespeare. The range of Shakespeare's plays runs the gamut from fantasy and satire to searing tragedy in plays such as *A Midsummer Night's Dream, Measure for Measure* and *Hamlet*. The live performance of plays became extremely popular during the reign of Elizabeth. This was a very flowery and elegant period of English prose, perhaps best illustrated in the works of William Shakespeare.

This period was followed by the Jacobean period, named in reference to the reign of James I of England (James VI of Scotland, 1603-25). Even at the end of Elizabeth's reign the mood of England had turned gloomy. This was obviously reflected in the literature. The style of writing became less elaborate. Francis Bacon introduced the essay form.[66] *The King James Version of the Bible* must also be mentioned here again as a mark of high literary achievement. Jacobean poetry is best represented by the works of Ben(jamin) Jonson and John Donne,[67] the latter being the most important

---

[66] **Francis Bacon** (22 January 1561 - 9 April 1626) was an English philosopher, statesman and essayist. He is also known as a proponent of the scientific revolution. He has been credited as the creator of the English essay. ("Francis Bacon" In *Wikipedia*. Retrieved July 31, 2008)

[67] **John Donne** (1572 - March 31, 1631) was a Jacobean poet and preacher, representative of the metaphysical poets of the period. His works, notable for their realistic and sensual style, include sonnets, love poetry, religious poems, Latin translations, epigrams, elegies, songs, satires and sermons. His poetry is noted for its vibrancy of language and inventiveness of metaphor, compared with that of his contemporaries. He is famous for his Holy Sonnets. ("John Donne" In *Wikipedia*. Retrieved July 31, 2008)

of the metaphysical poets.68) In fact, Shakespeare produced his finest work, i.e. his tragedies and romances, in the Jacobean period.

The 18th century opened with the Enlightenment, also known as the Age of Reason, which has some connection with such events as the French[69] and American Revolutions.[70] The 19th century sees the return of the romance, typified by the poetry of John Keats,[71] Percy Bysshe Shelley[72] and

---

68) **Metaphysical poets** were a loose group of British lyric poets of the 17th century, who shared an interest in metaphysical concerns and a common way of investigating them. The label "metaphysical" was given much later by Samuel Johnson in his *Life of Cowley*. These poets themselves did not form a school or start a movement; most of them did not even know or read each other. Their style was characterized by wit, subtle argumentations, "metaphysical conceits", and/or an unusual simile or metaphor. ("Metaphysical Poets" In *Wikipedia*. Retrieved July 31, 2008)

69) **The French Revolution** (1789 - 1799) was a period of political and social upheaval in the political history of France and Europe as a whole, during which the French governmental structure, previously an absolute monarchy with feudal privileges for the aristocracy and Catholic clergy, underwent radical change to forms based on Enlightenment principles of nationalism, citizenship and inalienable rights. ("French Revolution" In *Wikipedia*. Retrieved July 31, 2008)

70) **The American Revolution** refers to the period during the last half of the 18th century in which the Thirteen Colonies gained independence from the British Empire to become the United States of America. In this period, the Colonies united against the British Empire and entered a period of armed conflict known as the Revolutionary War (also, mostly in British usage, "American War of Independence"), between 1775 and 1783. This resulted in an American Declaration of Independence in 1776, and victory on the battlefield in October 1781. ("American Revolution" In *Wikipedia*. Retrieved July 31, 2008)

71) **John Keats** (31 October 1795 - 23 February 1821) was one of the principal poets of the English Romantic movement. During his short life, his work received constant critical attacks from the periodicals of the day, but his posthumous

William Wordsworth.

Since the ModE period spans a long time of about 300 years, we cannot deal with the literary achievements of the entire period in detail. But it is quite clear that at this time the English literature was advanced up to the position where it could make an important contribution to the world literature, just as England itself was becoming an Empire having its colonies all over the world.

---

influence on poets such as Alfred Tennyson has been immense. Elaborate word choice and sensual imagery characterize Keats's poetry, including a series of odes that were his masterpieces and which remain among the most popular poems in English literature. ("John Keats" In *Wikipedia*. Retrieved July 31, 2008)

72) **Percy Bysshe Shelley** (August 4, 1792 - July 8, 1822) was one of the major English Romantic poets and is widely considered to be among the finest lyric poets of the English language. He is perhaps most famous for such anthology pieces as *Ozymandias*, *Ode to the West Wind*, *To a Skylark* and *The Masque of Anarchy*. ("Percy Bysshe Shelley" In *Wikipedia*. Retrieved July 31, 2008)

07 Chapter

Expansion of English around the World[*]

7.1. Expansion of English within the British Isles and to Ireland

Now let us consider how and in what way English could spread around the world and gain the present status. For this matter, we have to go back to the OE period and start there.

In a sense, the English language has always been on the move. As soon as it arrived in England from northern Europe in the 5th century, it began to spread around the British Isles. However, English was spoken only in England during the Early OE period. But it spread to the west and to the north, entering parts of Wales,[1)] Cornwall,[2)] Cumbria[3)] and southern Scotland.

---

[*] This chapter is based on Crystal (1997a: 92-115; 1997b: 53-63; 2002: 233-63), Barber (1993: 234-42), Baugh and Cable (1993: 283-85), Svartvik and Leech (2006: 71-149) and Fisiak (1995: 134-35).

1) England still remained England even after the incorporation of Wales.

2) **Cornwall** (Cornish: *Kernow*) is a county in South West England, United Kingdom, on the peninsula that lies to the west of the River Tamar and Devon. The

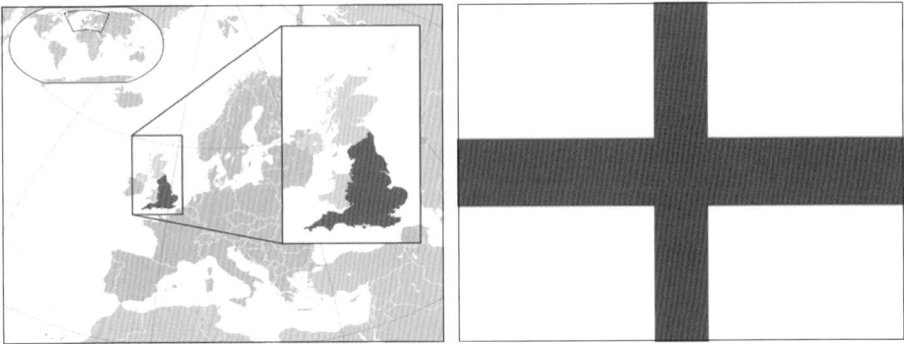

Figure 7.1. England and its Flag (St. George's Cross of England)

Figure 7.2. Wales and its Flag

Especially, English penetrated into southern Scotland at the Late OE times. Until c. 975, part of this country was under Anglo-Saxon rule. The border between Scotland and England that was established in the 10th century has not changed until today. After the French invasion of 1066, many English nobles became refugees, and fled north to Scotland, where they were

---

administrative center and only city is Truro.

3) **Cumbria** is a shire county in the extreme North West of England. The county consists of six districts. Cumbria is bound to the west by the Irish Sea, to the south by Lancashire, to the southeast by North Yorkshire, and to the east by County Durham and Northumberland. Scotland lies directly to the north.

welcomed (by the Scots king Malcolm III[4]). Eventually their language, English, could spread in this area.

Figure 7.3. Scotland and its Flag (St. Andrew's Cross of Scotland)

By the middle of the 17th century English was the normal language in the whole lowlands of Scotland, while many of the highlanders still kept their own language, Scottish Gaelic, which is one branch of Celtic languages. When in 1707 Scotland was formally united with England, English was regarded as the standard language and Scottish Gaelic and lowland Scots were reduced to the role of local dialects.[5] In particular, lowland Scots was

---

4) He is "most widely known as the slayer of Macbeth, as recounted by Shakespeare." (Crystal 2002: 234)
5) **Scots** is a kind of mixed language of English and Gaelic. Scots comprises the Anglic (i.e. English-like) varieties derived from early northern Middle English spoken in parts of Scotland and Northern Ireland. In Scotland Scots is sometimes called *Lowland Scots* (or *Lallans*) to distinguish it from *Scottish Gaelic*, traditionally spoken in the Highlands and Islands. Scots is also spoken in parts of Northern Ireland and border areas of the Republic of Ireland, where it is known in official circles as *Ulster Scots* or *Ullans*. ("Scots" In *Wikipedia*. Retrieved July 31, 2008)

kept alive as the literary language in the 18th century due to the works of Burns,[6] Ramsay,[7] Ferguson[8] and Walter Scott.[9] "The Scots English became increasingly different from that used in England, especially in pronunciation and vocabulary, and many of these differences are still heard today" (Crystal 2002: 234).

The Middle Ages witnessed the spread of English beyond Britain. Ireland became an English colony due to the invasion by the Anglo-Norman knights and the subsequent conquest by Henry II (1154-89). After that, the English administration, army and clergy began to arrive, bringing their language with them. At first English was spoken by only a handful of people but gradually its use began to spread as a result of administrative pressure. Only English was used in schools. And whoever spoke Irish Gaelic, which is a Celtic language and is the original language of the Irish people, were subject to severe punishment. Today, English is spoken everywhere, with Gaelic found only in certain rural parts of the west. And

---

6) **Robert Burns** (1759 - 1796) was a poet and a lyricist. He is widely regarded as the national poet of Scotland, and is celebrated worldwide. He is the best-known of the poets who have written in the Scots language, although much of his writing is also in English.

7) **Allan Ramsay** (1686 -1758) was a Scottish poet, born at Leadhills, Lanarkshire.

8) **Adam Ferguson**, also known as **Ferguson of Raith** (1723-1816) was a philosopher and historian of the Scottish Enlightenment.

9) **Sir Walter Scott** (15 August 1771 - 21 September 1832) was a prolific Scottish historical novelist and poet popular throughout Europe during his time. His novels and poetry are still read, and many of his works remain classics both of English-language literature and of Scottish literature. Famous titles include *Ivanhoe*, *Rob Roy*, *The Lady of the Lake*, *Waverley* and *The Heart of Midlothian*. ("Walter Scott" In *Wikipedia*. Retrieved July 31, 2008)

Ullster Scots (or Ullans) are spoken mainly in the northern area (cf. Footnote 15). The Irish English has something special, which has been given literary expression in the poetry of W. B. Yeats[10] and the novels of James Joyce[11] (Crystal 2002: 240).

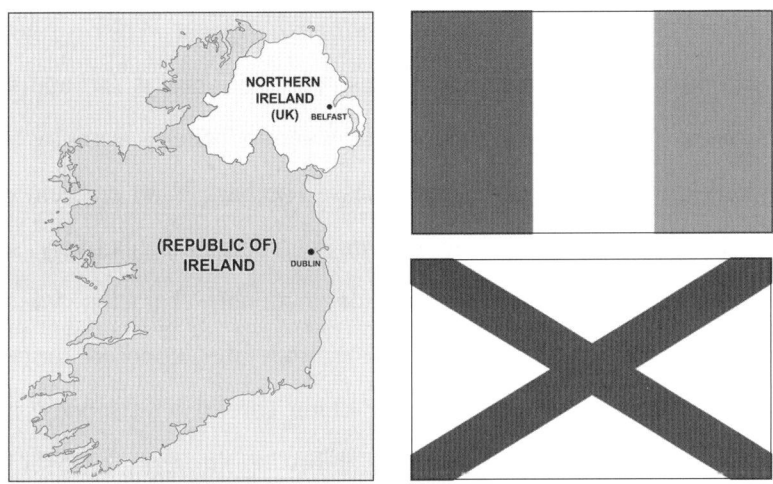

Figure 7.4. Ireland and its Flags
(St. Patrick's Cross of Ireland [Upper]
and the Flag of the Republic of Ireland [Lower])

---

10) **William Butler Yeats** (13 June 1865 - 28 January 1939) was an Irish poet and dramatist, and one of the foremost figures of 20th-century literature. ("William Butler Yeats" In *Wikipedia*. Retrieved July 31, 2008)

11) **James Augustine Aloysius Joyce** (2 February 1882 - 13 January 1941) was an Irish expatriate writer, widely considered to be one of the most influential writers of the 20th century. He is best known for his landmark novel *Ulysses* (1922) and its highly controversial successor *Finnegans Wake* (1939), as well as the short story collection *Dubliners* (1914) and the semi-autobiographical novel *A Portrait of the Artist as a Young Man* (1916). ("James Augustine Aloysius Joyce" In *Wikipedia*. Retrieved July 31, 2008)

In fact, Welsh, Scottish and Irish people feel their identity very strongly. There are some signs of national identity. For example, "the prefix *Mac* or *Mc* in surnames (such as *McCall, MacCarthy, MacDoanld*) is always either Scottish or Irish. The prefix *O* (as in *O'Brien, O'Hara*) is distinctively Irish. A very large number of surnames (e.g. *Davis, Evans, Jones, Lloyd, Morgan, Price, Rees, Williams)* suggest Welsh origin. First names can also be indicative. The Scottish form of *John* is *Ian* and its Irish form is *Sean*. And the kilt, a skirt with a tartan pattern worn by men, is a very well-known symbol of Scottishness. The harp is an emblem of both Wales and Ireland, while the bagpipes are regarded as distinctively Scottish. And there are certain stereotypes of national character which are well-known in Britain. For instance, the Irish are supposed to be great talkers, the Scots have a reputation for being careful with money, and the Welsh are renowned for their singing ability" (O'driscoll 1995: 11).

The spread of English to Wales, Scotland and Ireland was the movement on a very local scale - within the British Isles. And this spread resulted in the political unification from England to (Great) Britain and then to the United Kingdom. Although Wales was an actually occupied part of England since the Late OE times, it was officially merged with England only in 1536. The incorporation of Scotland into England was accomplished in 1707, much later than the real occupation and government by the English people. Thus Great Britain was born this year. The next step was the incorporation of Ireland, which was done by the Act of Union in 1800, after the long-standing resistance by the Irish people, when the Irish Parliament was joined with the Parliament of England, Scotland and Wales in Westminster. This incorporation resulted in the birth of the United

Kingdom (of Great Britain and Ireland). So the formation of the United Kingdom was a gradual process that took several hundred years. However, the Irish people could get independence in 1922,[12] establishing their own country again, the Republic of Ireland. The problem is that they could not have the whole island of Ireland as their territory. The northern Ireland is still the land of the United Kingdom, which became the land of the continuous conflict between the English and the Irish.

Table 7.1. The Formation of
The United Kingdom of Great Britain and Northern Ireland

	England (London)	Wales (Cardiff)	Scotland (Edinburgh)	Ireland (Dublin)	Northern Ireland (Belfast)
Date of Incorporation	5th century	in 1536	in 1707	in 1800	after the Irish independence in 1921[13]
State Name	England	England	Great Britain	The United Kingdom of Great Britain and Ireland	The United Kingdom of Great Britain and Northern Ireland

---

12) "When in 1800 the Irish Parliament was joined with the Parliament for England, Scotland and Wales in Westminster, the whole of the British Isles became a single state - the United Kingdom of Great Britain and Ireland. However, in 1922, most of Ireland became a separate state." (cf. O'driscoll (1995: 10))

13) Following the war of independence, Ireland was split into two parts in 1922: the newly independent **Irish Free State**, and **Northern Ireland** (which rejoined the United Kingdom). The Free State left the British Commonwealth to become a republic (i.e. the Republic of Ireland) in 1949.

- The UK = England (Germanic) + Scotland, Wales, and Northern Ireland (Celtic)

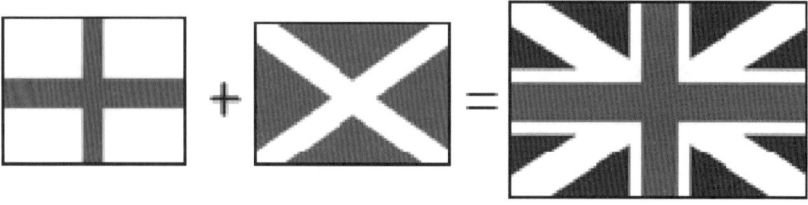

Flag of Great Britain (1707)

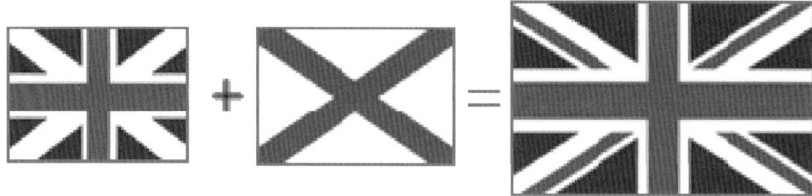

Flag of the UK, Union Jack (since 1800)

Figure 7.5. The Formation of *Union Jack*, the Flag of the United Kingdom

7.2. Expansion of English to America[14]

The most significant step towards its status as a world language took place with the cultivation of the American Colonies starting at the end of the 16th century because it is surely American political and economic power

---

14) The name *America* comes from Amerigo Vespucci, an Italian navigator who explored the Atlantic coast of today's South America around 1500. *America* or *the Americas* actually refers to the whole of the American continent, including North America, Central America and South America. But this broad *America* is sometimes used as the same term with *the United States of America*. *The United States of America* is a full and official name of this country, although the more common term is *the United States* (e.g. *The United States government*), or its abbreviation *the U.S.* (e.g. *a U.S. citizen*, usually written without periods in Britain: *the US*). A more informal term among Americans is *the States*. cf. Svartvik and Leech (2006: 85)

that accounts for the dominant position of English in the world today.[15]

The first expedition from England to the New World was sponsored by Walter Raleigh (?1552-1618) in 1584,[16] and turned out a failure.[17] A group of explorers landed near Roanoke Island, which now belongs to North Carolina, and established a small settlement. But they disappeared after several years, leaving a mystery. The first permanent English settlement dates from 1607, when an expedition arrived in Chesapeake Bay. Thus the English language was brought to America in the same year by these English colonists (approximately 120 people). The colonists called their settlement Jamestown (after James I of the English king (1603-1625) at the time) and the area Virginia[18] (after the 'Virgin Queen' Elizabeth I (1558-1603)). The further spread of English in the New World was due to the expansion of colonies and new arrivals of colonists in the following years.

In November 1620 the Mayflower brought a group of pilgrims,[19] later

---

[15] "For the role of English today as a world language, the single most important historical factor was surely the coming of the English language to America." (Svartvik and Leech 2006: 71)

[16] **Sir Walter Raleigh** (1552/1554 - 1618) was a famed English writer, poet, courtier and explorer. He was responsible for establishing the first English colony in the New World, on June 4, 1584, at Roanoke Island in present-day North Carolina. He is also famously known to have popularized two American products - tobacco and potato.

[17] When the settlement failed, the ultimate fate of the colonists was never authoritatively ascertained, and it became known as "The Lost Colony".

[18] The ending *-ia* has the meaning of 'land'. So *Virginia* is 'the land of a virgin'. Likewise, *Georgia,* a state of the USA, is 'the land of George'. *Geroge* again means a farmer because *geo-* means 'earth, land, territory', as can be seen in *geometry, geology* and *geography*.

[19] **Pilgrims** or **Pilgrim Fathers** is the name commonly applied to early settlers of the

known as the Pilgrim Fathers, (102 in all, a group of Puritans[20]) which comprised 35 members of the English Separatist Church and the company of 67 other settlers). They set up the Plymouth Colony in the north in Cape Cod Bay.[21] They had in common a new religious kingdom, free from persecution and 'purified' from the church practices they had experienced in England. In 1628 Puritans started the Massachusetts Bay Colony further to the north. A large Puritan migration began in 1630. The influx of colonists between 1620 and 1640 was on an unprecedented scale. The extent of migration can be judged as extraordinary, with 15,000 new arrivals at that time. The number of settlers reached 25,000 in 1640. Most of them established settlements around Massachusetts Bay.

    Plymouth Colony in present-day Massachusetts. First, they had fled from the East Midlands of England to the Netherlands to get the freedom of their religious belief. Concerned with losing their cultural identity even in the Netherlands, the group later arranged to establish a new colony in North America. The colonists faced a lengthy series of challenges. However, the colony was ultimately established in 1620. Their story has become a central theme in United States cultural identity.

20) **Puritan** of 16th and 17th century England was any person seeking "purity" of worship and doctrine. They rejected both the Roman Catholic Church and the Church of England (i.e. the Anglican Church). They sought to reform the liturgy and theology of the Roman Catholic Church and to be separated from the Church of England.

21) **Plymouth** is also the name of the port city in England, from which they departed England taking the ship *Mayflower*.

Figure 7.6. Changes of *Stars and Stripes*, the National Flag of the United States of America

"It is important to appreciate that the two settlements, the southern settlement of 1607 and the northern one of 1620, resulted in different linguistic consequences" (Crystal 2002: 241). For example, the southern explorers came mainly from the west country of England, so they pronounced the [r] after vowels, whereas the Puritans came from East Anglia and the surrounding counties, lacking an [r] after vowels.[22]

---

[22] For details, see Section 8.1.1.

7.3. Expansion of English to Canada[23]

After landing in New England, the English language was making progress further north. Before that, English reached Newfoundland area through the expedition by John Cabot as early as 1497.[24] John Cabot is said to have given Newfoundland its name. But he did not leave any permanent settlement there. Actually, the first European language in Canada was French. It reached the country with French colonists, e.g. the explorations of Jacques Cartier in the 1530s.[25] At first Canada was known as *New France* due to the French colonization. In fact, Canada derives its names from the word *kanata*, which meant 'village' or 'community' in Huron, an Iroquoian language.

---

23) **Canada** is a country occupying most of northern North America. It is the world's second-largest country by total area, and extends from the Atlantic Ocean to the Pacific Ocean and northward into the Arctic Ocean. Canada shares land borders with the United States to the northwest and south. Canada was founded in 1867 as a union of British colonies (some of which were formerly French colonies). It gained independence from the United Kingdom in 1982. It remains a Commonwealth Realm with Queen Elizabeth II as its head of state. Canada is a bilingual and multi-cultural country, with both English and French as official languages at the federal level. ("Canada" In *Wikipedia*. Retrieved July 31, 2008)

24) **Giovanni Caboto** (c.1450 - c.1499), known in English as **John Cabot**, and in French as **Jean Cabot**, was an Italian navigator and explorer. He is commonly credited as one of the first early modern Europeans to land on the North American mainland, in 1497.

25) **Jacques Cartier** (1491 - 1557) was a French navigator who first explored and described the Gulf of Saint Lawrence and the shores of the Saint Lawrence River, which he named Canada.

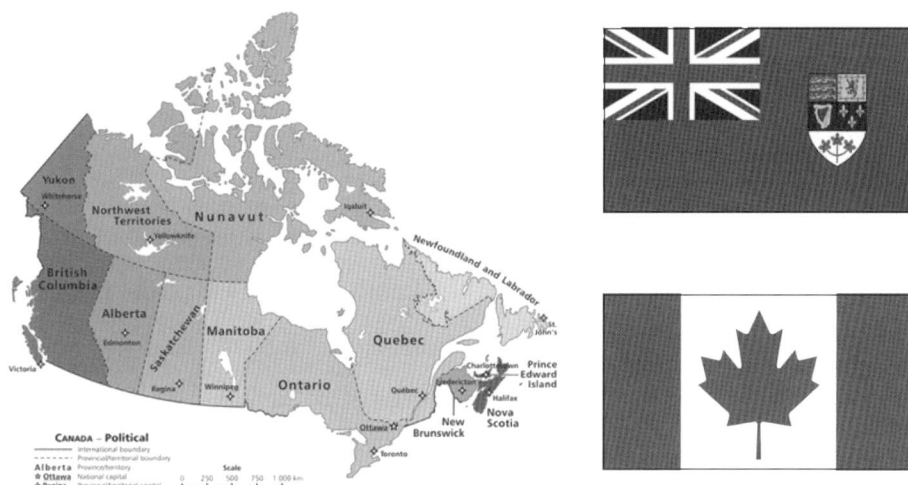

Figure 7.7. 10 Provinces and 3 Territories of Canada, its Flag [Right Upper] and the Old Flag before 1965 [Right Lower])

But the French language declined in Canada when the French settlers were defeated by the British Army in Queen Anne's War (1702-13)[26] and the French and Indian War (1754-63).[27] The result was that Canada became a

---

26) **Queen Anne's War** (1702-1713) was the second in a series of four French and Indian Wars fought between France and England (later France and Great Britain) in North America for control of North America. In addition to the two main combatants, the war also involved a number of American Indian tribes and Spain, which was allied with France. ("Queen Anne's War" In *Wikipedia*. Retrieved July 31, 2008)

27) **The French and Indian War** (1754 - 1763) was the North American chapter of the **Seven Years' War**. The name refers to the two main enemies of the British: the royal French forces and the various American Indian forces allied with them. The colonial war between the kingdoms of France and Great Britain resulted in the British conquest of all of New France east of the Mississippi River, as well as Spanish Florida. The outcome was one of the most significant developments in the persistent Anglo-French Second Hundred Years' War. To compensate its ally,

British colony in 1763. So British rule eventually prevailed in Canada and the English language became its national language. Although French is still spoken widely in Quebec province (e.g. in such cities as Montreal and Quebec City),[28] English is the main language across Canada. During the 1750s, about 6,000 speakers of French were deported from Acadia (modern Nova Scotia),[29] with most ending up in Louisiana. In their place thousands of English people moved to Canada from New England. And the people from Ireland, England and Scotland also came to Canada, mainly to Nova Scotia. The Canadian population figures also swelled after 1776 when American supporters of Britain, who advocated the government of the American colonies by the British king and so were called *Loyalists*, fled to escape the newly independent Untied States, and settled in Nova Scotia and then in the New Brunswick area. Thousands were attracted by the promise of cheap land in Upper Canada (beyond the Great Lakes and north of Montreal, present-day Ontario) and over 7,000 settlers had moved there by 1785. Due to the migration of the increasingly large number of Loyalists, Canada was divided into Upper Canada dominated by English-

---

Spain, for its loss of Florida, France ceded its control of French Louisiana west of the Mississippi. France's colonial presence north of the Caribbean was reduced to the tiny islands of Saint Pierre and Miquelon. ("French and Indian War" In *Wikipedia*. Retrieved July 31, 2008)

28) Canada is composed of 10 **provinces** (British Columbia, Albert, Saskatchewan, Manitoba, Ontario, Quebec, New Brunswick, Nova Scotia, Newfoundland and Labrador, and Prince Edward Island) and 3 **territories** (Yukon, Northwest Territory and Nunavut). The *province* is equivalent to a *state* in the US, while the *territory* is a *quasi-state*.

29) *Nova Scotia* means 'New Scotland' in Latin. It clearly shows the influence by the Scottish people who migrated there.

speaking colonists, and Lower Canada (present-day Quebec) which was inhabited mainly by French-speaking colonists.

Over the course of the 19th century settlement proceeded westwards, as it did in the United States, eventually reaching the Pacific coast. French-speakers by and large remained in the East (i.e. in Quebec area), however. The role of French in Quebec has until recently been supported by bilingual regulations governing the whole of Canada, but the position of French seems to have been slipping in recent years. Anyway, English could spread across Canada. Now English is spoken across the whole North America, including the US.

Canadian English shows the 'mixed' character of American and British English (Crystal 2002: 250; Parker and Riley 2005: 141). So "British people commonly mistake English-speaking Canadians for Americans, while many Americans identify a Canadian accent as British. Yet the Canadians themselves believe that both the American and British varieties are clearly distinguishable from their own" (Svartvik and Leech 2006: 95). For example, "the phrase *tire centre* uniquely Canadian. In the United States the phrase would be *tire center*; in England, it would be *tyre centre*."[30] "The vocabulary looks very 'mixed', with American and British items co-existing - such as *tap* (AmE *faucet*) and *porridge* (AmE *oatmeal*) alongside *gas(oline)* (BrE *petrol*) and *billboard* (BrE *hoarding*). Vehicle terms are typically American: *trucks* (BrE *lorries*), *fenders* (BrE *wings/mudguards*), *trunks* (BrE *boots*, of a car), *caboose* (BrE *guard's vans*), etc." Canadian spelling is also mixed. It sometimes patterns like British spelling: "for example, AmE *center*/Canadian *centre*, AmE

---

30) For the lexical and spelling differences between American and British English, see the next chapter.

check (banking item)/Canadian *cheque*, AmE *color*/Canadian *colour*, AmE *theater*/Canadian *theatre*. However, in other cases, Canadian spelling patterns like America spelling rather than British spelling: for example, AmE-Canadian *aluminum*/British *aluminium*, AmE-Canadian *tire*/British *tyre*." And "such words as *curb* (BrE *kerb*), *jail* (BrE *gaol*) and *tire* (BrE *tyre*) are also normally spelled in the American way." However, Canadian English shows its own usages, too. For example, lexical differences exist between AmE and Canadian English: *electoral district/riding, napkin/serviette, sofa/chesterfield, you know? right?/eh?,*[31] *zee* (name of letter Z)/*zed*.[32]

7.4. Expansion of English to Australia[33]

Towards the end of the 18th century, the continuing colonial expansion of

---

[31] "But there is a little word *eh* (pronounced /ei/) that is widely considered to be a marker of Canadian speech. Its use is fairly consistent across the country, and it occurs in cases like theses: *Nice day, eh?* (statement of opinion), *It goes over here, eh?* (statement of fact), *What a game, eh?* (exclamation), *Eh? What did you say?* (to mean 'pardon')." (Svartvik and Leech 2006: 97)

[32] "Most Canadians pronounce name of the letter Z as in British English, thus /zed/, not /ziː/." (Svartvik and Leech 2006: 96)

[33] The **Commonwealth of Australia** is a country in the Southern Hemisphere comprising the mainland of the world's smallest continent, the major island of Tasmania and a number of other islands in the Southern, Indian and Pacific Oceans. On 1 January 1901, the six colonies became a federation, and the Commonwealth of Australia was formed. Since federation, Australia has maintained a stable liberal democratic political system and remains a Commonwealth Realm. The capital city is Canberra, located in the Australian Capital Territory. The population is 20.8 million, and is concentrated mainly in the mainland state capitals of Sydney, Melbourne, Brisbane, Perth and Adelaide. ("Australia" In *Wikipedia*. Retrieved July 31, 2008)

Britain cultivated new colonies in the southern hemisphere. Although the number of people going there was not very large, the English language could be spoken in the Pacific areas, i.e. in Australia and New Zealand.

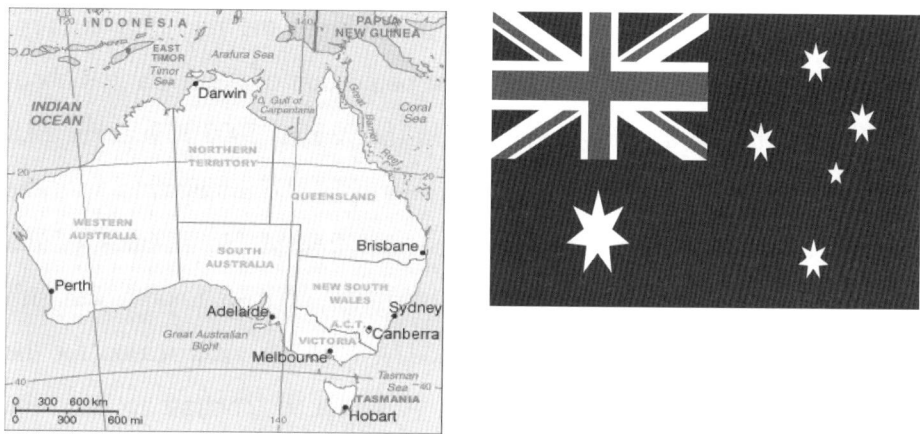

Figure 7.8. Australia and its Flag

"The first known Europeans to reach the continent we now call Australia were Portuguese and Dutch sailors in the 16th century. Initially, it was known as *Nova Hollandia* 'New Holland'; the name *Australia* is derived from Latin *terra australis incognita* 'unknown southern land'[34] (Svartvik and Leech 2006: 98).

Australia was visited by James Cook in 1770,[35] and after twenty years

---

34) "During the First World War *Aussie* (pronounced 'Ozzie') became an informal short form for the noun *Australian* (as in *a dinkum Aussie* 'a real Australian') and the adjective (as in *Aussie Rules* for a code of football which originated in Australia). these days there is also an informal name for Australia: Oz." (Svartvik and Leech 2006: 100)

35) Captain **James Cook** (1728 - 1779) was a British explorer, navigator and cartographer. Cook made three voyages to the Pacific Ocean, achieving the first

Chapter 7 | Expansion of English around the World   217

Britain had established its colony in Sydney in 1790. Sydney was developed as a penal colony to accommodate the overcrowding prisoners at their homeland. The number of the prisoners, who were called 'free' settlers, was not big at first, and then about 130,000 prisoners were transported during the following fifty years. From the mid-19th century, immigration was permitted. By 1850, the population of Australia was about 400,000 and by 1900 nearly 4 million. In the year of 2008 it is about 20.8 million. The British Isles provided the majority of the immigrants, with the largest proportion coming from London and Ireland. So features of the Cockney twang[36] of London and the brogue[37] of Irish English can still be noticed in the speech of Australia today. It is the main reason for the remarkable homogeneity nationwide in Australia, in contrast to, say, the United States or Canada.

Through the contact with indigenous peoples and their languages, English

---

European contact with the eastern coastline of Australia, the European discovery of the Hawaiian Islands, and the first recorded navigation and mapping of Newfoundland and New Zealand. He accurately charted many areas and recorded several islands and coastlines on European maps for the first time. He died in Hawaii in a fracas with Hawaiians during his third exploratory voyage in the Pacific in 1779.

36) The term **cockney** refers to working-class inhabitants of London, particularly east London, and the slang used by these people. It is also often used in reference to the "cockney accent", the accent common among London's working-class.

37) A **brogue** is a strong dialectal accent, notably in Irish dialects of the English language. It is from the Irish word "bróg", meaning "shoe". The term has been said to have been coined by an Englishman who met an Irishman whose accent was so thick that he spoke "as though he had a shoe in his mouth", but it more likely derives from the association of Irish workers with their rawhide shoes. ("Brogue" In *Wikipedia*. Retrieved July 31, 2008)

borrowed from them some lexical items referring to animals or cultural implements found only in Australia,[38] such as *kangaroo, boomerang, koala* and *willy-willy*. Many such words have also become loanwords in other languages beyond English. In recent years the influence of American English has been noticeable, so that Australian English shows a very mixed linguistic character, in some ways resembling that found in Canada. Thus we find American *truck* (BrE *lorry*), *elevator* (BrE *lift*) and *freeway* (BrE *motorway*), alongside British *petrol* (AmE *gas(oline)*), *boot* (of a car; AmE *trunk*) and *tap* (AmE *faucet*). (cf. Crystal (2002: 258))

7.5. Expansion of English to New Zealand[39]

Unlike Australia, New Zealand was not settled by prisoners.[40] In 1769

---

38) The indigenous people in Australia do not have a uniform name but accept the term **Aborigines**, derived from Latin *ab origine* meaning 'from the beginning'. (Svartvik and Leech 2006: 101)

39) **New Zealand** is a country in the south-western Pacific Ocean comprising two large islands (the North Island and the South Island) and numerous smaller islands. New Zealand is notable for its geographic isolation, being separated from Australia to the northwest, approximately 2000 kilometers across. Its closest neighbours to the north are New Caledonia, Fiji and Tonga. The population is mostly of European descent, with the indigenous Maori being the largest minority. Non-Maori Polynesian and Asian people are also significant minorities, especially in the cities. Elizabeth II, as the Queen of New Zealand, is the Head of State. The Queen 'reigns but does not rule'; she has no real political influence. Political power is held by the democratically-elected Parliament of New Zealand under the leadership of the Prime Minister, who is the Head of Government. ("New Zealand" In *Wikipedia*. Retrieved July 31, 2008)

40) New Zealand takes its name from the Dutch province *Zeeland*. It reflects the fact

Captain Cook found these islands, one year before arriving in Australia, and claimed the land for the British Crown.

Figure 7.9. The Flag of New Zealand [Left]
and the Silver Fern Flag of the 2015 Referendum [Right]

The settlement started from the 1790s, mainly by European whalers and traders. But the official colony was not established until 1840. After that, there was a rapid increase in European immigration. The total population in 2008 is about 4.2 million.

The New Zealand people (and its English) has its own characteristics (Crystal 1997b: 37). Firstly, in comparison with Australia, there has been a stronger sense of the historical relationship with Britain, and a greater sympathy for British values. That is, they are more sympathetic to the British than are the Australians. Their English also shows British influence. In fact, there is greater antipathy towards American English and American cultural influence in general than in Australia. Secondly, there has been a growing sense of national identity. So they like to assert their difference from Australians, contrary to the common misunderstanding that Australia and New Zealand will be the same in national characters. Rather, they have

that the first Europeans known to have reached New Zealand were Dutch explorers.

much in common with the Canadians. Nevertheless, New Zealand English has its own accent. Thirdly, there has been a fresh concern to take account of the rights and needs of the indigenous people (i.e. Maori people), who now form over 10 percent of the population. This fact has resulted in an increased use of Maori words,[41] thus forming the peculiar vocabulary of New Zealand English.

7.6. Expansion of English to Other Areas

We have seen the expansion of British colonialism and the consequent spread of the English language to the areas where English was established as the mother tongue; Scotland, Ireland, and then the American colony, Canada, Australia, and finally New Zealand. These countries are forming the Inner Circle of English. However, the expansion of English did not stop there. It also moved to the areas which were occupied by the British colonial power and where English became their second language along with the original language of the area. For example, English moved to India, Singapore, Malaysia, Hong Kong, Papua New Guinea, and many countries in Africa. In these regions English is still taught and used as the second language, and is accepted as an official language. These regions form the Outer Circle of English.

---

41) **Words of (New Zealand) Maori origin** have entered New Zealand English and are considered native words. Some of those words have in turn been exported from New Zealand English to other branches of the English language and to other languages. ("English Words of Maori Origin" In *Wikipedia*. Retrieved July 31, 2008) For example, *kiwi* is such a word, meaning 'the bird, a New Zealander, or sometimes (not in New Zealand) the kiwi fruit'.

Chapter 08

The American English

In Section 7.2 we reviewed how the English language was transmitted to America. The language that the British brought with them to America, beginning with the first settlement in Jamestown in 1607, is Early ModE. At this time the language was the same both in Britain and in America However, the language has developed differently in the two areas since then, resulting in the two quite different national varieties; British and American English.

Differences are still noticed. However, the differences are being reduced due to the temporal and spatial closeness between the two areas with the help of the modern technology. In a sense, we, as EFL speakers, need not know which is a British usage and which is an American one. But we have to bear in mind that English is not uniform and it permits wide varieties. It is controversial to decide which is standard and which is more acceptable. What is important to us is to realize that there are varieties of English and all such variations are fully acceptable as correct English. In this chapter we will see what variations English reveals for America and Britain.[1]

8.1. Language Variation in America

8.1.1. Diverse Backgrounds of the Early Settlers

American English begins in Elizabethan times, around the year 1600 when English-speaking settlers began to live on the Atlantic coast of the American continent. The language the American colonists used was the English they spoke and wrote at home; Early ModE of the 17th century. These first settlers had learned as children to speak and write English in the last quarter of the 16th century. The English they took with them to the new lands must therefore have been in a certain sense the language of Shakespeare, Marlowe and Queen Elizabeth I.

But the two settlements - one in Virginia to the south (through the expedition in 1607) and the other to the north, in present-day New England[2] (through the expedition in 1620) - had different linguistic backgrounds. The southern colonists came mainly from England's 'West Country', e.g. such counties as Somerset and Gloucestershire, and brought with them its characteristic linguistic features, e.g. the /r/ strongly pronounced after vowels.

---

1) This chapter is based on Pyles and Algeo (1993: 21-33), Baugh and Cable (1993: 345-400), Crystal (2002: 264-69), Strevens (1972), Carney (1997: 64-6), etc. For a more detailed treatment of American English, refer to Algeo (2001) and Tottie (2002).

2) New England is the northern area of the US, comprising the six states such as Maine, New Hampshire, Vermont, Massachusetts, Rhode Island, and Connecticut.

By contrast, many of the northern Plymouth colonists came from counties in the east of England, in particular, Lincolnshire, Northinghamshire, Essex, Kent, and London, with some from the Midlands. These eastern accents were rather different, notably, lacking an /r/ after vowels. The tendency 'not to pronounce the /r/' is still a feature of the speech of people from New England. As a result, the starting point for the development of what is now American English was not even a single, standardized form of English. It was a large collection of local accents and dialects.

8.1.2. Uniformity and Diversity of American English

It has been reported in numerous histories of the English language on the uniformity of American English in contrast to British English. Although America is much bigger than the British Isles, the regional variation is not big within it. There is no doubt today that, in comparison with British English, American English is remarkably uniform. However, it is not true that there is no language variation in America. The various regions of American English have dialect features that clearly set them off from each other. That is, there coexist both diversity and uniformity in American English. The diversity was already rooted in the colonization process, since different varieties of English were transmitted to the northen and southern colonies.

  Nevertheless, the dialects that developed in America are generally much more homogeneous than they are in Britain. This is partly because of the high degree of physical and geographical mobility possible during the settlement process, and partly because of the social mobility that contrasts with the relatively static class structure in Britain. Furthermore, the country does not have a long history enough to develop new regional variations inside, which are not easily made within several decades.

8.1.3. Dialects of American English

There are still a large number of documented regional dialects in the United States. We saw that there were two main dialects, Yankee (i.e. Northern)[3] and Southern at the beginning stage of the colonization. But the language later developed a three-way division in its dialect areas. "It is usual to recognize three main dialect areas, the Northern, the Midland and the Southern" (Crystal 2002: 237). The Midland area is again subdivided into the North Midland and the South Midland areas. That is, a new dialect, Midland dialect was made in its evolution at the new land.

In spite of the dialect division of American English, the differences are not large, compared with British English or even with the dialects found in any other language. What is more, this division in the dialects was based largely on lexical differences among the different regions, not on any signifiant linguistic (phonetic, morphological or syntactic) differences. The following brief list gives some examples of the lexical differences found diagnostic of particular regions (Parker and Riley (2005: 141)):

---

[3] The term *Yankee*, sometimes abbreviated to *Yank*, has several different but related meanings. It often refers to someone of Northern U.S. origin or heritage. Originally the term referred to residents of New England. During and after the American Civil War its meaning expanded to include any Northerner. Outside the United States, Yank or Yankee is a slang term, sometimes derogatory, for any U.S. citizen.

Table 8.1. Lexical Differences between Northern and Southern U.S.

Northern U.S.	Southern U.S.
pail	*bucket*
bag	*sack*
faucet	*spigot*
quarter of four	*quarter to four*
sick to my stomach	*sick at my stomach*
(*cherry*) *pit*	(*cherry*) *seed*

Because our main concern is the higher-level division of British and American English, we will ignore the differences of this kind here.

8.2. Differences between British and American English

Now let us consider the differences between British and American English in terms of vocabulary, spelling, pronunciation and grammar.[4] Here, only the Present-day Standard English and (as far as speech is concerned) "nonlocal" pronunciations will be considered for both sides. In each case we shall consider similarities and differences.

---

4) Svartvik and Leech (2006: 157) say that, when we study the main standardized varieties of AmE and BrE, we come to the following conclusions:
   i. in grammar, they are very similar;
   ii. in spelling they are very similar (in spite of those changes Webster promoted);
   iii. in vocabulary they are different in some areas, but strikingly the same in core vocabulary;
   iv. in pronunciation they are clearly different, but generally mutually intelligible.

8.2.1. Differences of Vocabulary

The vocabulary difference is most easily noticeable as the differences of British and American English. That is, there are far more examples of British and American differences in vocabulary than in grammar. But we should keep in mind that the difference in vocabulary must not be taken too seriously, because both American words and British ones are understood in both sides in most cases. For example, such American words as *automobile*, *mailman* (or *letter carrier*), *railroad*, *baggage* and *mad* are fully understood in Britain, too, along with its British counterparts like (*motor*) *car*, *postman*, *railway*, *luggage* and *angry*. So what is important is not to distinguish which is American or British but to know that both words or expressions are indiscriminately used as a kind of synonymy. And we should not forget that the greater proportion of English words are common to both British and American English.

Actually, there are three types of vocabulary difference existing between American and British usage, which are discussed below.

1) Different Words for the Same Meaning

The first category comprises a fairly large number of cases where different words are used to denote the same idea or object. In this case, we have simply to know that there are more than two words or expressions denoting the same thing without memorizing which is British and which is American.

The broad semantic areas in which British-American lexical differences are especially noticeable are food/cooking, fashion/clothing, transportation and education. First, consider the lexical differences in the area of food and cooking. The differences are quite natural, considering the fact that new foods and new ways of processing and cooking foods have arisen since the separation of the two nations:

Table 8.2. Lexical Differences in the Area of Food and Cooking[5]

AmE	BrE	AmE	BrE
cookie, cracker	*biscuit*[6]	*dessert*	*sweets, pudding*
french fries	*chips*	*biscuit*	*scone*
potato chips	*crisps*[7]	*broil*	*grill*
candy	*sweets*	*custard*	*egg custard*
peanuts	*monkey nuts*	*eggplant*	*aubergine*
oatmeal	*porridge*	*Jello*	*jelly*
bar, tavern	*pub*	*jelly*	*jam*
corn	*maize, sweet corn*	*zucchini*	*courgette*

The vagaries of fashion have also caused difference in the vocabulary of clothing:

---

5) The examples are mostly from Crystal (2002: 268-69).
6) "In Britain biscuits are small flat thin pieces of pastry, as in *chocolate biscuits*, eaten as a snack; in the US biscuits are little breakfast breads and part of a meal, not a snack." (Svartvik and Leech 2006: 153)
7) So the word *chips* may be understood differently in Britain and America, meaning 'potato chips' in America and 'french fries' in Britain as the famous British food 'fish and chips' indicates. *Chips* and *crisps* are used in its pluralized form as the food names.

Table 8.3. Lexical Differences in the Area of Fashion

AmE	BrE	AmE	BrE
pants	trousers	underpants, shorts	pants
vest[8]	waistcoat	suspenders	braces
undershirt, T-shirt	vest	garter	suspender
pantyhose	tights	sneakers	trainers

The many differences in the terminology of transportation were also caused after the separation of the US and Great Britain. The following list shows some examples:

Table 8.4. Lexical Differences in the Area of Transportation

AmE	BrE	AmE	BrE
hood	bonnet	shoulder	verge
trunk	boot	fender	wing, mudguard
freeway, highway,[9] expressway	motorway	(pedestrian) crossing[10] crosswalk	zebra (crossing)
main street	high street	automobile	(motor) car
truck	lorry	baby buggy, carriage	pram
bus	coach	cab	taxi
gas(oline)	petrol	traffic circle	roundabout
trailer	caravan	railroad	railway
one-way ticket	single ticket	gearshift	gear lever
round-trip ticket	return ticket	freight	goods
intersection	crossroads	transportation	transport
muffler	silencer	sidewalk	pavement

---

8) So *pants* and *vest* are understood differently in Britain and America. In these confusing cases, we should know which is British and which is American.
9) Meanwhile, there is another American word *turnpike*, meaning the *motorway*. A *turnpike* is a motorway which you usually have to pay to use (e.g. *The New Jersey*

Differences in the organization of education in Britain and America lead to different terms.[11] The word *school* is differently understood in both countries; the word is used in Britain mainly on primary and secondary levels, while it is used for any educational system in America. So an American can say "Stanford is a pretty good school", but the word *school* is not used to refer to a university or other college of higher education in Britain. A *public school* in Britain is in fact a *private school*, whereas the American *public school* is a *state school* in Britain. The American *grade school* or *elementary school* is equivalent to British *primary school*.[12] An American high school *student graduates*: a British secondary school *pupil* (never *student*) *leaves school*. To *graduate* is possible only from a university, polytechnic or college of education, and *graduating* entails taking a degree in British usage. British universities have three *terms*; American universities have two *semesters* (or in some recent years, four *quarters*). A British university student takes three years, in the typical case, to get his degree: these are known as the first, second and final years. The American university student typically takes four years, known as *freshman*,

---

Turnpike).
10) Simple *crossing* can denote the *railway crossing*, so the word *pedestrian* is sometimes added before *crossing* when meaning the *zebra*.
11) This paragraph on the terms of education is mostly the quotation from Strevens (1972: 56-7).
12) *Elementary school* is the preferred term in some countries, particularly those in North America. *Primary school* is the preferred term in the United Kingdom, India, Pakistan, Australia, Latin America, South Africa and New Zealand. *Elementary schools* in the United States are also sometimes called *grade schools*, especially in the northern states.

sophomore, *junior* and *senior* years. ... The British student who has already taken a first degree is a *postgraduate*; the American equivalent is a *graduate*. In American universities, those who teach are known as the *faculty*; in Britain they are the *staff*, possibly dignified as the *academic staff*" (Strevens 1972: 56-7). The university hierarchy of teaching posts is also differently termed as follows (Strevens 1972: 57):

Table 8.5. The University Hierarchy of Teaching Posts

American	British
(Full) Professor (T)[13]	Professor (T)
Associate Professor (T)	Reader (T)
Assistant Professor	Senior Lecturer (T)
	Lecturer (T)

There are some other miscellaneous differences. The following list contains some examples which we need know:

---

13) (T) means 'normally having security of tenure'.

Table 8.6. Miscellaneous Lexical Differences

AmE	BrE	AmE	BrE
elevator	*lift*	*subway*	*underground, tube*
apartment	*flat*	*underground*	*subway*
zero	*nil*	*vacation*	*holiday*
line	*queue*	*public school*	*state school*
zipper	*zip*	*second floor*	*first floor*
downtown	*city centre*	*pharmacy*	*chemist*
pacifier	*dummy*	*closet*	*cupboard*
trashcan	*dustbin*	*yard*	*garden*
liquor store	*off-license store*	*trash*	*rubbish*
intermission	*interval*	*mailbox, letter box*	*pillar-box*
briefcase	*portfolio*	*vending machine*	*slot machine*
attorney[14]	*solicitor, barrister*	*band-aid*	*sticking plaster*
stairway[15]	*staircase*	*sick*[16]	*ill*
package	*parcel*[17]	*faucet, spigot*	*tap*
insane	*mental*	*fall*	*autumn*
alumnus	*graduate*	*ballpoint*	*biro*
can	*tin*	*couch*	*sofa*
call (phone)	*ring*	*purse*	*handbag*
raise	*rise*	*realtor*	*estate agent*
flashlight	*torch*	*mail*	*post*
movie	*film*	*schedule*	*timetable*
term paper	*essay*	*yield (road sign)*	*give way*
cell(ular) phone	*mobile (phone)*	*bill*	*note*
mad	*angry*	*crazy, insane*	*mad*
parking lot	*car park*	*period*	*full stop*

14) The neutral term is *lawyer*.
15) Now *stairs* is the usual term in both countries.
16) In Britain, *sick* means only 'nauseated', as in *Lucy felt sick the morning after the party*.
17) The British words *parcel* and *post* are also widely used among Americans, who send

2) Same Words for the Different Meaning

The second category covers words which are used in both British and American English, but with a difference of meaning. However, several American English words and expressions come to be used in British English in recent years:

Table 8.7. Same Words for the Different Meaning
(Crystal 2002: 268)

Words	AmE Meaning	BrE Meaning
dumb	stupid, mute	mute
homely	plain (people)	domestic
nervy	cheeky	nervous
pants	trousers	underpants
vest	undershirt, T-shirt	waistcoat
subway	underground urban railroad	underground tunnel or passage
underground	underground tunnel or passage	underground urban railroad
pavement	any paved surface	pedestrian path
mad	angry	crazy, insane
sick	ill, nauseated	ill

3) Words with No Counterparts

"The third category covers words for ideas or objects which have no counterparts in the other country. An obvious group of examples would be words for geographical features or plants or animals found only in America (AmE *everglades, bayou, canyon, caribou, gopher, sequoia, sagebrush,*

---

packages by the *parcel post*, not by the *package mail*.

etc.); or words for games and sports not shared between the British and the Americans. Examples are BrE *wicket, fast bowler, silly mid-off* (all terms from the cricket game), and AmE *pitcher, home run, doubleheader* (terms from the baseball game). British English retains the vocabulary of a monarchy (BrE *princess, duchess,* etc.), but these terms are clearly part of English as a whole. Meanwhile, the American vocabulary of presidential government is more restricted to American society: AmE *precinct* (a political constituency), *primary* (election for the selection of Presidential candidates), *ticket* (set of political aims, or names), etc."[18] There are certain semantic fields where groups of lexical differences cluster.

4) American Slangs

American slangs clearly show the lexical differences from British English. Many British speakers do not understand American slangs. Nevertheless, slangs are widely used in American English, so we should be equipped with the proper knowledge of slang expressions to understand American English. Of course, it is not recommended to use these slang expressions yourself. But slangs are not always bad words. To know slangs (especially inoffensive ones) is sometimes essential to understand the American speech. You can get a useful and practical list of American slangs at the site of Dave's ESL cafe (http://www.eslcafe.com/slang/a.html).

There exist more differences in the use of words other than those that were mentioned above, but, as far as everyday speech is concerned, they are not

---

18) This is the quotation from Strevens (1972: 59).

really very numerous or very significant. The differences are being intermingled, so the formerly national differences are being reduced to the simple lexical choice. That is, the use of any term is acceptable and fully understood in most cases.

8.2.2. Differences of Spelling

Another differences between British and American English are found in their spelling conventions. However, some American spellings are now in use in Britain, and, conversely, some British spellings are used in America, too:

(1) Americans use <-ize> instead of the <-ise> forms,[19] as in *baptize, criticize, organize, sympathize, capitalize, dramatize, regularize, naturalize*, etc.[20] Meanwhile, the ending <-ise> is more frequent in BrE, although both <-ise> and <-ize> forms occur even in BrE.

(2) Americans write *honor, humor, color, favor, armor, flavor, behavior, harbor, labor, neighbor, mold, smolder*, and others without the <u> of British *honour, humour,*[21] *colour, favour, armour, flavour, behaviour, harbour, labour, neighbour, mould, smoulder*, etc.[22]

---

19) Likewise, Americans use <-yze> instead of the <-yse> forms, as in *analyze* and *paralyze*.
20) But some words are always spelled <-ise> in both AmE and BrE: *advertise, advise, comprise, compromise, disguise, despise, devise, disguise, exercise, improvise, revise, rise, supervise, surprise*.
21) British spelling has *humour* but *humorous* and *humorist*. It has *vapour* but *vaporise* and *evaporate*. That is, the <-u-> disappears when certain suffixes are added. But it is not uniform, e.g. *colourful, colouring* and *colourist*.

(3) Americans use only one consonant letter where the British write two: *traveler - traveller, counselor - counsellor, canceling - cancelling, leveled - levelled, programed - programmed, kidnaper - kidnapper, worshiping - worshipping, libelous - libellous, jewelry - jewellery, woolen - woollen, wagon - waggon, instalment - installment*, etc.[23]

(4) Superfluous letters have been cut in AmE spelling in several other cases. The BrE diagraph spellings <ae> and <oe> for [i:] in Greek and Latin loanwords have been reduced to simple <e> in AmE spelling;[24] *an(a)emia, an(a)esthetic, encyclop(a)edia, medi(a)eval, p(a)ediatrics / am(o)eba, diarrh(o)ea, f(o)etus, man(o)euver* and *(o)estrogen*.

(5) The ending <-ogue> in *analogue, catalogue, dialogue, epilogue, monologue, travelogue*, has been simplified to <-og> in American English, giving *analog* and others. There is a similar reduction in *abridgement* and *acknowledgement*, etc., giving *abridgment* and others.

---

22) But it is not the case that all <-or> words have the corresponding <-our> words. Some agent nouns like *author, doctor, emperor, governor, collector* and *senator* are spelled as <-or> even in BrE. There are other nouns ending in <-or> in BrE, like *horror, mirror, rigor, stupor, pallor, terror, tenor, languor* and *squalor*. Conversely, AmE has *glamour*.
23) Conversely, the single <l> at the end of BrE *appal, enthral, instil, fulfil,* is doubled in AmE to give *appall*, etc.
24) Latin had a pair of diphthongs [ae] and [oe], and the Greek had a similar pair, [ai] and [oi], which are conventionally rendered in Latin and English as [ae] and [oe]. (Trask 2010: 141)

(6) Americans write <-er> instead of <-re> in such words as *fiber, center, theater, (kilo)meter, liter, somber, caliber, maneuver* and *scepter*.[25]

(7) Americans prefer an <-s-> in words like *defense, offense, pretense, license, recompense,* and similar words, instead of BrE <-c->.[26]

(8) Americans use <-i-> instead of the <-y-> forms, as in *cider, cipher, tire* vs. *cyder, cypher, tyre*.

(9) Americans use the <-ction> ending instead of BrE <-xion> forms, as in *connection, inflection,* etc.[27]

(10) Americans use the <in-> prefix instead of the British <en-> in some words like *incase, inclose, indorse, inquire/inquiry, insure,* and others.[28]

Besides the systematic differences given above, there are some idiosyncratic

---

[25] Exceptions are *acre* and *lucre*, since *acer and *lucer would be pronounced as, e.g. [éisər] not as [éikər]. The spelling <c> is pronounced as [s] in front of the front vowels such as [i] (as in *city*) and [e] (as in *certain*).
[26] But *fence*, which is simply an aphetic form of *defense* (or *defence*), is not spelled as *fense* even in America.
[27] The British forms such as *connexion, inflexion,* etc, are etymologically correct, since they are all Latin loanwords. The Latin forms are *connexiōn(em)* and *inflexiōn(em)*. But such forms do not show clearly the relation with the verbs like *connect* and *inflect*.
[28] This does not apply to all <en-> words. Such words as *encamp, enchant, endow* are found in AmE, too.

differences, too, as in the following table:[29]

Table 8.8. Idiosyncratic Spelling Differences

AmE	BrE	AmE	BrE
aluminum	*aluminium*	*ax*	*axe*
plow	*plough*	*story*	*storey*
czar	*tsar*	*jail*	*gaol*
specialty	*speciality*	*pajamas*	*pyjamas*[30]
curb	*kerb*	*program*	*programme*
mustache	*moustache*	*sulfur*	*sulphur*
draft	*draught*	*artefact*	*artifact*
check	*cheque*	*mold*	*mould*
skeptical	*sceptical*	*gray*	*grey*

These differences often passed unnoticed. It is because both spellings, i.e. the conservative British spellings and the innovative American ones, are indis criminately used on both sides of the Atlantic.

What should be mentioned here is that the most innovations in American spellings were due to one person's advocacy for them and the incorporation of them in his dictionary. The person is Noah Webster (1758-1843).[31] He

---

[29] "Non-standard spellings are much more in public use in American English in advertisements, shop signs, road signs, etc.: *donuts, hi/lo, tonite, thru, thruway, kool.*" (Crystal 2002: 266)

[30] There is no pronunciation difference between *pajamas* and *pyjamas*, i.e. [pədʒáːməz].

[31] **Noah Webster** (October 16, 1758 - May 28, 1843) was an American lexicographer, textbook author, spelling reformer, political writer, word enthusiast and editor. He has been called the "Father of American Scholarship and Education". His Blue-backed Speller books taught five generations of children in the United States how to spell and read, and (in the US) his name became synonymous with "dictionary", especially the modern Merriam-Webster dictionary that was first

lived in the time of the American Independence War (1775-1783).[32] With a war against the British waged and later political independence achieved, many of the colonists (or citizens of a new country) revealed a distaste for anything British, including its language. Noah Webster expressed this attitude more vigorously than any other. Although he majored in law at Yale, he turned to teaching after graduation. Especially, he was interested in the language matter. His credo was that the English language in America should be a distinctly American thing, developing along its own lines, and deserving to be considered from an independent, American point of view. He advocated forming and using the American language, not the English language. He also wanted to weld the 13 colonies into a unified nation through their own linguistic identity.[33] The culmination of his efforts to

published in 1828 as *An American Dictionary of the English Language*. ("Noah Webster" In *Wikipedia*. Retrieved July 31, 2008)

32) In 1775, the American colonies began their struggle for independence from the British Empire. On July 4, 1776, the Declaration of Independence was issued as colonists attempted to sever ties with Britain. Revolt led to revolution and war. On October 19, 1781, the British, led by Lord Cornwallis, surrendered at Yorktown, Virginia. This ended the war and assured the independence of the US. The peace treaty was signed in Paris on September 3, 1783. Britain agreed to give the US all territory to the south of what is now Canada, north of Florida, and west to the Mississippi River.

33) The 13 colonies at the time of independence are as follows;

  I) New England Colonies; New Hampshire, Massachusetts, Connecticut, Rhode Island
  II) Middle Colonies; New York, Pennsylvania, New Jersey, Delaware
  III) Southern Colonies; Maryland, Virginia, North Carolina, South Carolina, Georgia

promote the idea of the American language was the publication of *An American Dictionary of the English Language* in 1828.

But the language was still English, not American. He and Americans could not introduce a new language. In any way their language was (from) English. Nevertheless, they wanted to have some differences, along with the inevitable sameness. Webster's way to achieve this aim was to stress American usage and American pronunciations by adopting a number of distinctive spellings.

Ultimately the differences in spelling between British and American usage are due either to American innovations or to deliberate policy. Since Webster, there have been a number of efforts to reform English spellings in both countries, with somewhat more success in America than in Britain.[34]

The general direction of the American spelling reform was the omission of all superfluous or silent letters. Webster proposed to delete the letters such as the <a> in *bre<u>a</u>d, fe<u>a</u>ther* and the <e> in *giv<u>e</u>*. He also proposed to substitute <ee> for the vowels in *m<u>ea</u>n, sp<u>ea</u>k, gr<u>ie</u>ve, k<u>ey</u>,* etc., and to use <oo> for <ou> in *gr<u>ou</u>p* and *s<u>ou</u>p*, and also to use <k> for <ch> in such words as had a [k] sound (e.g. *<u>ch</u>aracter, <u>ch</u>orus*). But these proposals were not accepted, which proves that the radical reform, in particular, led by a few people, cannot be successful in language matters. One of the reason

---

The States of Maine and Vermont were not the colonies at that time. Maine was a part of Massachusetts and Vermont was established as a state much later.

34) Webster was not the only person who advocated the spelling reform of the English spoken in America. For example, Benjamin Franklin also took an interest in the spelling reform. In the early years of the last century, Andrew Carnegie and President Theodore Roosevelt also actively supported the spelling reforms of (American) English.

for the failure is that the morphological form, which reveals the etymology of the word, is as important as the pronunciation. If we change the word *sign* into *sin* or *sine* by eliminating the silent <g>,35) the resulting new form will not be understood as its original word, and will not show any morphological and etymological relation with such words as *signature, signify* and *signal*. In the case of *signature, signify* and *signal*, <g> is pronounced and so cannot be deleted. Ultimately, all the silent letters cannot be deleted. In addition to that, there are variations of pronunciation, especially of vowel sounds. The pronunciation itself is changing. Therefore, some principles are necessary for the successful spelling reform. Otherwise, the reforms would rather perplex than ease the learner. Even Webster's reforms were partly successful.36)

8.2.3. Differences of Pronunciation

As in word choices and spelling differences, there is no fundamental

---

35) To indicate the length of the vowel, the word-final silent <e> is often added, as in *scrape* (vs. *scrap*), *pipe* (vs. *pip*) and *cope* (vs. *cop*). This is another example showing why all silent letters should not be deleted. Meanwhile, Webster proposed to drop off the final <-e> of *-ine, ite* and *ive*, recommending to use such spellings as *determin, examin, doctrin, medicin, definit, fugitiv*, etc. It was because the vowel of the final syllable are all short here and so the <-e> is not necessary. Nevertheless, the attempt turned out to be a failure. Language is not an object of logic.

36) Some reforms by Webster were accepted even to British English. For example, he proposed to eliminate the final <k> in such words as *music, physic, logic, traffic, public, almanac*, etc. Today, the spellings like *musick, physick, logick, traffick, publick, almanack*, etc. are not found any more even in Britain.

differences in pronunciation between British and American English. Otherwise, American and British people would have a big trouble in communication, which is contrary to fact. Nevertheless, when a native speaker speaks English, even we, a non-native speaker of English, can often notice with ease whether it is American English pronunciation or British one. It is because there are some characteristic pronunciations of each variation.

For pronunciation, there are so many variations even within one national variant that we cannot compare all the differences together. Instead, we will focus on the standard pronunciations of each national variant. It is traditional to refer to the pronunciation of Standard British English as Received Pronunciation, or, more shortly RP. Its American equivalent is General American (GA) pronunciation. We will suggest some systematic differences between RP and GA in this section. The differences are mostly found in vowel values. But there exist a few consonantal differences, too

1) Consonants

The inventory of consonants is identical to both RP and GA. The only differences between the two variants lie in the distribution of the phonemes[37]

---

37) A **phoneme** is the basic form of sound and a contrastive phonological segment in a language. A phoneme is not a sound actually spoken and heard. That is, phonemes are not the physical segments themselves, but mental abstractions of them. A phoneme could be thought of as a family of related phones, called allophones, that the speakers of a language think of, and hear or see, as being categorically the same and differing only in the phonetic environment in which they occur.

and in their allophonic realizations.38)

The first difference is about the pronunciation of [r]. RP is non-rhotic (*r*-less).39) So [r] is not pronounced when it appears before a consonant or at the end of a word.40) To non-rhotic speakers, such word pairs as *fa*r*ther/father* and *lo*r*e/law* have the same pronunciations.41) However, it is

---

38) In phonetics, an **allophone** is one of several similar phones that belong to the same phoneme. A phone is a sound that has a definite shape as a sound wave, while a phoneme is a basic group of sounds that can distinguish words (i.e. changing one phoneme in a word can produce another word); speakers of a particular language perceive a phoneme as a single distinctive sound in that language. Thus an allophone is a phone considered as a member of one phoneme.

39) **Rho**, whose adjective is *rhotic*, is the name of one of Greek alphabet which is equivalent to English alphabet <r>. There is a sound change in English called **Rhotacism**. It is the change of [s] to [r] before a vowel sound, as in the alternations like *ru*s*tic-ru*r*al, ju*s*tice-ju*r*y* and *agno*s*tic-igno*r*ant*.

40) "More precisely speaking, non-rhotic pronunciations are typical of the southeast of England, of the Midlands, of Wales and of much of northen England; they are also typical of Australia, New Zealand, South Africa and the east coast (New England and New York City) and the coastal south of the US. Rhotic accents, in contrast, are usual in the southwest of England, in Scotland and parts of northern England, in Ireland and in most of the US and Canada." (Trask 1994: 26)

41) "The difference in the pronunciation of [r] is due to the history of English (expansion). Several centuries ago, all speakers of English used a rhotic pronunciation. This type of pronunciation was therefore carried to North America in the 17th century. In the 18th century, however, the new, non-rhotic style of pronunciation appeared in the southeast of England and became fashionable and this new pronunciation began to spread over England and Wales. The West County, Scotland and Ireland, for whatever reason, declined to accept the new fashion and continued to use their traditional rhotic speech. Australia, New Zealand and South Africa were largely settled in the 19th century by immigrants

retained when the following word begins with a vowel (for instance, *near it* [nɪr ɪt]) even in a non-rhotic area.42)

Secondly, the pronunciation of the intervocalic <t> is not the same. <t> is not voiced in RP and so is strongly pronounced, whereas it is voiced into [d] or sometimes a [r]-similar sound in GA pronunciation. It means that [t] has [d] or [r] as its allophones in GA.43) But the voicing of <t> is confined to the environment where it is positioned between vowels and the stress falls on the syllable before <t>. Here, the location of the stress is important. So *wáiter* is voiced, while *detér* is not.

Thirdly, RP does not distinguish [hw] from [w].44) Therefore,

---

from England, who took with them the new non-rhotic style. Non-rhotic speech was also carried across the Atlantic to the coastal cities of the United States, which were in fairly close contact with the mother country, but the new fashion failed to across the Appalachian Mountains, and most of the mainland of North America retained its rhotic style." (Trask 1994: 26)

"In England, non-rhotic speech is now generally regarded as more prestigious than rhotic, ... In the US, however, the situation is reversed: there rhotic pronunciation is generally regarded as more prestigious ..." (Trask 1994: 26)

42) An unnecessary [r] is sometimes added between a word ending in a vowel and another word beginning with a vowel (for instance, *idea of* [ɑɪdɪərəv]). This sound is called an intrusive [r].

43) Another allophonic sound of [t] is the glottal stop [ʔ]. But it is normally limited to the end of syllables before another consonant, as in *button* or *kitten*. The glottal stop is the sound made when the vocal cords are pressed together to stop the flow of air and then released; for example, the break separating the syllables of the interjection *uh-oh*.

44) Some phoneticians prefer to use the symbol [ʍ] instead of [hw] to indicate that the sound is a separate single distinctive sound, not the combination of two consecutive sounds [h] and [w].

which/witch and *whether/weather* are homophones.[45]

Finally, in RP the semivowel[46] [j] appears after alveolars[47] and before [u] in many words (known as yod-dropping, for example, *new* [nu:], *tune* [tu:n], *assume* [əsú:m], *due* [du:] in GA, cf. *new* [nju:], *tune* [tju:n], *assume* [əsjú:m], *due* [dju:] in RP).

2) Vowels

A vowel is unstable in its phonetic quality, so there are much more variations than consonants. Furthermore, the phoneticians employed their own phonetic alphabets to indicate the vowel sounds, and the number of the vowel sounds are not the same among scholars. In particular, British

---

45) A **homophone** is a word that is pronounced the same as another word but differs in meaning. The words may be spelled the same, such as *rose* 'flower' and *rose* 'past tense of *rise*', or differently, such as *carat, caret* and *carrot*, or *your* and *you're*. A homophone is a specific type of **homonym**, which is one of a group of words that share the same spelling or pronunciation (or both) but have different meanings. Examples are *stalk* (which can mean either part of a plant or to follow someone around) and the trio of words *to, too* and *two*.

46) **Semivowels** are defined as the vowel-like sounds that correspond phonetically to specific close vowels. The semivowel is considered by some to be the same as a vowel but the semivowel is a little different from a vowel. English semivowels are two: [j] corresponding to [i], and [w] for [u], as in *boy* [bɔi, bɔj] and *bow* [bau̯, bau̯]. The sound [j] represents a vowel sound [i] when it appears after a vowel sound, as in *boy* [bɔi, bɔj] and *clay* [klei, klej]. When it appears before a vowel, however, it represents a consonantal sound, as in *yes* [jes] and *year* [jiər]. Some scholars prefer to use [y] instead of [j]; [bɔy] and [yes] instead of [bɔj] and [jes].

47) **Alveolars** are the sounds that are pronounced with the tongue raised in various ways to the alveolar ridge. English has seven alveolar sounds, [t, d, n, s, z, l, r].

and American linguists have traditionally used dissimilar methods to analyze the vowel system because the inventory of the vowels is different between British and American English.

The first and the most familiar difference between RP and GA vowel sounds is probably the RP use of [ɑː] (as opposed to GA [æ]) before some fricatives[48] and nasals,[49] as follows:

Table 8.9. Pronunciations of RP [ɑː] and GA [æ]

Neighboring Sound	Examples
_ [s]	*ask, basket, brass, castle, fast, glass, last, master*
_ [f]	*after, calf, craft, draft, draught, half, laugh, shaft*
_ [θ]	*bath, path, lath*
_ [m]+C	*example, sample*
_ [n]+C	*advance, answer, aunt, branch, can't, chance*

That is, American speakers use [æ] sound in such words.[50] Although there was an opinion that [ɑː] sound has a higher social standing than [æ], it is

---

48) **Fricatives** (or **spirants**) are consonants produced by forcing air through a narrow channel made by placing two articulators close together. English has about ten fricative sounds [f, v, θ, ð, s, z, ʃ, ʒ, h, x]. The sound [x] is heard only in some forms of Scottish English. For example, the final sound of *loch*, meaning 'lake', is [x].

49) A **nasal consonant** is produced when the velum (the fleshy part of the palate near the back) is lowered, allowing air to escape freely through the nose. The oral cavity still acts as a resonance chamber for the sound, but the air does not escape through the mouth as it is blocked by the tongue. English has three nasal consonants [m, n, ŋ].

50) But [ɑː] is heard even in American pronunciation before *r* (as in *far*), *lm* (as in *calm*), and in *father*.

just a prejudice. Even the speakers of standard British English do not use the expected [ɑː] sound all the time (cf. Pyles and Algeo (1993: 224)). For example, such words as *cl_a_ssic, cl_a_ssical, cl_a_ssicism, cl_a_ssify, p_a_ssage, p_a_ssenger* and *p_a_ssive* have [æ] even in British English, in contrast to the [ɑː] of *cl_a_ss, gl_a_ss, gr_a_ss* and *p_a_ss*. *_A_mple* has [æ], but *ex_a_mple* and *s_a_mple* have [ɑː]; *f_a_ncy* and *rom_a_nce* have [æ], but *ch_a_nce, d_a_nce* and *gl_a_nce* have [ɑː]; *m_a_scot, m_a_ssacre* and *p_a_stel* have [æ], but *b_a_sket, m_a_ster* and *n_a_sty* have [ɑː], and *b_a_stard, m_a_squerade* and *m_a_stiff* may have either [æ] or [ɑː].

The next vowel difference is about the pronunciation of the <o> spelling. For the most part, British English has a lightly rounded vowel symbolized by [ɒ] in such words as *p_o_t, t_o_p, r_o_d*, and others,[51] while Americans use the sound [ɑː]:

---

51) The vowels [uː, u, ou, ɔ] in *b_oo_t, p_u_t, b_oa_t* and *b_o_re* are rounded vowels. They are produced with pursed or rounded lips, so the round vowels are all back and non-low (i.e. mid and high) vowels. It should be mentioned here that British English employs another round vowel, [ɒ], which is a low back round vowel. It sounds quite similar to [ɔ], only differing in tongue height.

Table 8.10. Pronunciations of RP [ɒ] and GA [ɑː] (or [ɔː])

Neighboring Sound	Examples
_ [p]	*stop, cop, drop, pop, top*
_ [t]	*bottle, hot, motto, lot, Scot*
_ [k]	*box, doctor, knock, lock, pocket*
_ [b]	*Bob, hobby, lobby, Robert, snob*
_ [d]	*cod, fodder, God, model, rod*
_ [m]	*bomb, comma, mom, pomp, Tom*
_ [n]	*bond, honest, honor, John, pond*
_ [l]	*college, doll, holiday, solid*
_ [tʃ]	*blotch, notch, Scotch*
_ [dʒ]	*dodge, lodge, Roger*
_ [ʃ]	*gosh, Joshua*
_ [v]	*novel, poverty*
_ [z]	*closet, Moslem*
_ [ð]	*bother, mother*

It has been reported that "an increasingly large number of Americans do not distinguish between [ɑː] and [ɔː]" (Pyles and Algeo 1993: 32). For them, *caught* and *cot* are homophones, i.e. pronounced in the same way. The word pairs such as *taught* and *tot*, *dawn* and *don*, *gaud* and *God*, *pawed* and *pod*, *walk* and *wok*, and *maul* and *moll*, are all alike. Then these speakers will pronounce the words given above with either [ɑː] or [ɔː] indiscriminately. As a result, Americans have two sets of correspondences for RP [ɒ], i.e. [ɑː] or [ɔː].[52] Furthermore, some American speakers also use the British [ɒ] sound, which can be heard in western Pennsylvania and eastern New England.

---

[52] Because there are two sounds in GA for RP /ɒ/, there is considerable variation in GA between the two vowels.

3) Individual Differences

Apart from the regular differences, like the ones shown above, there are some more words that have different pronunciations in RP and GA. But these words do not show any patterned difference. Here are some of the frequently used ones (from Crystal (2002: 264-65)).

(1) *Schedule* begins with two consonants in AmE (as in *skin*), but with one in BrE (as in *shin*).

(2) The middle vowel of *tomato* rhymes only with *car* in BrE, but also with *mate* in AmE.

(3) The first syllable of *lever* rhymes only with *leaver* in BrE, but also with that of *level* in AmE.

(4) Conversely, the first syllable of *leisure* rhymes only with the vowel of *let* in BrE, but also rhymes with *lee* in AmE.

(5) *Route* rhymes with *out* for many AmE speakers; it is always like *root* in BrE.

(6) *Vase* rhymes only with *cars* in BrE, but also with *days* in AmE.

(7) *Docile* is 'doss-ile' in AmE, but 'doe-sile' in BrE. The <-ile> ending regularly changes in this way: *missile* is often pronounced like *missal* in AmE, and similarly *fertile, hostile, fragile, tactile,*

volatile, ster<u>ile</u>, etc.53)

(8) *Herb* is pronounced without the initial <h> in AmE, but with the <h> in BrE; however, some <herb-> words do have <h> in AmE, such as *herbivore, herbicide*.

The following table shows more examples of such words:54)

Table 8.11. Pronunciation Differences of Individual Words

Example Words	GA	RP
Anthony	[ǽnəəni]	[ǽntəni]
ate	[eit]	[ɛt]
been	[bin]	[biːn]
buffet	[bəféi]	[búfei]
clerk	[klɚk]	[klɑk]
figure	[figjɚ]	[figə]
shone	[ʃoun]	[ʃɔn]
vitamin	[váitəmin]	[vítəmin]
either	[iðə]	[aiðə]

4) Stress

Both RP and GA have a stress-timed rhythm. Both have at least three levels of stress for syllables: primary, secondary, and tertiary (or) minimal stress.55)

---

53) Even here there are exceptions: *rep<u>tile</u>, serv<u>ile</u>* and *juven<u>ile</u>* are often pronounced with [ail] in the US, and *mob<u>ile</u>* can be [-əl], [-ail], or even [-il].
54) This list can be extended. The different pronunciations of the words such as *evolution, medicine, nephew, process, trait, tryst, valet, zenith*, and more, can be added to the list.

In polysyllabic words, however, RP tends to use minimal stress on many syllables that have secondary stress in GA. In particular, the endings such as <-ary>, <-ery> or <-ory> usually have a secondary stress in GA but not in RP. For example, *secondary* is pronounced in RP as /sékəndrĭ/, but its American pronunciation is /sékəndèrĭ/. Other examples are *auditory, territory, cemetery, monastery, legendary, secretary* and *dictionary*.[56]

As in the following list, some words show the difference in the position of the main stress. But the two variants are used in both British and American English. Especially, the American stress pattern is penetrated into British English:

Table 8.12. Stress Differences of Individual Words

GA	RP	GA	RP
áddress	*addréss*	*ballét*	*bállet*
café	*cáfe*	*cigarétte*	*cígarette*
frontíer	*fróntier*	*garáge*	*gárage*
mágazine	*magazíne*	*místache*	*moustáche*
príncess	*princéss*	*résearch*	*reséarch*
tránslate	*transláte*	*wéekend*	*weekénd*

---

55) Four-level distinction of stress is also possible: primary (marked as ´ [an acute mark]), secondary (marked as ` [a grave mark]), tertiary (marked as ˘ [a breve mark]) and quaternary (or minimal) stress (marked as ˆ [a circumflex mark] or no mark at all). It should be noted that the tertiary stress can have no mark in the three-level distinction, like the quaternary stress in the four-level distinction.
56) The city name, *Birmingham*, is the same; the British pronunciation is [bə́:miŋhəm], while the American counterpart is [bə́:rmiŋhæm].

8.2.4. Differences of Grammar[57]

There are some differences between AmE and BrE in the field of grammar.[58] However, grammatical differences are in fact rather few and their nature seems to be trivial. So the differences do not cause any difficulty in the communication between American speakers and British speakers. Still, a few differences do exist. Here will be given some prominent examples.

1) Differences of Verbs

In both British and American English, the verbs *have* and *get* are among the most frequent, especially in speech. As a result, differences of usage in these verbs are easily noticed.

(1) *do you have* (AmE) vs. *have you got* (BrE): In British English *have* acted as an auxiliary, so such question was (still is in the restricted area) possible as <u>Have</u> *you a pencil I can borrow*? A negative sentence like *We <u>haven't</u> a house of our own* was also possible. But through the comparison with such construction as <u>Have</u> *you ever met*

---

57) This section is based on Strevens (1972: 47-53).
58) I will label variants AmE and BrE for what is typically American or British English, but this does not mean that a particular form could never be used in the other variety. In the area of grammar, British English is nowadays being influenced by American English, and that several grammatical features that used to be regarded as typical of American English are now no longer exclusively American (cf. Americanization, Leech *et al.* (2009: 252-59)).

John before?, where *have* is an auxiliary, the *have* in <u>Have</u> *you a pencil I can borrow?* could be misunderstood as an auxiliary having no lexical meaning ('possession'). So a new verb *got* was added to strengthen the weakened 'possession' meaning, and the original verb *have* became a kind of auxiliary.59) The form *have got* always deliver the meaning of 'possession' only.60) Thus, **I usually <u>have</u> <u>got</u> a sandwich for lunch*, meaning 'I usually <u>eat</u> a sandwich for lunch' is wrong. (cf. *I'<u>ve</u> <u>got</u> some sandwiches. Would you like one?*)

(2) *Did you meet ...?* (AmE) vs. *Have you met ...?* (BrE): This is a difference between British and American usage for asking a question in the past. In American English the simple past form is used instead of the expected traditional present perfect(ive) form. Thus the adverbs such as *ever, never, yet, just* and *already* can be used with the simple past in American English.61)

---

59) The auxiliary status of *have* in *have got* is easily evidenced in questions and negative sentences; <u>Have</u> *you got a pencil I can borrow?* (cf. <u>Do</u> *you have a pencil I can borrow?*) and *I <u>have</u> not got a pencil to lend you* (*I <u>do</u> not have a pencil to lend you*).

60) One exception is *have <u>got</u> to*. *Got* is inserted here although *have* does not deliver the 'possession' meaning here. This form was accepted into American English, where the original verb *have* almost disappeared, leaving the form *got to* (*gotta* or *gorra*).

61) We have some examples as follows (from Murphy (2001: 14, 16)):

<Past Action with Current Relevance>

i. He told me his name, but *I've forgotten* it (=but *I forgot* it). (so I can't remember it now.)

ii. "Is Kimberly here?" "No, *she's gone* out." ("No, she *went* out.") (so she is out now.)

<A Recent Happening>

(3) Mandative subjunctive (AmE)[62] vs. 'Quasi-subjunctive' use of *Should* or Present tense form (BrE): AmE prefers to use the subjunctive verb (i.e. the same form with the base verb form) after such verbs as *recommend, insist, demand, require, propose* and *suggest,* after some nouns like *recommendation, requirement, demand* and *necessity,* or after some adjectives like *important, necessary* and *imperative,*[63] while BrE uses *should.* The use of the non-subjunctive present tense form, the third option, is found in BrE but it is not acceptable in AmE:

e.g. The doctor recommended that she *rest* for a few days.
(preferred in AmE, now on the increase in BrE)
The doctor recommended that she *should rest* for a few days.
(preferred in BrE)

---

iii. "Are you hungry?" "No, I've *just had* lunch." ("No, I *just had* lunch.")
iv. Don't forget to mail the letter. "I've *already mailed* it." ("I *already mailed* it.")
v. Has it *stopped* raining *yet*? (*Did* it *stop* raining *yet*?)
vi. I wrote the letter, but I *haven't mailed* it *yet*. (but I *didn't mail* it *yet*.)

However, the present perfective cannot be always replaced by the simple past even in American English. The simple past cannot express the activity which is still happening nor the actions that are repeated over a period of time. For example, *It has been raining* is not synonymous with *It was raining.* And *Debbie is a very good tennis player. She's been playing since she was eight* cannot be replaced with **She was playing since she was eight.*

62) *Mandative* indicates that it occurs in constructions expressing wishes, orders or requirements.
63) Note the following subjunctive examples:

i. They insisted that he *not bring* them a present.
ii. The chairperson proposed that the plans *be changed.*

254 The External History of English: Stories of English

The doctor recommended that she *rests* for a few days. (in BrE, not accepted in AmE)

(4) Singular agreement with a collective noun (AmE) vs. Plural agreement (BrE): Collective nouns such as *team, audience, board, cabinet, council, committee* and *government,* and the names of sports clubs are generally regarded as singular in AmE, but they are treated as plural in BrE:

e.g. Manchester United *defeats* Arsenal. (AmE)
Manchester United *defeat* Arsenal. (BrE)
Buffalo *has* signed a new tight end. (AmE)
Liverpool *have* signed a new midfielder. (BrE) (Trask 2010: 126)
The government *has* decided that *it has* to launch a campaign. (AmE)
The government *have* decided that *they have* to launch a campaign. (BrE) (Tottie 2002: 149)

(5) *gotten* (AmE) vs. *got* (BrE): American speakers say *I've just gotten* [gátn] *a letter*, British speakers say *I've got* [gɒt] *a letter*.[64] That is, British English use has no past participle *gotten*. Formerly, *gotten* was only used in the sense of 'acquired or obtained'. It is increasingly used in other meanings, too, as in *I wish I could have gotten* ('arrived') *here sooner* or *She's gotten into trouble in school.*

---

64) In BrE, therefore, *I've got a letter* can have two different interpretations: either 'I have a letter (simple present)' or 'I have received a letter (present perfective).'

(6) *dare* and *need*: *Dare* and *need* are fairly unusual verbs with modal meanings. Sometimes they behave like modals in negative sentences and questions, and sometimes not, as follows:

Table 8.13. *Dare* and *Need*

		Negation	Question
Dare	as an Auxiliary	I *daren't* do it.	*Dare* he do it?
	as a Lexical Verb	I *don't dare to* do it.	Does he *dare to* do it?
Need	as an Auxiliary	You *needn't* come in today.	*Need* he answer?
	as a Lexical Verb	You *don't need to* come in today.	Does he *need to* answer?

The general tendency is that BrE uses *dare* and *need* as auxiliaries more often than AmE. But both constructions are acceptable in the two national varieties.

(7) *be going to*: *Be going to* is used to express future meaning in both varieties but is more common in AmE than in BrE. The form *gonna* for *going to* is also more common in AmE but it is on the increase in BrE and is sometimes found in written representations of spoken language in both varieties:

e.g. He's *going to* be twenty next year. (AmE > BrE)
She's *gonna* win this game. (AmE > BrE)

2) Differences of Nouns and Pronouns

(1) Modifiers for a person: In British English, when a person is named, any attributing modifiers that may be stated about him tend to follow

the name, whereas they tend to precede it in American English:

e.g. Bearded 30-year old property millionaire Edward Johnson ... (AmE, pseudo-title construction)[65]
Mr. Edward Johnson, (the) bearded 30-year old property millionaire ... (BrE, appositive construction)

(2) *One ... he* (AmE) vs. *one ... one* (BrE): Another clear grammatical difference is in the treatment of a repeated subject after *one*. *One* is very rarely used at all in either variety and only in rather formal styles. In BrE, however, *one* is somewhat more frequent than in AmE and the possessive form of *one* is *one's*. Meanwhile, the tradition is to use *his* after *one* in AmE:

e.g. When *one* has seen the size of the problem, *he* realizes ... (AmE)
When *one* has seen the size of the problem, *one* realizes ... (BrE)[66]

---

65) A pseudo-title is defined as any construction containing an initial unit (such as *city employee* in *city employee Mark Smith*) that provides descriptive information about an individual and that cannot be classified into any of the real titles. Real titles are such categories as Professional (*Doctor, Professor*), Political (*President, Senator*), Religious (*Bishop, Cardinal*), Honors (*Dame, Earl*), Military (*General, Corporal*), Police (*Constable, Detective-Sergeant*) and Foreign (*Monsieur, Senorita*). Meanwhile, the appositive considered equivalent to a pseudo-title occurs after, not before, the noun phrase it is related to and a determiner is optional (e.g. *Mark Smith, (the) city employee*). For the newly-appearing pseudo-title construction, refer to Meyer (1992, 2002: Chapter 5).
66) British usage has an advantage of avoiding the controversial 'generic' or 'epicene' *he*. The *he* here may refer to females, too, so the masculine *he* is clumsy. Instead,

(3) New plural forms for *you* (AmE): After the loss of the <th-> forms like *thou / thy-thine / thee*, English lost a useful way to distinguish the number for the second person pronoun. So it tried to devise new plural forms, like *yous(e)*, *you-uns* (that is, *you ones*), *you-all* (or *y'all*), and the recent *you guys* '*you people*'. But these forms are mostly used in AmE and not regarded as standard in BrE (e.g. *you all* or *y'all* - in the South of the US, *yous(e)* in the Northeast of the US, especially New York City)

(4) Indefinite pronouns: Pronouns ending in *-body* (*anybody, everybody, somebody, nobody*) are preferred in AmE to those ending in *-one* (*anyone, everyone, someone, no one / none*) according to Biber *et al.* (1999: 352)

3) Differences of Adverbs and Adjectives

(1) Use of adjectives (AmE) instead of the grammatically more acceptable adverbs (BrE): AmE tends to use adjective forms instead of the grammatically expected adverbs as in BrE:

---

the singular *they* is widely used these days, as in *When one has seen the size of the problem, they realizes* ...

i. ... and I was talking to *someone* about this the other day / and *they* said ah yes (SEU, S-7-1; telephone conversation, 1961, Wales (1996: 129))
ii. *Whoever ran into that tree* must have really hurt *themselves/themself.*
iii. *The patient* should be told at the outset how much *they* will be required to pay.
iv. But *a journalist* should not be forced to reveal *their* sources.

e.g.67) They pay them pretty *good* (AmE) / *well* (BrE).

You'll have to speak *slow* (AmE) / *slowly* (BrE).

She's *awful* (AmE) / *awfully* (BrE) thin.

I *sure* (AmE) / *certainly* (BrE) hope it's temporary.

4) Differences of Prepositions

(1) *different from* vs. *different than* or *different to*: The official standard form is *different from* in both countries. The colloquial form is *different than* in AmE, but *different to* in BrE.

(2) Different phrasal verbs: A number of phrasal verbs of the type [Verb+Preposition] use a different preposition in British and American English. There seems to be no clear pattern.

e.g. I'll *check out* the brake. (AmE)

I'll *check up on* the brake. (BrE)

to *talk with* somebody (AmE)

to *talk to* somebody (BrE)

to *visit with* neighbors (AmE)

to *call on* (or just *visit*) neighbors (BrE)

(3) Preposition with dates, days of the week: Another clear distinction occurs here. British English requires *on* before a day of the week or a specific date. American English frequently dispenses with *on* here.

---

67) The examples are all from Svartvik and Leech (2006: 168).

e.g. The new air service begins *on* January 1(st). (BrE)
The new air service begins January 1(st). (AmE)
On Mondays we take the bus. (BrE)
Mondays we take the bus. (AmE)

(4) *days; nights* (AmE) vs. *by day; by/at night* (BrE): Somewhat parallel but less clear-cut is the American English use of *days* and *nights* where BE would have *by day* or *by/at night* or an alternative expression.

e.g. I work *nights* as a bar-tender. (AmE)
I work *by/at night* as a barman. (BrE)

(5) *home* (AmE) vs. *at home* (BrE): In American English the word *home* is used largely as in British English, except that it serves alone also where British English requires *at home*.

e.g. Let's stay *home* this evening. (AmE)
Let's stay *at home* this evening. (BrE)

(6) *all of the* (AmE) vs. *all the* (BrE): Until recently, British English invariably had *all the* (as in <u>all the</u> time) while American English invariably has *all of the* (as in <u>all of the</u> time). Written usage still retains this characteristic distinction, but in the speech of younger people it is increasingly common to hear both forms in British English, too.

(7) *from ... through* (AmE) vs. *from ... to* (BrE): Different prepositions are used to express a period of time:

e.g. The tour lasted *from* January *through* June. (AmE)
The tour lasted *from* January *to* June. (BrE)

In AmE, *through* clearly signifies 'up to and including', but, in the BrE construction, it is often confusing if June is included or not. So *inclusive* is sometimes expressed together to clarify the inclusion: *from* January *to* June <u>*inclusive*</u>.

(8) Other prepositions:

e.g. I live *on* Walnut Street. (AmE)
I live *in* Broad Street. (BrE)
John is *in* school, and Mary is *in* college. (AmE)
John is *at* school, and Mary is *at* college.
(BrE and AmE, cf. *at/in Keimyung University*)
In the back of the house was a yard to play in. (AmE)
Behind the house was a yard to play in. (AmE and BrE)

5) Differences of Conjunctions

(1) *Like* (AmE) vs. *As if* (or *as though*, BrE): *As if* (or *as though*) is used to say how somebody or something looks, sounds, feels, etc. But *like* can be used instead of *as if* in AmE:

e.g. Ann sounded *as if / as though / like* (AmE only) she had a cold.[68]

(2) *the way*: *the way* (not followed by *in which* or *that*) is often used as a conjunction meaning 'as,' as in *Do it the way I do it*. This usage is common in informal language in both AmE and BrE, but in AmE, it is also widespread in newspapers and other written registers:

e.g. He talked *the way* he always talked. (AmE > BrE)
Shopping at Jim's is shopping *the way* it used to be. (AmE > BrE)

(3) *Directly* and *immediately*: *Directly* and *immediately* are not used as conjunctions in AmE but have to be followed by *after*:

e.g. John left *directly after* Mary arrived. (AmE)
John left *directly* Mary arrived. (BrE)
Mary left *immediately after* she heard about it. (AmE)
Mary left *immediately* she heard about it. (BrE)

Crystal (2002: 266-67) gives the following list that shows the differences of the grammar of individual lexical items between the two English varieties:

---

68) After *as if / like* we sometimes use the past when we are talking about the present, since the idea is not real:

i. I don't like Norma. She talks *as of / like* she *knew* everything.

Table 8.14. Other Grammatical Differences

AmE	BrE
twenty of four	*twenty to four*
five after eight	*five past eight*
Hudson River	River Thames
a half hour	*half an hour*
in the future	*in future*
I burned it.	*I burnt it.*
I snuck out quietly.	*I sneaked out quietly.*
I won't (will not) tell anyone.	*I shan't (shall not) tell anyone.*
I'll go get the car.	*I'll go and get the car.*
Come take a look.	*Come and take a look.*
I asked that he leave.	*I asked him to leave.*
I want out.	*I want to get out.*
There were six million.	*There were six millions.*
He is in the hospital.	*He is in hospital.*
I'll see you over the weekend.	*I'll see you at the weekend.*
Look out the window.	*Look out of the window.*
I'll go momentarily.	*I'll go in a moment.*
I haven't seen her in ages.	*I haven't seen her for ages.*
September first	*September the first*

There are much more grammatical differences between American and British English than the ones illustrated here. But differences are minor, in the sense that they seldom seriously impede communication between speakers from different English varieties. Furthermore, differences are for the most part not systematic - that is, matters of general rules, but rather involve collocability and co-occurrence restrictions for individual words. These differences are the kind that dictionaries, not the grammar books, should record.

Cited Bibliography

\# I apologize for any possible infringement of copyright. I have tried to reveal the primary sources of the quotations, but it was limited and not always possible.

Algeo, J. (ed). 2001. *The Cambridge History of the English Language, Vol VI: English in North America.* Cambridge: Cambridge University Press.

Angermeyer, P. and J. Singler. 2003. The Case for Politeness: Pronoun Variation in Co-ordinate NPs in Object Position in English. *Language Variation and Change* 15, 171-209.

Aremo, W. B. 2005. On Some Uses of Singular Collective Nouns. *English Today* 81, Vol 21, No. 1, 52-55.

Barber, C. 1993. *The English Language: a Historical Introduction.* Cambridge: Cambridge University Press.

Bauer, L. 1994. *Watching English Change: An Introduction to the Study of Linguistics Change in Standard Englishes in the Twentieth Century.* London and New York: Longman.

_____. 2002. Hitting a Moving Target. *English Today* 72, Vol 18, No. 4, 55-59.

Baugh, A. and T. Cable. 1993. *A History of the English Language*, 4th edition. London: Routledge.

Biber, D., S. Johansson, G. Leech, S. Conrad and E. Finegan. 1999. *Longman Grammar of Spoken and Written English.* London: Longman.

Bloomfield, M. and L. Newmark 1963. *A Linguistic Introduction to the History of English.* New York: Knopf.

Bolton, W. F. (selected and edited). 1966. *The English Language: Essays by English and American Men of Letters.* Cambridge: Cambridge University Press.

Buck, R. A. 2003. Why? and How? - Teaching the History of the English Language in Our New Millenium. *English Today* 73, Vol 19, No. 1,

44-49.

Cambridge International Dictionary of English. 1995. Cambridge: Cambridge University Press.

Carney, E. 1997. *English Spelling*. London and New York: Routledge.

Crystal, D. 1997a. *The Cambridge Encyclopedia of the English Language*. Cambridge: Cambridge University Press.

_____. 1997b. *English as a Global Language*. Cambridge: Cambridge University Press.

_____. 2002. *The English Language: A Guided Tour of the Language*, 2nd edition. London: Penguin Books.

Culpeper, J. 1997. *History of English*. London and New York: Routledge.

Davidson, K. 2007. The Nature and Significance of English as a Global Language. *English Today* 89, Vol 23, No. 1, 48-50.

Denison, D. 1996. The Case of Unmarked Pronoun. Britton, D (ed). *English Historical Linguistics* 1994 Papers from the 8th International Conference on English Historical Linguistics: Edinburgh, 19-23 September 1994. (Current Issues in Linguistic Theory, 135.), 287-299. Amsterdam: John Benjamins.

Erling, E. 2005. The Many Names of English. *English Today* 81, Vol 21, No. 1, 40-44.

Fisiak, J. 1995. *An Outline History of English*, Vol 1. Poznan: Kantor Wydawniczy Saww.

Hogg, R. (ed). 1992. *The Cambridge History of the English Language*, Vol 1. Cambridge: Cambridge University Press.

Hook, D. 2002. On English, its Simplicity and Great Usefulness. *English Today* 72, Vol 18, No. 4, 35-38.

Jespersen, O. 1909-49. *A Modern English Grammar on Historical Principles*. London: Allen & Unwin.

_____. 1954. *Growth and Structure of the English Language*, 9th edition. Oxford: Blackwell.

Johannessen, J. 1998. *Coordination*. Oxford: Oxford University Press.

Kachru, B. 1985. Standards, Codification and Sociolinguistic Realism: the English

Language in the Outer Circle. Quirk, R. and H. G. Widdowson (eds). *English in the World*, 11-30. Cambridge: Cambridge University Press.ll.

Lee, P. H. 1999a. *English Diachronic Syntax* (in Korean). Seoul: Hankookmunhwasa.

_____. 1999b. The Progressive Passives and the Extension of English Verbal Group: Functionalism vs. Formalism (in Korean). *History of English* 8, 63-92.

_____. 2005. Morphological Implications on Preposition Stranding and Split Infinitives. *The Linguistic Association of Korea Journal* 13(2), 43-67.

_____. 2006. For Gender Neutral English - With Special Reference to Pronoun Usage (in Korean). *The New Studies of English Language & Literature* 34, 247-275.

_____. 2007. *Syntactic Changes in English* (in Korean). Seoul: Hankookmunhwasa.

_____. 2009. On the Usage-expansion of *Who* and the Demise of *Whom*. *English Language and Linguistics* 27, 41-68.

Leech, G., M. Hundt, C. Mair and N. Smith. 2009. Change in Contemporary English: A Grammatical Study. Cambridge: Cambridge University Press.

Mair, C. and G. Leech. 2006. Current Changes in English Syntax. Aarts, B. and A. McMahon (eds). *The Handbook of English Linguistics*, 318-342. Oxford: Blackwell.

McArthur, T. 2004. Is it world or international or global English, and does it matter? *English Today* 79, Vol 20, No. 3, 3-15.

Merriam-Webster's Dictionary of English Usage. 1994. Gilman, W. (ed). Springfield, MA: Merriam-Webster

Mesthrie, R. 2008. English Circling the Globe. *English Today* 93, Vol 24, No. 1, 28-32.

Meyer, C. 1992. *Apposition in Contemporary English*. Cambridge: Cambridge University Press.

_____. 2002. *English Corpus Linguistics: An Introduction*. Cambridge: Cambridge University Press.

Murphy, R. 2001. *Grammar in Use: Intermediate*, 2nd edition/2nd printing. Cambridge: Cambridge University Press.

Nevalainen, T. and H. Raumolin-Brunberg. 2003. *Historical Sociolinguistics*. London: Longman.

O'driscoll, J. 1995. *Britain - The Country and its People: An Introduction for Learners of English*. Oxford: Oxford University Press.

Oxford English Dictionary = 1992 CD-ROM version. Oxford: Clarendon.

Parker, F. and K. Riley. 2005. *Linguistics for Non-linguists*, 4th edition. Boston: Pearson.

Pyles, T. and J. Algeo. 1993. *The Origins and Development of the English Language*, 4th edition. New York: Harcourt Brace Jovanovich.

Rastall, P. 2002. English in a Historical Perspective - a Neglected Inheritance. *English Today* 70, Vol 18, No. 2, 28-32.

Redfern, R. 1994. Is *between you and I* Good English? Little, G. and M. Montgomery (eds). *Centennial Usage Studies*, 187-193. Tuscaloosa: University of Alabama Press.

Robinson, F. C. 1994. Old English. Asher, R. (ed). *Encyclopedia of Language and Linguistics*, 2868-71. Oxford: Pergamon Press.

Smith, J. J. 1994. Middle English. Asher, R. (ed). *Encyclopedia of Language and Linguistics*, 2487-91. Oxford: Pergamon Press.

Smith, R. 2005. Global English: Gift or Curse? *English Today* 82, Vol 21, No. 2, 56-62.

Stewart, R. 2003. A Decline in Spoken English. *English Today* 75, Vol 19, No. 3, 57-58.

Strevens, P. 1972. *British and American English*. London: Collier-Macmillan.

Svartvik, J. and G. Leech. 2006. *English: One tongue, Many Voices*. New York: Palgrave MacMillan.

Tottie, G. 2002. *An Introduction to American English*. Oxford: Blackwell.

Wales, K. 1996. *Personal Pronouns in Present-day English*. Cambridge: Cambridge University Press.

Wikipedia, the Free Encyclopedia. http://en.wikipedia.org/wiki.

Index

a

Afrikaans	93
agglutinative languages	98
Alfred	120, 132, 139
American Dictionary of the English Language	240
American English	222, 224, 233
American Independence War	239
American slangs	234
American spellings	235
Angles	106, 111
Anglian	123
Anglo-Norman	155
Anglo-Saxon Chronicle	113, 131
Anglo-Saxon Heptarchy	117

b

Battle of Hastings	144
Battle of Maldon	134
Bede	111, 139
Beowulf	138
Black Death	154
Breton	96
Britain	107, 115
British	106
British Celts	109, 110, 135
British English	233
British Isles	18, 19, 111, 206
brogue	218

c

Cambridge	159
Canadian English	215
Canterbury	126
Canterbury Tales	160, 163
Celtic languages	95
Celtic peoples	106
Centum languages	88
Charles I	187
Charles the Simple	145
Chaucer	160, 163
Christianity	119, 126, 162
Christopher Marlowe	169, 198
Claudius	107
Cockney twang	218
cognates	81
comparative linguists	84
Cornish	96
Cromwell	187

d

Danelaw	133
Danish	93, 94
dative case	101
dead languages	173
dictionaries	178
Dutch	93

e

East Anglia 117
East Germanic 93
Ecclesiastical History of the English People
.... 111
Edward the Confessor 135, 143
Elizabeth I 166, 167, 173, 209
endings 99
England 18
English as a foreign language 19
English as a native language 19
English as a second language 19
English Civil War 167
English Revolution 186
Essex 117
external history 42

f

Flemish 93
Frisian 93
Frisians 106, 111

g

General American 242
genitive case 101
Germanic Conquest 110, 111
Germanic language 90
global language 14
Gothic 94
Great Britain 18
Greek 173, 175
Gregory 125, 139
Guthrum 132

h

Hadrian 107
Hadrian's Wall 108
Hamlet 76, 198
Harold 143
Henry VIII 167
heteronyms 31
High German 93
Hundred Years' War 152

i

incorporative language 98
Indo-European homeland 83
Indo-European languages 84, 86
inflectional simplicity 26
inflective languages 98
internal history 42
international language 14
Ireland 18
Irish Gaelic 96, 109, 204
isolating languages 98
Italian 96

j

Jacques Cartier 212
James Cook 217
Jamestown 167, 209
Jarrow 120
Joan of Arc 153
John Cabot 212
John Calvin 197
John Hart 185
John Wycliffe 50, 163
Jonathan Swift 193
Joyce 205
Julius Caesar 106
Jutes 106, 111

k

Kent 117
Kentish 122, 157
King James Bible 51, 168
King John 151

l

Language family 82
Latin ··· 97, 109, 111, 172, 173, 175
Latin alphabet 127
Layamon 162
Lindley Murray 184
loanwords 136, 176
London 159
loss of Normandy 150
Low German 93

m

Manx 96
Maori 221
Martin Luther 197
Mercia 117, 126
Mercian 122, 157
Middle English 44, 141
Middle English dialects ... 155, 158
Modern English 44

n

New Zealand English 221
Noah Webster 238
nominative case 101
Norman Conquest 44, 141, 143, 146, 165
Normandy 145, 151
North Germanic 93
Northumbria 117, 126

Northumbrian 122, 157
Norwegian 93, 94

o

objective case 63
Old English 44, 105
Old English dialects 121
Old Norse 136
Oxford 159
Oxford English Dictionary 180

p

parchment 127
Picts 110
Pilgrim Fathers 210
Plymouth 224
Plymouth Colony 210
Portuguese 96
Pre-Old English Period 80
prescriptive grammar 189, 191
printing 45, 160, 171
Protestant Reformation 167
Proto-Indo-European 83, 100
puritans 210

q

Quebec 214, 215
Queen Anne's War 213

r

Received Pronunciation 242
reconstructed language 83
Renaissance 168, 196
Republic of Ireland 18, 207
Richard Mulcaster 185
Robert Cawdrey 179

Robert Lowth ················· 184
Roman Empire ········ 97, 106, 127
Romance languages ·········· 89, 96
Rumanian ······················· 96
Runes ·························· 128

S

Samuel Johnson's Dictionary ········· 180
Satem languages ················ 88
Saxons ···················· 106, 111
Scandinavian invasions ·········· 130
Scots ··························· 110
Scottish Gaelic ········ 96, 109, 203
Shakespeare ········ 76, 169, 173, 198, 199, 223
Spanish ························· 96
spelling Reforms ················ 183
St. Augustine ··············· 119, 125
Standard English ················ 158
Stuarts ······················ 166, 187
subjective case ················· 63
Sussex ·························· 117
Swedish ···················· 93, 94

t

the French and Indian War ······· 213
Thor ··························· 131
thou ···························· 77

Tudors ························· 166

u

United Kingdom ············ 18, 206

v

Vikings ···················· 131, 134
Virginia ··················· 209, 223

w

Wales ······················ 18, 206
Walter Releigh ················· 209
Welsh ······················ 96, 109
Wessex ···················· 117, 132
West Germanic ·················· 93
West Saxon ················· 122, 157
William Bullokar ················ 183
William Caxton ············· 161, 171
William Wordsworth ············· 200
Winchester ····················· 124
Woden ························· 131
world language ·················· 14
Wulfila ························· 94

y

Yiddish ························· 94

Index 271